The Renaissance
and Reformation
in Germany

The Renaissance and Reformation in Germany

AN INTRODUCTION

Edited by Gerhart Hoffmeister

FREDERICK UNGAR PUBLISHING CO.
New York

To Henri Stegemeier,
distinguished humanist, teacher and scholar

Library of Congress Cataloging in Publication Data

Main entry under title:

The Renaissance and Reformation in Germany.

   Bibliography: p.
   Includes index.
   1. Reformation—Germany—Addresses, essays,
lectures.   2. Renaissance—Germany—Addresses,
essays, lectures.   3. Germany—Intellectual life—
Addresses, essays, lectures.   I. Hoffmeister,
Gerhart.
DD176.R44   943′.02   77–5429
ISBN 0–8044–1391–6
ISBN 0–8044–6272–0 pbk.

Contents

Contents

Preface

This collection of essays is intended as an introduction to the long neglected field of the Renaissance and Reformation in Germany. A study of this period should be exciting and rewarding because our own time has many of its roots in that transitional age of turmoil and spiritual rebirth. The theocentric world view of the Middle Ages was gradually giving way to a secular attitude. This massive reshaping of the Western mind found expression in religious upheaval, the rise of capitalism, the great Peasants' Revolt, and the Copernican revolution. Profoundly distressed at the velocity of change, some called for a return to the old ways (Sebastian Brant in his *Ship of Fools*) and others looked to the pagan and the occult (as, for example, Faustus).

This book provides the necessary background information to enable both teacher and student to have a better grasp of the period. One result should be an appreciation of some outstanding literary works, written mostly by German-born humanists and reformers. These works were best sellers in their day and are still regarded as masterpieces of world literature.

The idea for this arrangement and spectrum of topics came to the editor some years ago when he participated in teaching an interdisciplinary course on "Humanism and Antihumanism in Europe between 1300 and 1650." His students expressed the need for a textbook to help them in their studies. Some anthologies and several interpretive books dealing with the period are available, but none of them meets the expectations of a reader seeking a guidebook that might cover both Renaissance humanism and the Reformation, both the background and the literary contributions of the epoch.

The present volume attempts to fill this gap and will prove to be a welcome aid for classwork, whether in interdisciplinary, comparative literature, or literature in translation courses on the undergraduate or graduate level, taught in German or English.

The editor is responsible for the general framework of the book and the topics selected. The responsibility for any shortcomings should be his. His appeal for contributions from scholars —established or young—throughout the United States met with an immediate and positive response. Without the advice and, of course, contributions of his colleagues, especially the valuable suggestions of Professors Wayne Rebhorn, University of Texas, and Frank Borchardt, Duke University, this enterprise would not have come to fruition. To them the editor expresses his sincere thanks.

May this book turn out to be a useful tool for and a persuasive invitation to more detailed and successful studies in this area.

Gerhart Hoffmeister

University of California
Santa Barbara

1

First Contacts with Italy

Frank L. Borchardt

The vanguard of Italy's cultural rebirth knocked at the gates of Prague. Its ruler, Charles IV (1316–1378), king of Bohemia and Holy Roman Emperor, bemused and surely uncomprehending, granted admission. But the men bearing the new ideas soon departed, disappointed at their failure to win Charles to their grand designs. Disappointed perhaps, but they were also admired and imitated; although only superficially understood or misunderstood altogether, they left behind an indelible impression. The encounter might have proved to be a mere episode, isolated and without consequence, but the future was preparing an important role for the new ideas. Once Charles had opened the gate, there was no closing it.

The first to knock was Cola di Rienzo (1313–1354), commonly known as Rienzi. He was one of those half patriotic, half opportunistic popular leaders hurled into power on a wave of Roman anarchy, only to drown in it. Rienzi had drunk the heady waters of Roman antiquity at the source, one of the first to do so. Perhaps because he was only the son of a Roman innkeeper, Rienzi found it expedient to claim to Charles IV that he had been fathered by Henry VII, Charles's grandfather and the emperor in whom the great Dante had once placed his hopes for Italy. This claim made Rienzi twice imperial: Roman-born and the son of an emperor. Soon after Rienzi's birth his mother died, and his innkeeper father sent him to relatives in the countryside around Anagni to be raised. Rienzi thus grew to manhood in the shadow of the fortress that had humiliated the papacy in the person of Boniface VIII (1217–1303), given victory to the Roman barons, driven the pope to Avignon, and plunged Rome into feudal anarchy, that collapse of restraining authority which the barons relished and required for their petty tyrannies. Upon his father's death, the impressionable young man returned to Rome. There he saw all about him the ruins of the ancient city. He began to read the ancient historians, especially Livy, or what was then known of his work. He collected carved gems, those that had engraved upon them the images of ancient Roman patriots and leaders such as Scipio and Caesar. Rienzi studied the crumbling inscriptions, generally ignored, on the buildings, arches, and columns of Rome that spoke to him of the lost grandeur of antiquity. He was indeed later acknowledged as the expert at deciphering the obscure inscriptions.

His splendid oratory during an embassy to the pope in Avignon won Rienzi an office in the municipal government of Rome (1344). For three years he exploited his office to draw attention to himself. He staged the unveiling of a newly discovered Roman ruin to remind the people of past glories. He held orations before the mob, terrifying them with the prospects of the end of the world in the form of a huge picture painted for the occasion on the outside walls of the Roman Senate. Under papal protection he harangued the marauding nobles with impunity. And in secret he organized an elaborate conspiracy.

On the feast of Pentecost, May 19, 1347, Rienzi heard the mass of the Holy Spirit in the Church of Sant' Angelo in Pescheria. The senatorial militia under Stefano Colonna, the mightiest of the barons, had left the city for Corneto to convoy a shipment of grain back to Rome. Rienzi met with his fellow

conspirators, sent heralds throughout the city to summon the
populace to the Capitol, and made his way there himself. Before
a vast crowd Rienzi proclaimed the restoration of the Roman
Republic. The mob ratified the proclamation with frenzied approval and accepted Rienzi as dictator with unlimited political
powers. Rienzi kept the papal vicar, Raimondo Orvieto, at his
side, to give the impression, largely genuine, that the revolution
enjoyed ecclesiastical approval.

Rienzi called a general Italian parliament to Rome. Many
of the municipalities, particularly those with democratic governments, heeded his call. He clearly aimed at unifying his tragically
fragmented country and giving a new birth to Roman glory. But
he had many and powerful enemies. The barons trembled in
rage and terror at his summary justice, which reached inside
their very houses. In Rome their plots and ambushes consistently
met failure. In Avignon, however, things were different.

Even as enthusiasm waned—and it was bound to—Rienzi retained popular support. Perhaps to rekindle enthusiasm or to act
out his dreams of antiquity, Rienzi performed spectacular ceremonies. He bathed in the baptismal font in which, as legend had
it, the pope had baptized Constantine, curing him of leprosy,
and receiving from the emperor as a mark of his gratitude the
Donation of Constantine, the notorious forgery by which the
popes claimed political sovereignty in the West. On that occasion
Rienzi styled himself Knight of the Holy Spirit and first instructed the German rivals for the empire—which included
Charles IV—to submit to the judgment of the people of Rome.
Two weeks later he assumed the ancient Roman title Tribune,
carried by the protector of the plebeians, and again summoned
the Germans to his tribunal.

These and similar extravagances played into the hands of
the barons who were undermining Rienzi's position in Avignon.
He had maneuvered the timid papal vicar into the background.
Pope Clement VI, who had launched Rienzi on his public career,
began to see that Rienzi's patriotic visions threatened papal sovereignty in Italy. Clement flung charges of heresy and usurpation
at Rienzi (December 3, 1347)—charges that did less to threaten

Rienzi's authority among the people than to erode his self-confidence and sense of mission. Rienzi became indecisive. When his worst enemies fell into his hands, he hesitated. They were not executed, though Rienzi felt they richly deserved such punishment, but merely humiliated and released, only to become more resentful and dangerous. When an adventurer with a handful of soldiers stormed his quarters (December 15, 1347) Rienzi was convinced that it was the Roman mob. He fled to the Castell Sant' Angelo, the refuge of many a deposed Roman despot. From there he vanished into the mountains amidst a company of visionary hermits. His stunned supporters watched Rome revert to anarchy. The Black Death soon followed, then a series of earthquakes. And Rienzi revitalized his shattered spirits on the words of mystics and prophets.

These visionary hermits had withdrawn from the world to await the apocalyptic events of the final days. They brooded over the teachings of Joachim of Fiore (ca. 1135–1202), or a confused version of them that foresaw a total reform of Christendom by a fabled monarch, the "just and peaceful king" (*rex iustus et pacificus*). Their leader, Fra Angelo, persuaded Rienzi that Charles fit the prophecy. Thus persuaded, Rienzi searched him out, the king he had so recently and insultingly commanded to Rome.

At every step of his development Rienzi combined two strains of revival, rebirth, renaissance. The one arose out of the ruins of classical antiquity and expected a revival of that golden age. The other arose at the outer fringes of medieval piety and anticipated a universal spiritual rebirth. Himself reborn among the hermits, Rienzi journeyed quietly to Prague. Charles received him honorably and thrice gave him audience. Rienzi delivered an impassioned oration before the court, naming Charles as the chosen emperor, the monarch of prophecy destined to restore the grandeur of Rome and to lead in the final days with a just and peaceful reign. He placed before the king a vision of imperial Rome to remind Charles of the dignity he would wear and the duties attached to it by history.

But Charles was not to be won over. One aspect of the

Italian Renaissance, the treachery and ruthlessness of Italian city politics, thoroughly disenchanted Charles. As a very young man he had gained his first political experience in Italy. Charles's frivolous father, John of Luxemburg, King of Bohemia, preferred the joust to the duties of government and assigned to his adolescent son the pacification of the north Italian cities. Charles extricated himself from the morass of Italian politics only after he had narrowly escaped poisoning. Members of his retinue died in agony, while he was spared by the sheer chance of a communion fast. Charles used some trickery of his own when he had Rienzi commit his speeches to writing and then promptly placed him under arrest.

Rienzi had become an explosive commodity. Clement VI demanded his extradition to Avignon. Charles was negotiating his Roman coronation with the very reluctant pope and had no intention of giving away such a valuable knight, at least not without some sort of concession. Rienzi represented little more than a useful political accident to Charles, but the court seemed dazzled by this revolutionary and his brilliant rhetoric. The imperial chancellor, Johannes von Neumarkt, initiated a friendly correspondence with the imprisoned Rienzi and collected everything he could find of Rienzi's writings. Archbishop Ernest of Prague also took up a correspondence, but more cautiously than Neumarkt. Courageously Rienzi persisted in his pleas to Charles, detailing his program for the great rebirth and Charles's crucial role in it. His daring and persuasiveness caused his friends at court to worry for his safety in Prague, even while captive. And so the Archbishop had him removed to his fortress at Raudnitz on the Elbe. Here Rienzi grew discouraged, prepared his will, and wrote many letters—which passed through the hands of the admiring chancellor. The elegance of Rienzi's style conquered Prague as his visionary policies never could. Charles himself had Rienzi's style employed in a response to an emotional appeal from Rienzi's friend, the first Renaissance man of letters, Francesco Petrarca (1304–1374).

Rienzi's end was no less dramatic than his earlier career. Charles eventually surrendered him to Avignon. A new pope,

Innocent VI, more interested in pacifying Rome than in punishing Rienzi, sent him to govern the city. On the anniversary of the declaration of his knighthood (August 1, 1354), he entered Rome triumphantly. The last extant letter from his hands enthusiastically congratulates Charles on the start of his Roman journey and the forthcoming imperial coronation in the city of the Caesars. Within a week of the letter (October 8) Rienzi was murdered by an agent of the Colonna family, his corpse exposed to public ridicule, then burned on dry thistles, the ashes scattered to the winds.

At the beginning of Rienzi's public life, during his embassy to Avignon (1343–1344), he became acquainted with the singer of the praises of Laura, the sonneteer, the most famous scholar and antiquary of his time, Petrarch. Their common love for the ancients and their common sorrow at the desolation of Rome made them fast friends. Petrarch applauded Rienzi's victories and lamented his defeats. They were of one mind on the fate of Italy. When Petrarch took up contact with the imperial court, it was wholly in the spirit of Rienzi's fire-breathing patriotism, and he was identically committed to the rebirth of ancient grandeur. Like Rienzi, Petrarch thrust the imperial past before Charles as a glorious model and a damning reproach.

The full force of historical and legal tradition made the medieval German emperor the successor of the Caesars. Charles understood that perfectly. He was acutely sensitive to the aura of his office, the importance of ritual and splendor, the countless intangibles that constitute majesty. He made them servants, not masters, of his policy. Petrarch's appeals could never convince Charles to sacrifice his state for an impossible dream, but they did provide him with an opportunity to borrow the prestige of genius. Petrarch, then at the height of his fame, had no serious rival in all of Europe as the prince of poets and scholars. Charles had already brought to Prague the best jurists, architects, theologians, artists, and physicians he could find for his new university (1348) and the construction of his new cathedral. To attract Petrarch to Prague would have crowned Charles's cultural politics with glory.

Charles's letter of response to Petrarch politely declines the honor of pacifying Italy but does so wholly in humanistic style, replete with references to classical antiquity. The letter marks a watershed. Henceforth Charles's correspondence and that of the imperial chancellery would gradually abandon medieval Latin and begin to follow the new rhetoric of the Italian humanists. Charles's chancellor, Johannes von Neumarkt, whose job was the conduct of the epistolary business of the empire, doubtless determined the adoption of the new style. He engaged Petrarch in correspondence, as he had Rienzi, and included select letters from both correspondences in his official book of models for letter writing, the *Summa Cancellariae*. It survives in some nineteen manuscripts from all over Germany and moved to Austria with the imperial chancellery when the Hapsburgs succeeded to the empire in the next century. As though the authority of the imperial chancellery would not be enough to guarantee the influence of the new style, Neumarkt sponsored a school that taught it to future civil servants.

Officials conducted their business not only in Latin, but also in the various vernaculars of the empire, including German. Neumarkt himself had an obvious interest in the vernacular. The poems of Heinrich von Meissen, called *Frauenlob* (ca. 1250–1318), appear among Neumarkt's writings. He translated a series of religious works into a form of German that can be read today, without special philological training, by any modern German speaker. At a time when the standard literary form of the language was still strictly medieval, Neumarkt was writing the earliest form of modern German. This language was clearly taught in his school and, within a generation, produced a small masterpiece in *Der Ackermann aus Böhmen* (The Plowman from Bohemia).

Neumarkt's language reforms were no small accomplishment. Even Petrarch noted the Latin results and cordially commended the chancellor for restoring the ancient dignity of the official imperial correspondence. Petrarch's letters to the chancellor consistently demonstrate pleasure that the New Learning has found admirers in the barbaric north. Neumarkt was not alone in his admiration. He shared news about Petrarch with teachers in the city. Empress Anna exchanged letters with the master. The fashion spread eastward to the court of Jost of Moravia, who maintained active personal contact with the first generation of Petrarch's pupils.

Personal contact between Petrarch and the court had to await Charles's Roman journey. Some two months after the fall of Rienzi, Charles reached Mantua and there he received Petrarch (December 15, 1354). The two enjoyed conversation long into the night. Charles invited Petrarch to attend his coronation in Rome as an honored guest and to teach him the meaning of antiquity. Petrarch was, despite himself, enormously flattered by the imperial attentions. A few weeks later in Milan the two met again. Charles, fresh from his coronation with the Iron Crown of the Lombards (January 6, 1355), renewed his invitation. Petrarch had to refuse for political reasons, but accompanied the court for fifty miles past the walls of the city of Piacenza.

On this same journey, at Pisa, Charles met the most famous jurist of the age, Bartolo Sassoferrato (1314–1357), named him to his court, invited him to his table, and gave his family a coat-of-arms. Roman law, which Sassoferrato represented at its most sophisticated, slowly took over the German courts, but the story of its reception belongs to the fifteenth and sixteenth centuries. Within memory of his meeting with Sassoferrato, Charles promulgated the Golden Bull (December 25, 1356), which provided the empire with a constitution, regulated imperial elections, fixed the electors in their privileges, and helped shape German history until the dissolution of the empire in 1806. The Italian jurist may or may not have influenced its composition directly, but the Golden Bull does cite Roman law (chapter 24) and reflects the authority of the Italian law schools, which educated so many northern jurists.

In the next years Charles repeatedly offered Petrarch the hospitality of Prague and seriously hoped he would settle permanently in the court. In July of 1356, Petrarch appeared in Prague on a diplomatic mission for the Visconti of Milan. The mission failed, but Petrarch won even more admirers in Charles's capital, particularly the Archbishop. Archbishop Ernest was one of the northern jurists educated in the Italian schools. He had spent some fourteen years in Italy before returning to Prague as its first archbishop.

The city did have certain attractions. For one, the climate was healthy. The Black Death that devastated the rest of Europe largely bypassed Prague. Charles's cultural policies had already populated Prague with Petrarch's countrymen, among them the apothecary Angelo of Florence, who gave Prague the first botanical garden in the north. The flourishing university had numerous professors called from Italy. Charles supported it every way he could. He placed students and professors under his special protection and exempted them from tolls and customs whenever they traveled through his realm. Toward the end of his life there were thousands of students in Prague. When a collection of books came on the market and to Charles's attention, he bought it and donated it to the university.

In addition to the university, Charles undertook two other major building projects to give lasting evidence of the grandeur of his reign: the cathedral of Prague to house the relics of Saint Wenzel (good King Wenceslas) and the massive fortress at Karlstein to house the royal and imperial regalia. His patronage drew artists and artisans of great craftsmanship to Prague. The sculpture in the cathedral, the murals there and at Karlstein, the miniatures in the ceremonial manuscripts of the time, the paintings of the Bohemian school, now dispersed across Europe (the best collection is at the Dahlem Museum in West Berlin)—all this suggests that Petrarch would not have been at a loss for talented company. Charles had brought the pope's architect, Mathias of Arras, from Avignon to lay the foundations of the cathedral and design the Karlstein fortress. The Parler brothers from Swabia came to finish the task. Charles commissioned no fewer than five historians to uncover the past of his kingdom. One of them was the renowned Italian traveler Giovanni Marignola, just returned from China and Ceylon. Charles himself tried his hand at history by writing a political autobiography of his young years, particularly the bitter lessons of his Italian experience.

This and much more indicates a considerable cultural flowering at the time of Charles IV. Not all of it was connected to Italy, not all of it was housed in Prague, not all of it was Charles's doing. General medical and scientific works of the Middle Ages became available in German translation, as did minor works from classical antiquity and political tracts of some importance. The most modern political thinkers of the time, Marsilius of Padua (ca. 1275–1343) and William of Ockham (ca. 1290–1349) —who proclaimed such revolutionary doctrines as the sovereignty of the people and the legitimacy of tyrannicide—worked and died in Munich at the court of Charles's rival, Louis the Bavarian (ca. 1278–1347). The writing of history in German, as opposed to Latin, arose far from Prague, in the western cities, toward whose independence and power Charles was not favorably disposed. Parenthetically, German city chronicles indicate that Cola di Rienzo's appeal was general and extended well beyond the imperial court. Other universities began to rival that of Prague: Vienna (1365), Heidelberg (1386), Cologne (1388), Erfurt (1392). The most distinguished German among the scholars at the University of Paris, Heinrich von Langenstein (1323–1397), moved to Vienna to reorganize the university there, even though he also had an offer from Prague.

With this diffusion the Germans built a hedge against the vicissitudes of history. The unforeseeable future was to condemn the Prague flowering, splendid as it was, to wither under a storm of events. As Charles approached the end of his reign, a quiet monk became Pope Gregory XI. He fulfilled the dreams of Italian patriots by returning the papacy to the city of Peter. He died there (March 27, 1378). When Charles died some months later (November 29), there was one pope in Rome and one in Avignon. The Great Schism (1378–1415) was on. The disastrous division of Christendom was only compounded in the empire by Charles's incompetent son and successor, Wenzel (bad King Wenceslas). The honored tradition of fiery preaching from the pulpit of the Tyn Church in Prague suddenly exploded as Jan Hus voiced a violent Bohemian rejection of German cultural and political hegemony. Within fifty years of Charles's death Prague had turned into a Czech city that could not serve as capital of a transnational empire, let alone of a German nation. What had begun in Prague, the German reception of Italian humanism, scattered to the winds. It might have vanished without a trace had Germany depended upon a single cultural center so cosmopolitan as to make the competition provincial. When the seeds sowed at Prague struck lasting roots in Germany, they did so at various courts (Hapsburg, the Palatinate), universities (Heidelberg, Vienna, Ingolstadt), monasteries (Sponheim, Maria Laach), and, above all, in the cities (Nürnberg, Augsburg, Strassburg, Basel, Breslau). The roots spread so wide and went so deep that even the cataclysms of the Reformation and Counterreformation could not shake the tree.

The tree was Italian in ancestry. The climate of Germany's cultural history, of course, gave it a distinct shape. The revival of classical antiquity comfortably suited the essential patriotic and ethical aspirations of the Italian humanists. This would not do for the Germans. The superior airs of certain Italians (among them Enea Silvio Piccolomini, later to become Pope Pius II, and Antonio Campano, papal diplomat and friend of Enea Silvio) so annoyed many Germans (including the imperial chancellor Gregor von Heimburg, an enemy of Enea Silvio, and the humanist publicists and historians Jacob Wimpheling and Franciscus Irenicus) that they reacted with a patriotism of their own, almost unprecedented and, until then, thoroughly uncharacteristic of the Germans. The result was an intense investigation of the German national past, an attempt to revive an alternative antiquity as a rival to Rome. The spiritual needs of the Italians, despite such puritanical outbursts as the fanatical monk Savonarola (1452–1498) visited on Florence, seemed generally satisfied by the Roman Church, while the Italian humanists subtly reinterpreted Christian ethics on the model of the good man as they saw him in classical antiquity. To many Germans (e.g., Ulrich von Hutten) the Roman Church had become an Italian Church, hostile and subversive. And the Italian humanist model of the good man, with its stress on the active life and involvement in the affairs of state, proved to be profoundly alien to German sensibilities, which inclined toward the private, personal, and contemplative. The northern response to this ethic has acquired the name "Christian Humanism" to distinguish it from the Italian prototype.

But none of these seemed to satisfy the spiritual needs of the Germans. With the Reformation, another attempt was made to revive an alternative antiquity, primitive Christianity, as a rival to Rome. The aspect of revival displays itself distinctly in the radical Reformation. But even the middle-of-the-road reformers (Melanchthon, Luther's closest collaborator, and Mathias Flacius Illyricus, author of the *Magdeburg Centuries*, the pioneering work of Protestant historiography) sought in history noble models they genuinely believed they were reviving.

How can anything as ostentatiously German as national history and the Reformation possibly have Italian antecedents? Strip away the German surface and one finds the characteristic veneration of the past, the will to rescue it from oblivion, the compulsion to reach back to the sources, the gradual development from enthusiastic misinterpretation of the past to the threshold of critical understanding. And there is more to demonstrate the closeness of the relationship. Even classical antiquity —as unserviceable as it was for German patriotism and as alien to the Germans' sense of Christian values—retained in Italy and Germany both, a towering authority as the measure of civilization. In that role it haunted Germany well into modern times. And then the two cultures shared one great portal that opened on the past: the love of language. Language in all its aspects, as art and science, as poetry, eloquence, and style preoccupied the thinkers regardless of differences in geography. The sciences of language distinguished between the ancient and the modern, the true and the false, the authentic and the interpolated, whether in classical or biblical texts. These same studies recognized that time and place determined the word and that the word revealed time and place—all of this long before similar insights passed on to other fields of human learning.

The study of language, the love of the word, philology, survived the Renaissance to become an intellectual force as powerful and formative as its predecessor, theology, and its heirs apparent, science and technology. From the reform of the schools by Luther's humanist, Melanchthon, and by the Jesuits in Catholic Germany, to the end of the nineteenth century, perhaps even until a generation or two ago, philology gave education its form and substance. The love of the word may not have been the most important message of Italian humanism, but it was the most long-lived. When the Renaissance was still an infant, its eloquence was as much as a few open-minded courtiers in Prague could grasp. Grasp it they did and then grafted it onto the German heritage, there to flourish in all adversity down to our own century.

Selected Bibliography

PRIMARY SOURCES

Bishop, Morris, transl. *Letters from Petrarch*. Bloomington: Indiana University Press, 1966.

Blaschka, Anton, transl. *Kaiser Karl IV. Jugendleben und St. Wenzels-Legende*. In *Geschichtsschreiber der deutschen Vorzeit*, Dritte Gesamtausgabe, 83. Weimar: Böhlau, 1956.

Burdach, Konrad, ed. *Aus Petrarcas ältestem deutschen Schülerkreis*. In *Vom Mittelalter zur Reformation*, 4. Berlin: Weidmann, 1929.

———. *Briefwechsel des Cola di Rienzo*. In *Vom Mittelalter zur Reformation*, 2. Berlin: Weidmann, 1912–31.

———. *Vom Mittelalter zur Reformation*. 11 vols. in 17. Berlin: Weidmann, 1893–1939.

Cosenza, Mario E. *Francesco Petrarca and the Revolution of Cola di Rienzo*. Chicago: University of Chicago Press, 1913. (Contains English translations of texts throughout.)

Jarrett, Bede. *The Emperor Charles IV*. New York: Sheed and Ward, 1935. (Contains abridged English translation of Charles's autobiography, pp. 33–68.)

Klapper, Joseph. *Johann von Neumarkt, Bischof und Hofkanzler: Re-*

ligiöse Frührenaissance in Böhmen zur Zeit Kaiser Karls IV. In *Erfurter theologische Studien,* 17. Leipzig: St. Benno, 1964. (Contains texts, pp. 54–166.)

Müller, Konrad, ed. *Die Goldene Bulle Kaiser Karls IV. 1356.* In *Quellen zur neueren Geschichte,* 25. Bern: Lang, 1970.

Piur, Paul, ed. *Petrarcas Briefwechsel mit deutschen Zeitgenossen.* In *Vom Mittelalter zur Reformation,* 7. Berlin: Weidmann, 1933.

Voigt, Klaus, transl. *Italienische Berichte aus dem spätmittelalterlichen Deutschland: Von Francesco Petrarca zu Andrea de' Franceschi (1333–1492).* In *Kieler Historische Studien,* 17. Stuttgart: Klett, 1973.

Zacour, Norman P., transl. *Petrarch's Book without a Name: A Translation of the Liber sine Nomine.* Toronto: Pontifical Institute, 1973.

SECONDARY SOURCES

Borchardt, Frank L. *German Antiquity in Renaissance Myth.* Baltimore: The Johns Hopkins Press, 1971.

———. "Petrarch: The German Connection," in *Francis Petrarch Six Centuries Later: A Symposium,* Aldo Scaglione, ed. Chapel Hill: N.C. Studies in Romance Langs., 3, 1975, pp. 418–31.

Burdach, Konrad. *Reformation, Renaissance, Humanismus: Zwei Abhandlungen über die Grundlage moderner Bildung und Sprachkunst.* 3rd ed. Darmstadt: Wissenschaftliche Buchgesellschaft, 1963.

———. *Vorspiel: Gesammelte Schriften zur Geschichte des deutschen Geistes,* vol. 1, pt. 2: *Reformation und Renaissance.* In *Deutsche Vierteljahrsschrift für Literaturwissenschaft und Geistesgeschichte,* Buchreihe, 2. Halle: Niemeyer, 1925.

Friedjung, Heinrich. *Kaiser Karl IV. und sein Antheil am geistigen Leben seiner Zeit.* Vienna: Braumüller, 1876.

Gregorovius, Ferdinand. *Geschichte der Stadt Rom im Mittelalter.* 3 vols. 1953–57; rpt. Darmstadt: Wissenschaftliche Buchgesellschaft, 1963. (Gregorovius's masterpiece, originally published 1859–70, is divided into books, of which the eleventh treats Petrarch and Rienzi.)

Gray, Hanna H. "Renaissance Humanism: The Pursuit of Eloquence." *Journal of the History of Ideas,* 24 (1963), pp. 497–514.

Irmscher, Johannes, ed. *Renaissance und Humanismus in Mittel- und Osteuropa: Eine Sammlung von Materialien.* 2 vols. In Deutsche Akademie der Wissenchaften, Sektion für Altertumswissenschaft, *Schriften,* 32. Berlin: Akademie, 1962.

Joachimsen, Paul. *Vom Mittelalter zur Reformation*. Reihe Libelli, 50. Darmstadt: Wissenschaftliche Buchgesellschaft, 1959. Rpt. from *Historische Vierteljahrschrift*, 20 (1920–21), 426–70. (Most important for an alternative opinion of the Prague Renaissance. Joachimsen launches a many-sided attack on Burdach, with whose perspective my contribution to this volume conforms.)

Piur, Paul. *Cola di Rienzo: Darstellung seines Lebens und seines Geistes.* Vienna: Seidel, 1931.

Wilkins, Ernest Hatch. *Life of Petrarch*. Chicago: University of Chicago Press, 1961.

Winter, Eduard. *Frühhumanismus: Seine Entwicklung in Böhmen*. In Deutsche Historiker-Gesellschaft, *Beiträge zur Geschichte des religiösen und wissenschaftlichen Denkens*, 3. Berlin: Akademie, 1964.

BACKGROUND MATERIALS AND BIBLIOGRAPHIES

Andreas, Willi. *Deutschland vor der Reformation: Eine Zeitwende*. 4th ed. Stuttgart: Deutsche Verlags-Anstalt, 1943.

Burger, Heinz-Otto. *Renaissance, Humanismus, Reformation: Deutsche Literatur im europäischen Kontext*. In *Frankfurter Beiträge zur Germanistik*, 7. Bad Homburg: Gehlen, 1969.

Engel, James E. *Renaissance, Humanismus, Reformation*. In *Handbuch der deutschen Literaturgeschichte*, Zweite Abteilung, Bibilographien, 4. Bern: Francke, 1969.

Jantz, Harold. "German Renaissance Literature." *MLN*, 81 (1966), 398–436.

Jones, George F. *Spätes Mittelalter, 1300–1450*. In *Handbuch der deutschen Literaturgeschichte*, Zweite Abteilung, Bibliographien, 4. Bern: Francke, 1971.

Lorenz, Ottokar. *Deutschlands Geschichtsquellen im Mittelalter seit der Mitte des dreizehnten Jahrhunderts*. 3rd ed. 2 vols. 1886–87; rpt. Graz: Akademische Druck- und Verlagsanstalt, 1966.

Rupprich, Hans. *Vom späten Mittelalter bis zum Barock*. 2 vols. In *Geschichte der deutschen Literatur*, 4. Munich: Beck, 1970–73.

———. *Das Wiener Schrifttum des ausgehenden Mittelalters*, Österreichische Akademie der Wissenschaften, philosophisch-historische Klasse, *Sitzungsberichte*, 228, Abhandlung, 5. Vienna: Rohrer, 1954.

Stammler, Wolfgang. *Die deutsche Dichtung von der Mystik zum Barock*. 2nd ed. In *Epochen der deutschen Literatur*, 2, 1. Stuttgart: Metzler, 1950.

Strauss, Gerald, ed. *Pre-Reformation Germany.* New York: Harper and Row, 1972.

Taylor, Archer. *Problems in German Literary History of the Fifteenth and Sixteenth Centuries.* In Modern Language Association of America, General Series, 7. 1939; rpt. New York: Kraus, 1966.

——. *Renaissance Guides to Books: An Inventory and Some Conclusions.* Berkeley and Los Angeles: University of California Press, 1945.

Wuttke, Dieter. *Deutsche Germanistik und Renaissance-Forschung.* In *Respublica Literaria,* 3. Bad Homburg: Gehlen, 1968.

2

The Plowman from Bohemia

Antonín Hrubý

The reader who confronts *The Plowman from Bohemia* for the first time can hardly fail to notice the formal, poetic, and linguistic beauty of the work. If he studies the intellectual wealth of this meditation on death with a background of personal experience and sensitivity, he will understand why this debate between man and Death has been called "the best and most noteworthy example of poetic prose before Goethe's *Werther*."

The Plowman must have been popular during the fifteenth and sixteenth centuries—whether because of its form or its engaging content—since no fewer than sixteen manuscripts and seventeen old printed editions have been preserved from this period. Around the middle of the eighteenth century Johann Christoph Gottsched reclaimed *The Plowman* for literary criticism, and at the beginning of our own century, Burdach (see bibliography), who recognized the debate as the source of earlier Bohemian humanism, spoke of it as the oldest example of the new humanistic spirit in Germany. In fact, Latin and German stylistic traditions join forces to produce the striking formal qual-

ities as well as the unique linguistic beauty of this short work; its
ideas and content reflect centuries of Jewish, Arabic, and Christian speculation on the nature of God, and its ideal of humanity
breathes a spirit of human dignity that one does not find in such
concentration until the early Renaissance. *The Plowman* can
thus correctly be seen as heir of the entire Western cultural tradition.

To a certain extent, the popularity of *The Plowman* also
derives from its subject: the theme of death has always occupied
mankind. Clear evidence of the fascination that death has held
for man is provided by the honoring of the dead among primitive peoples as well as by the consecration of graves or magic
rituals in more civilized societies, by the myths of Osiris or Hel as
well as by the philosophies of Plato, Augustine, or Heidegger.
Death is in a special sense a topic of philosophical inquiry, since
man, when confronted with the incomprehensible reality of
death, necessarily feels compelled to question his relationship to
God, the nature of time and eternity, the meaning of existence
and of his own life.

Moreover, the depiction of death in art and literature has
been a recurring theme throughout the history of Western civilization. And the iconography of death has varied greatly. In
Greece death was represented as a charming youth, whereas
modern times prefer the macabre skeleton. The Middle Ages
represented death as a corpse, but also as judge, hunter, reaper,
grave-digger, even as king and minstrel. Images of death are to be
found in private prayer-books and on playing cards as well as on
monumental frescoes; dances of death and portrayals of the
apocalyptic triumph of death can be found not only in the ceme-
teries and churches of Paris, Basel, Lübeck, Pisa, or Clusone, but
also in the Palazzo Sclafani in Palermo and the imperial castle
near Prague. Dürer's and Holbein's visions of death are just as
present to modern consciousness as Picasso's *Guernica*. The
former present death as part of the human situation; the latter,
however, presents a human crime. Boccaccio's portrayal of the
pestilence in Florence moves us no less immediately than the
description of Nana's corpse in Zola's famous novel or Albert

Camus's chronicle of the plague. The concept of death in Chau-
cer's *Pardoner's Tale* is just as relevant to us as the depiction of
disintegration and death in *Death in Venice*. For human life is
nothing but a constant meditation on death, a *commentatio
mortis*.

The topic of death was especially alive in the Middle Ages,
for all of earthly human life was then understood as a preparation for true life in eternity. The descendants of Adam, who was
driven out of Paradise and burdened with original sin and personal guilt, remain forever in danger of spiritual death as long as
they make their way through the miseries of the world. The
death of the body completes the *status viatoris*, the return to
one's origin. With God's grace man is reborn and given the hope
of immortality and a return to the eternal homeland of earthly
paradise. This doctrine, first found in the writings of the church
fathers, and later of the Scholastics, subsequently found expression in monastic poetry and finally was carried over by preachers
and reformers into the popular genres of vernacular literatures.

In the Middle Ages the topic of death is treated in various
verse and prose forms—as philosophical treatise, topic for the
school debate, poem, letter, dialogue, drama, and disputation.
The oldest examples of monastic poetry dealing with the subject
of death are the *Memento mori*, written by the Hirsau monk
Notker around 1070, the *Erinnerung an den Tod* (ca. 1160)
written by the lay brother Heinrich of the monastery at Melk,
and the French *Vers de la mort*, written a quarter of a century
later by the Cistercian Hélinant de Froidmont. These poems
warn of the wicked *mundus* that tricks us out of salvation, or
they condemn the corruption of the higher classes, threatening
their readers with death, the inexorable leveler. In *Vers de la
mort* death is even portrayed as God's messenger to Hélinant's
aristocratic friends.

In the thirteenth century numerous dialogues between man
and death were born of the ascetic spirit and monastic imagination of the times. Among these dialogues is a short poem,
Tractatus de crudelitate mortis (Treatise on the Cruelty of
Death) as well as the Latin treatise of Pope Innocent III on the

misery of human existence, composed shortly before 1298 and, judging from the many preserved manuscripts and the printed copy of 1575, widely read throughout the Renaissance. Because of its pessimistic disdain for the world, Innocent's treatise became known as *De contemptu mundi*. Additional examples of literature dealing with death are offered by the dances of death beginning in the fourteenth century. These pieces reached a wider audience than the earlier monastic literature, as they were eventually printed in the vernacular and illustrated with wood cuts.

Though all these works were important in one way or another as precursors to *The Plowman*, they are now familiar only to specialists, whereas *The Plowman* has been translated into many languages and has achieved the status of world literature. We must therefore seek the reason for this difference between *The Plowman* and its predecessors in the manner in which its author treats his subject matter and not in the subject itself.

Often the word "form" is understood as meaning external form alone. In the case of *The Plowman* the internal form (or structure) requires particular attention; for example, the specific formulation of the problem of mortality, the poet's views on the relationships between life, love, suffering, loyalty, and human worth, or his thoughts on the relationship of justice and God, order in the world, and the justification of death. In *The Plowman*, as in every true work of art, the form is an expression of the underlying idea, so that its external characteristics are a reflection of its inner meaning.

The fact that Johannes of Teplá (also known as Johannes von Saaz), generally accepted as the author of *The Plowman*, emphasized in a dedicatory letter to his friend Peter Rothirsch of Prague the significance of stylistic devices and rhetorical figures, does not imply that the poet was not interested in the philosophical content of his work. The prose debate, however, is neither a mere stylistic exercise, as a number of recent critics claim, nor simply a philosophical treatise, as Hübner (see bibliography) has correctly pointed out. It is, rather, true poetry. Philosophical poetry, to be sure, in the truest sense of the word, since *The Plowman* is concerned with a philosophical subject par excellence, with man's "inescapable fate, death," to cite the dedicatory letter itself. And like every artist, the author so orders his material that even the discrete elements of his poetry are imbued with special meaning and are able to express matters of emotional and existential experience far exceeding the limits of everyday language.

The Plowman was written at the beginning of the fifteenth century at a time when the foundations of the medieval world based on the Augustinian *Weltanschauung* were crumbling. Twelfth- and thirteenth-century Scholastic thought experienced the powerful influence of Hellenistic, Arabic, and Aristotelian philosophy, all of which Thomas Aquinas attempted to incorporate into the Christian system of thought. But the new philosophy led nevertheless to ideas that were condemned in 1277 in Paris, as, for example, the doctrine that the world was not created by God, and therefore God did not possess the power to stop the eternal revolution of heavenly bodies or the permanent transformation of earthly phenomena. Serious political and spiritual crises threatened the authority of the church. The fourteenth century was familiar with simony and the outrageous luxury of the princes of the church; one witnessed the Babylonian captivity of the papacy (as Petrarch called it), the excommunication of the emperor, the declaration of the pope as heretic and anti-Christ, and finally, the schism that led to the establishment of two and even three opposing popes.

The people questioned religious truths and feared damnation; their doubts were only increased by the Black Death and many other outbreaks of pestilence. Flagellants wandered through Europe and pogroms against the Jews were instigated. Waldensians, Beghards, Lollards, and other heretic sects appeared everywhere. Such radical thinkers as William of Ockham and John Wyclif in England and Matthias of Janov, a precursor of Jan Hus, were writing; in Prague the reformers Konrad of Waldhausen, Milíč of Kroměříž, and Jan Hus were preaching. And the Hussite revolution broke out as a result of Hus's burning at the stake.

At the same time, a new spirit was awakening and a new

epoch was beginning. After the disintegration of knighthood, economic power and cultural activity gradually shifted to the patricians, and the prosperous commercial cities of Italy evolved into new political and cultural centers. In the midst of plenty, however, the ideal of poverty was preached, and Francis of Assisi once again became a model worthy of imitation. The demand of the times was for a religious and moral rebirth, a demand that the people's tribune, Cola di Rienzo,* extended to a political level as well. Poet-philosophers such as Dante, Petrarch, and Boccaccio formulated a new humanistic ideal which, under the steadily growing influence of the art and philosophy of antiquity, was to give rise to the Renaissance view of man.

The difficult question whether *The Plowman* belongs to the medieval world of ideas or whether the poet was influenced by the thoughts and artistic concepts of early humanism, cannot be answered unequivocally. Konrad Burdach (see bibliography), who saw signs of the new spirit in *The Plowman*, devoted much of his scholarship to identifying various humanistic features in the work. He pointed to the fact that the dynastic and European policies of the ruling Přemyslides brought Bohemia into contact with France, England, and Italy, and that close communication with Germany and the colonists, on the other hand, required the development of a standardized language for use in the chancelleries. Burdach asserted that this official language was later to develop into the standard form of written German. This official language began to evolve at the imperial chancellery in Prague with the early advent of Italian scribes who brought with them the Latin epistolary style and the art of rhetoric after the example of Pietro delle Vigne, chancellor under Frederick II.

Emperor Charles IV was in tune with European political and intellectual developments, having been brought up in Paris and having managed his father's urban estate in northern Italy for a brief period. Under Charles the Prague chancellery was headed by the enlightened John of Středa, more generally known

---

* See the articles by Frank L. Borchardt and Gerhart Hoffmeister in this volume.

as Johannes von Neumarkt. The imperial chancellor, like many other late medieval church magnates, was an open-minded intellectual, far ahead of his times in his private religious and artistic views. He was a master of Latin chancellery style, of ornamental prose, and of rhythmic sentence cadences. He quoted Dante in the original and was in contact, both personally and through correspondence, with various Italian humanists, including Petrarch and Cola di Rienzo, who even came to Prague. From Italy the chancellor brought examples of the new learning, and his translations of several of these documents—the pseudo-Augustinian *Liber soliloquiorum* (The Book of Soliloquies), the spurious Hieronymous letters, and the mystical Franciscan treatise *Stimulus amoris* (The Sting of Love)—became models of rhetorical German prose.

The main proof of the authorship of *The Plowman* by Johannes of Teplá is provided by the dedicatory letter to Peter Rothirsch, a citizen of Prague, found in the Freiburg *Formelbuch* (a collection of stylistic models) and by biographical information presented in several documents from Žatec (Saaz) and Prague. By reason of his profession, education, and literary activity Johannes of Teplá was well acquainted with the efforts of the chancellor and his circle. We find the signatures Iohannes de Tepla or Iohannes Henslini de Šitboř, and from the latter and other information we surmise that he was born around 1350 in Šitboř (Schüttwa), a village in the northern part of the Bohemian forest, where his father, Henslin, served as parson. It is impossible to determine with any certainty whether Johannes studied abroad or at the University of Prague, whether he ever earned the title of magister, or whether he taught at the Latin school in Tepl. It is certain, however, that by 1383 at the latest he was serving as city scribe and school rector in Žatec, and that he was named to the post of imperial notary some three years later. He was a prosperous member of the bourgeoisie whose income derived from commerce in spirits and from a butchery tax; he owned a house in Žatec, and later, another in Prague. In 1411 he moved to Prague, where he served as city scribe and notary of the New Town until his death. His widow, called Klara in early documents, is thought to be his second wife, since *The Plowman* speaks of a wife named Margaretha, who died August 1, 1400.

Johannes knew both national languages, as is made clear by occasional verses in Czech. He also wrote a short dedicatory stanza in German. With the exception of these few verses (poor ones at that), all of Johannes's other works are in Latin; *The Plowman* is thus—with its revolutionary transformation of German prose style and its unequaled force of language—an almost inexplicable and unique masterpiece in comparison with Johannes's other works.

Although Burdach generally supported his theory with adequate documentation, his theses and many of his conclusions have been repeatedly questioned, particularly in more recent scholarship. Philologists have shown that the development of the language proceeded in a much more complex manner than Burdach had assumed. Literary historians have especially questioned his conclusion that *The Plowman* represents the first work of German humanism.

This criticism is justifiable in so far as, stylistically and formally, *The Plowman*'s roots are to be found in medieval rhetoric and in the language of German mysticism and the German sermon. According to theme and use of motifs, it developed from courtly love poetry as well as from the poetry of the mastersingers. Scholastic, and especially Peripatetic, elements are in evidence. Quite clearly *The Plowman* continues the medieval tradition of philosophical speculation on death and the afterlife and belongs to the previously mentioned corpus of literature dealing with death. We may certainly say that all its stylistic mannerisms, all its form and genre features, its concepts and ideas, its motifs, topoi and themes, can be found in earlier works of the Middle Ages. Yet it would be wrong to consider *The Plowman* simply a medieval work, for it not only anticipates a future development but also carries a timeless message.

The Plowman consists of thirty-two chapters of dialogue between a man and Death; in the thirty-third God pronounces judgment, and in the thirty-fourth a man, identified in an acrostic as Johannes, asks for the salvation of his wife, whom he calls Margaretha. In the third chapter the man identifies himself as a professional scribe when he presents himself allegorically as a plowman who works with a plow made of "the clothing of a bird"—with a quill, that is. The man, whose wife has recently died, complains of the loss of his loved one and accuses Death, before God's tribunal, of being an unjust arbiter, an enemy of mankind and of God, of purposefully destroying the divine order of the world by allowing the evil to live and snatching away the just.

At first Death calmly and arrogantly rejects the accusations of the plaintiff; he warns the plowman of his invincible power and claims that, as the necessary ordering principle of universal mortality, Death's authority encompasses all of natural creation. According to Death, the plowman's complaint that Death is partial is also an unjust one, since he in fact takes away everyone without making any distinction, thus functioning as a just tool of God, who created him in Paradise after the Fall and granted him unlimited dominion over the world. This argument fills the first sixteen chapters.

In the second part of the work the man persists in his accusation that Death acted arbitrarily in taking away his virtuous wife; he demands compensation for his loss or advice on how to find comfort and overcome his suffering. But in this part Death takes off the mask of the calm philosopher and reveals himself rather as an abominable denier of life, a nihilistic reviler of man, who offers nothing but forgetfulness, resignation, contempt for the world, and scorn for art, knowledge, happiness, and all human values. The plaintiff rebels against Death's suggestions and defends life. Deeply moved, he praises the joys of the world, sport, marriage, feminine manners, and especially the dignity of man that derives from his likeness to God. Man is God's most sublime creation, argues the plowman, because he alone was given the noble gift of reason and intelligence. He is thus the only free creature possessing the capacity to comprehend the nature of God.

When Death becomes so carried away as to assert that life

was created only for the sake of dying, and finally even explains that Death will rule the world after all of mankind has perished, the plaintiff denies Death's claims emphatically and banishes Death to hell. In his last words the plowman expresses the conviction that all of Death's assertions are only lies designed to find fault with the perfection of God's creation and to convince the accuser of Death's mastery over life. He refers to Plato and other prophets who taught the principle of eternal return, claiming that the world, with its recurrent revolutions of the heavens and planets and the never-ending change of earthly phenomena, is eternal. The plowman thus insists on his original accusation and asks God to punish and destroy Death.

Death, too, perseveres in his conviction that the world has become vain, empty, futile, and fickle as a result of man's lust, avarice, and wickedness, and that the only way to do good and maintain a clear conscience is to withdraw entirely from this evil world. Death insists that God Himself should be the one to vindicate his counsel. But God's judgment favors neither the plowman nor Death, or rather, it favors both of them. The plowman, according to the judgment pronounced, complains and makes accusation because of the loss of his wife as if he had a hereditary claim to her. And Death boasts of sovereign authority, although both life and the power of death were granted only temporarily by God.

The debate is nevertheless, according to God, not without meaning, for the plaintiff's suffering forces him to make his complaint and the accusation forces Death to tell the truth. Thus God grants the plaintiff the honor and Death the victory, since each man is bound to give his life to death, his body to the earth, and his soul to God.

This ending leaves the reader with many unanswered questions, for, like other great poetic works, *The Plowman* presents multiple levels of meaning and does not lend itself to any single, rigid interpretation. Was Death telling the truth when he advised the plowman to turn away from the world's vanity and gain a clear conscience? Was his assertion correct that on account of the Fall all of life on earth is destined to suffer decay and destruction? The doctrine of original sin and the portrayal of the Judgment Day in the New Testament, especially in the second epistle of Saint Peter, would certainly allow for such an interpretation of the victory of death. Why, then, does the ending also state that the power of death is only a gift of God, recallable at any time? And who is the plaintiff? Does he represent mankind, as the plow allegory seems to suggest? Is he the reincarnation of Adam who, when driven out of Paradise, turned his plow to the cursed fields of the earth, doomed to eat bread earned from the sweat of his brow until he in turn was returned to the earth? Or is he the poet himself, as the acrostic of the concluding prayer and the encoded name of the city of Žatec in the fourth chapter lead one to believe?

If the poet himself is speaking, then his despairing defiance of Death would be the expression of the sorrowing heart of a widower, and the debate would represent the first piece of experiential poetry in the history of German literature. To whom, though, does God promise honor? To the poet, to the fictitious plaintiff, who defended life so well, or to man, for his capacity for suffering and his likeness to God? And how can God grant to man the right to make his accusation and still concede the victory to Death?

All possible answers to these questions have been suggested by critics, none of whom have been either completely wrong or wholly right. The poet surely wanted to leave the great questions of this dialogue open, since there is no simple answer to questions dealing with the justification of death, man's claim to immortality, the existence of suffering and of evil, and the demand for heavenly justice. Thus God's judgment remains a mystery in offering us no certain knowledge of man's fate at death. God does not promise to take away Death's power in order to reunite body and soul and return man as a whole to the lost homeland of an earthly paradise and to a state of immortality. But it was just this belief in the eschatological promises of the Bible, the return of Christ, the regaining of an earthly paradise, and the immortality of the just that caused the plowman to curse Death as an enemy of God and man. For whenever Death allows evil persons to prosper and takes the lives of the good who, like the plowman's wife, could plead for and earn the grace of God, he delays, indeed denies, the possibility for the return of a heavenly kingdom on earth.

This certainty of a personal immortality, and not the unquestionable eternity of the soul, was the plowman's main concern when he turned to God, requesting Him to destroy Death, the greatest scandal of creation. God, however, does not grant this certainty to human creatures plagued by existential doubts. In his judgment he asserts that it is God who will determine the fate of the soul and that Death will appear as victor in the temporal order of the world. And this incomprehensible paradox of creation finds its only justification, according to the judgment, in God's omnipotence, in which it finds its resolution. The God of *The Plowman* is thus the source of the power of creation and at the same time the unrevealed center of the world, *deus absconditus*, the hidden and incomprehensible God, whose goodness and justice will forever remain unknown to the suffering creature, man.

When Johannes of Teplá selected as organizational principle of the entire dialogue the polar interdependence of the irreconcilable opposites of life and death, transcience and immortality, he gave formal expression to his dialectic conception of the world. An observant reader will readily notice that the dialectic of accusation and justification of death, which thematically unifies the topoi and motifs of the first sixteen chapters, also appears in the first and the sixteenth chapters as opening and conclusion. When the plowman calls on God and all of creation to curse, punish, and condemn Death, and when Death, on the other hand, finally justifies his own existence on the grounds that he was created by God, the two chapters mirror one another. Their opposition exemplifies, in an abbreviated form, the contrapuntal thematic texture of the entire debate. The reader thereby feels compelled to recall the many themes of the work and tends to perceive simultaneously the polyphony of this circular, canonlike piece.

Attempts have been made to interpret the composition of

The Plowman according to its graphic form or number symbolism (as a cross, for example, or in terms of the thirty-three
years in Christ's life). Since the Middle Ages favored an allegorical world view, it is entirely possible that the author of *The
Plowman*, like the architect of a cathedral, did have Christian
symbolism in mind. But for today's reader it is more informative
to realize that a cathedral's buttresses and framework, the
symmetry of its arches, and the numbering of its columns, once
ordered symbolically, can now just as well be understood in
terms of tectonic function; the beauty of the edifice remains just
as impressive outside the historically limited scope of a Christian
esthetics.

A similar observation can be made on the overall formal
principle of *The Plowman* that divides each period and each
word of the work into rhythmically varied triads, and places
various groups of triads in polar opposition to one another. This,
too, remains valid today and comprehensible in terms of its
communicative function. The chiastic form which supplies every
sentence with an opposite is in reality the external expression of
the uncertainty of late medieval man, whose faith in justice and
in the visible order of the world had been deeply shaken: "For
all things have become reversed; what was behind is now in
front, what was in front now behind, the things underneath are
on top, that which was on top underneath; the great mass of the
people has turned wrong into right."

The dialectic form of *The Plowman* expresses the same uncertainty, since each dialogue is both question and answer, with
the result that one can repeatedly come full circle without ever
finding answers to the questions posed. To be sure, the world's
incomprehensible opposites are reconciled in God, the hidden
center of creation, but they can never be reconciled in this world.
Thus the accusation of Death must ultimately be transformed
into a prayer, the most intimate dialogue of the soul with God.

The hotly debated question, then, whether *The Plowman*
belongs to the Middle Ages or, in fact, reflects the new spirit of
humanism, is largely academic, not directly affecting today's
reader, however meaningful and interesting it may be for the

history of ideas. As far as the work itself is concerned, the most important fact is that *The Plowman* remained influential far beyond its own time. To be sure, its form derives from medieval poetics and contains syntactic, verbal, and rhythmic figures developed in the letters of the papal and royal chancelleries. The stylistic intent, however, anticipates in some respects the style of later humanistic prose and poetry.

Similarly, the ideological contours of the work are neither strictly medieval nor humanistic. Its defense of life is deeply rooted in the Scholastic, theological, and biblical traditions of the Middle Ages. Its vision of the eternal revolution of the heavens and the permanent change of earthly phenomena is Peripatetic. The concept of Death as archenemy of mankind can be traced back to Augustine. From St. Paul derives the idea of the hope of overcoming sin, and from the apocalyptic prophecies of the Apostle John the belief in regaining Paradise and winning immortality.

It is true that in comparison to Nicholas of Cusa's philosophical concept of death or Giovanni Pico's humanistic ideal, *The Plowman* can by no means be considered a work of the Renaissance. But *The Plowman*'s answer to the problem of death and its concept of man do represent a significant break with the tradition of the Middle Ages. When comparing *The Plowman* with the works of the humanists, however, we should not overlook the fact that Nicholas of Cusa's or Pico's speculations on immortality, and even those of the Italian humanist Ficino, were no less indebted to Scholasticism and Aristotelianism than *The Plowman*, in spite of their new use of Platonism. And in attempting to solve the problem of death and existence, the humanists were just as bound to Christian doctrine as was the author of *The Plowman*.

Important for a modern understanding of *The Plowman* is the fact that the problem of death—separated into Death's nihilism and the plowman's optimism—as well as the ambiguity of God's judgment anticipate the later development of Reformation and Renaissance. Death's pessimistic words damning all of mankind foreshadow the later doctrines of predestination. The plowman's disavowal of the power of Death and his declaration of Death as the enemy of God's order, on the other hand, open the way for man's personal obligation to battle evil and death—a concept that first found clear expression in the theology of Luther, or, on the level of artistic experience, in the graphic works of Dürer and the writings of Ulrich von Hutten.

The truly revolutionary aspect of *The Plowman*, however, is to be found in its apocalyptic belief in the eternity of the world and personal immortality. This idea, too, has its roots far in the past, but *The Plowman* again anticipates the future by approaching the problem of death in a similar way to the dialogue *De dignitate et excellentia hominis* (On the Dignity and Excellence of Man) by Gianozzo Manetti. Modern man considers death as somehow unseemly, as an infirmity that man's immortal nature will eventually conquer and remove from the world. In the works of both Johannes of Teplá and Manetti the answer still remains orthodox. But in both the stress has changed; instead of the concern with the eternal salvation of the soul in the hereafter, the yearning for the reattainment of the earthly paradise and the hope for physical immortality on earth are manifested. This is a *novum* which, because it sets as man's objective a renewed life in the temporal sphere, not only announces the profane-metaphysical concept of life, formulated by the Renaissance, but also points the way to the development of our own profane and materialistic life-utopia.

Translated by Jill McDonald

Selected Bibliography

PRIMARY SOURCES

Johannes von Saaz. *Der Ackermann aus Böhmen.* Günther Jungbluth, ed. vol. 1. Heidelberg, 1969. (This edition lists all the manuscripts as well as the entire secondary literature until 1968.)

Johann von Tepl. *Der Ackermann aus Böhmen.* Keith Spalding, ed. Oxford, 1950. (German text with English introduction, notes, and glossary.)

Johannes von Tepl. *Der Ackermann aus Böhmen*. M. O'C. Walshe,
M.A., ed. London, 1951 (German text with English introduction,
notes, and glossary.)

Johannes von Tepl. *Der ackerman*. Willy Krogmann, ed. Wiesbaden,
1953. (German text with German introduction and notes, bibliography on pp. 249–64.)

————. *Der Ackermann aus Böhmen*. transl. and ed. by Felix Genzmer.
Stuttgart: Reclam, 1969.

Johannes de Tepla. *Death and the Plowman*. Transl. by E. N. Kirrmann.
In *Studies in the Germanic Languages and Literatures*. Chapel Hill,
1958.

Johannes von Saaz. *The Plowman from Bohemia*. Transl. by A. and E.
Henderson. New York: Ungar, 1966. (Bilingual edition.)

SECONDARY SOURCES

Bacon, J. "A Survey of the Changes in the Interpretation of *Ackermann aus Böhmen*." *Studies in Philology*, 53 (1956), pp. 101ff.

Bäuml, F. H. "*Der Ackermann aus Böhmen* and the Destiny of Man."
The Germanic Review, 33 (1958), pp. 223ff.

Burdach, Konrad. *Der Dichter des* Ackermann aus Böhmen *und seine
Zeit*. In *Vom Mittelalter zur Reformation*, 3. Berlin, 1926–32.

Hübner, Arthur. "Deutsches Mittelalter und italienische Renaissance
im *Ackermann aus Böhmen*." *Zeitschrift für Deutschkunde*, 51
(1937), pp. 225 ff.

Philippson, E. A. "*Der Ackermann aus Böhmen*: A Summary of Recent
Research and an Appreciation." *Modern Language Quarterly*, 2
(1941), pp. 263ff.

Swinburne, H. "Echoes of the *De consolatione Philosophiae* in the
Ackermann aus Böhmen." *The Modern Language Review*, 52
(1957), pp. 88ff.

Walshe, M. O'C. "*Der Ackermann aus Böhmen* and Its Latin Dedication." *The Modern Language Review*, 47 (1952), pp. 211ff.

————. "*Der Ackermann aus Böhmen*: A Structural Interpretation."
Classica et Mediaevalia, 15 (1954), pp. 130ff.

3

Nicholas of Cusa:
Precursor of Humanism

Robert Joda, S.J.

History has shown that little-known, out-of-the-way hamlets can produce individuals whose contributions to life and letters bring those small towns out of obscurity. The village of Cues on the Moselle river, about seventy-five miles west of Koblentz on the Rhine, is one such town. Though the surrounding vineyards are known the world over for their delicate Moselle wines, Cues also offers the visitor an attraction whose worth increases with the years. Situated not far from the river bank is the building housing the chapel, library, and hospice for the elderly erected by Nicholas of Cusa, who has been acclaimed by historians as the greatest representative of northern humanism during the fifteenth century.

Whether one views Nicholas as the inaugurator of modern philosophical thought; as a writer of scientific treatises on motion, mathematics, and the solar system; as a papal diplomat working tirelessly for church reform and the reunification of the Greek Orthodox church with Rome; as a classical scholar hunting out manuscripts; or as an author of mystical works, one must conclude that Cusanus was the universal man of his century. The historian Paul Joachimsen summarized aptly when he stated that if Germany could boast a Renaissance mentality, it would be best exemplified in Cardinal Nicholas of Cusa.

Nicholas's contribution to his own mid-fifteenth-century world, and his influence on later northern humanists, can only be appreciated in the context of the complex structural changes that occurred between the years 1300 and 1600. To understand the cultural history of Europe during these three centuries is a complicated task, because this was a transitional period, a bridge between the Middle Ages and the modern era. The task is made more difficult by the changing interpretations given these centuries by historians and variously labeled the Renaissance, humanism, or Renaissance humanism. These designations are often further divided into the Italian Renaissance and northern humanism.

The continuing debate about the interpretation of Renaissance humanism has as its point of departure the studies of two nineteenth-century historians, the German Georg Voight and the Swiss Jacob Burckhardt. Voight viewed Renaissance humanism as a rather sudden, clear departure in attitudes and interests from the preceding Middle Ages, coupled with a marked rejection of scholasticism. In their place, argued Voight, the Italian humanists set up the cultures of ancient Greece and Rome, particularly the classical form and content of their literatures, as sources of the spirit of individualism that was to characterize modern man. Burckhardt's more widely read work, *The Civilization of the Renaissance in Italy*, which still dominates the debate on Renaissance interpretation, considered the total civilization of Renaissance Italy—he did not deal with other countries—and did not emphasize classical literatures as formative factors to the extent Voight had done. Significant for Burckhardt's interpretation was the abrupt, clear distinction he found between the total Renaissance civilization of Italy and all that had preceded it. He pointed to the heightened interest in human personality and external nature, and to the irreligious and immoral tone of the age, all of which reflected a new concern for the individual person. Underlying the sudden change from the Middle Ages was, according to Burckhardt, the political anarchy that ruled the Italian peninsula during the thirteenth century.

The rather rigid and static interpretations of Burckhardt and Voight did not go unchallenged. As new material was discovered and synthesized at the beginning of the twentieth century, historians in specialized areas began to revise their views. Some twenty years ago a new consensus emerged on Renaissance humanism. These more recent interpretations show a flexibility and an awareness of the complexity of the problem of interpretation, something lacking in the earlier dogmatic views.

Representative of this more recent scholarship are the interpretations of Paul Oskar Kristeller and Wallace K. Ferguson. According to these historians, Renaissance humanism is best viewed as an age of transition from medieval to modern civilization, marked by a gradual but decisive change in the intellectual climate of all Western European countries. This pervasive change occurred in the two institutions that dominated the social structure and the ideological content of medieval civilization: the feudal system and the omnipresent church.

By the twelfth century the landholding economy of feudalism began to break down as commerce and skilled industry developed, resulting in the growth of cities and an expansion of a money-based economy. The moral prestige and the authority of the church were badly shaken by the growing wealth and political power of the national states and by internal crises over the papal Avignon Captivity and the Western Schism. These changes in the social, political, and economic spheres opened careers to laymen trained in law and administration and, at the same time, afforded the middle and upper classes an opportunity to cultivate and patronize literature and the arts. As the educated public increased in size, intellectual leadership began to shift from the clergy to the laity, whose interests were understandably more secular than those of the medieval churchmen bound by clerical traditions.

These cultural changes and shifts in educational objectives did not occur simultaneously or with the same directional emphasis in all European countries. Renaissance humanism assumed different features in each major country, usually paralleling the specific qualities that had characterized the Middle Ages in that country. In Italy, where most historians agree that Renaissance humanism had its beginning, the movement was dominated by lay scholars, who were often employed by the wealthy independent city-states. Petrarch (1304–1374) is usually considered the first significant writer to show the kind of enthusiasm for Greek and Latin literature that was to typify many subsequent generations of Italian humanists. Their interests focused on making the classics of Greece and Rome accessible by devising an educational curriculum that stressed literature, formal eloquence in speech and writing, history, ethics, and the visual arts. These professional teachers of the humanities were by no means irreligious men, but they did concentrate their efforts on promoting those values that would enhance life in the secular city.

Although the first phases of German enthusiasm for classical formal eloquence derived from Italian literary scholars such as Petrarch and his pupil Boccaccio, by way of the imperial chancellery under Emperor Charles IV at Prague (see opening article by Frank L. Borchardt), northern humanistic thought was by no means limited to the cultivation of classical literary forms. The northern countries had inherited from the Middle Ages an intellectual, political, and social climate markedly different from that of their southern neighbors. The northern mentality clung longer to codes of courtly chivalry and felt more closely bound to the hierarchical character of the Christian church and the Holy Roman Empire than did its Italian counterpart. Because of this love of tradition and the need for strong leadership in church and state, northern humanism suffered a severe setback when the church hierarchy was divided during the Western Schism (1378–1417).

The Council of Constance (1414–1418) ended the schism by invoking the theory of conciliarism, which held that the highest power of ecclesiastical jurisdiction lay in a general assembly of bishops acting independently of the pope. At Constance, the three claimants to the papacy were deposed, and a Roman cardinal, who took the name of Martin V, was elected. It was at the next general council, at Basel in 1431, that Nicholas of Cusa came to prominence on the European scene.

From his monument in the Church of Saint Peter in Chains at Rome, we learn that Nicholas was born in 1401. His father, Johan Krebs, may have been a boatman by trade or may have belonged to a group of merchant shippers. Because of his middle-class origin, Nicholas seems to have harbored some feelings of inferiority well into his mature years. In an autobiographical sketch composed in 1449 he wrote: "A boatman from Cues sired him, but the boatman's offspring achieved great things, and his achievements were finally recognized by the popes by his eleva-tion to the cardinalate. And all recognize that the Church does not look upon the origins of birth, but is the most generous rewarder of virtue. For this reason this cardinal has written this story, to the praise of God." As if struggling with this feeling of inferiority, young Nicholas determined to get the best possible education.

As did several other northern humanists after him, Nicholas received his elementary education under the Brethren of the Common Life at Deventer in Holland. Years later he wrote with affection about his early training and about the emphasis on mysticism that formed an important part of the education at the schools of the Brethren. This mystical orientation made a deep impression on the young student, for his library at Cues shows Bonaventure's *Journey of the Soul* and Gerson's *Mystical Theol-ogy* to be among the first of his acquisitions.

At the age of fifteen, Nicholas began to study the traditional liberal arts at the University of Heidelberg. This was not an exceptionally early age for that period. What was unusual was that after a stay of only one year at this center of nominalism, Nicholas earned his bachelor's degree, an example of extraordi-nary precocity. His next decision, to study for a doctorate in church law at the University of Padua in Italy, was to have far-reaching consequences.

By the early fifteenth century Padua had become a leading intellectual center, particularly after it was absorbed into the Venetian state in 1405. At the University of Padua the scions of

Venetian aristocracy mixed with Germans and Poles, Greeks and Englishmen. In law Padua rivaled Bologna, but in medicine Padua was without peer. Even more important, the university became the leading Renaissance center for the study of Aristotle. Here a secular interpretation of Aristotle flourished, largely unhampered by the theologians who dominated Paris and Oxford. The radical interpretation of Aristotle by the Arab Averroës found many disciples, while other scholars preferred to follow the ancient Greek commentators. Interest centered on the immortality of the soul and on the scientific works of Aristotle. Many early leaders of the scientific revolution—Copernicus, Vesalius, Galileo, and Harvey—studied and taught at Padua.

During his six years at Padua, Cusanus made important contacts that later advanced his career as churchman and diplomat, among them Cardinal Guliano Cesarini, the future president of the Council of Basel. Equally important were the intellectual influences on Nicholas, notably that of Marsigilio of Padua, whose famous *Defensor Pacis* (Defender of the Peace) of 1324 radicalized earlier theories of the control that councils should exercise over the Church. Marsigilio argued that all governing power, ecclesiastical and civic, was vested primarily in the total community, and only secondarily in the ruler chosen by the community. He denied the divine origin of the papacy and held that the highest authority in matters of faith resided in a general council of the church. Marsigilio's theory of conciliarism was still very much alive at Padua when Nicholas studied at the university and was later reflected in the great church reformatory work that Nicholas presented to the Council of Basel.

From the six years spent in Italy Nicholas brought back to Germany something just as valuable as his doctorate in church law, namely, many first-hand impressions of the increasing interest in all branches of learning. With his formal education completed, Nicholas returned home to his native Cues in 1425. Shortly thereafter, he accepted several part-time minor positions in the local chancellery before his appointment to the faculty of ecclesiastical law at the University of Cologne.

As professor of church law and legal counselor of bishops,

Nicholas was much admired and sought after. He specialized in the history of church law, and his painstaking research into the university archives and the library vaults of the cathedral resulted in discoveries of inestimable importance for the humanistic movement. One such discovery was a manuscript that has come to be known as the *Codex Carolinus*. This astonishing document contained letters written by the popes to the Frankish kings, who had reigned centuries before Charlemagne, and official reports of provincial parliaments held in the vicinity of Arles in 417–418. Such discoveries anticipated the cultivation of romantic nationalism, an outlook characterized by exhalting German history and German achievements, in claiming, for example, that the ancient *imperium romanum* (Roman rule) had passed over to the Germanic peoples in the Holy Roman Empire of German nations. These discoveries also added to Cusanus's reputation as legal historian. Such discoveries anticipated the cultivation of romantic nationalism among later German humanists such as Conrad Celtis, increased Nicholas's reputation as a legal historian, and were instrumental in his being offered the chair of historian of church law at the newly founded university of Louvain, a position Nicholas twice refused.

Another such discovery started a flurry of correspondence among the Italian humanists. At the beginning of the fifteenth century, only eight plays by Plautus, along with Terence one of ancient Rome's two important dramatists of comedy, were known to Renaissance scholars. The first announcement of the existence of a manuscript containing the twenty complete plays that we now possess appeared in a letter written by Poggio Bracciolini in 1429. Poggio, secretary to Pope Martin V, informed his fellow humanist Niccolò Niccoli in Florence that their mutual friend Nicholas of Cusa in Germany had discovered manuscripts for several hitherto unknown classical works, among them a volume containing twenty plays by Plautus. The manuscript actually contained only sixteen plays, but twelve of these had been unknown up to that time.

In a second letter written some months later, Poggio announced that Nicholas had arrived in Rome with the precious document and had handed it over to Cardinal Orsini. Orsini was the papal delegate to Germany and had consulted with Nicholas in Cologne on some points of church law. As a result of this one brief meeting, Nicholas accepted the position of private secretary to this most influential papal diplomat. In his letter Poggio expressed some concern that Orsini had not yet had the manuscript transcribed. And in yet another letter, Poggio wrote that he hoped the transcription would be done carefully, and not, as had happened so often in the past, with the words all run together.

A short time later the manuscript was brought to Florence at the explicit request of Lorenzo de Medici, and there a copy of it was made by the humanist scholar Niccolò Niccoli himself. Having made a name for himself among the Italian humanists, and secure in the patronage of Orsini, Nicholas was prepared to make his own contribution to Renaissance thought as a legal historian. The Council of Basel (1431–1437) provided him with the opportunity.

Originally Nicholas had come before the council delegates to represent the dubious claim of one Ulrich von Manderschied for the vacant diocese of Trier. Since the council put off the decision of the case until the final sessions, Nicholas concerned himself with the basic questions of the council and had himself appointed to the Committee Concerning the Articles of Faith, whose main task was to determine the relationship between a universal church council and the authority of the pope.

At Constance in 1418 Pope Martin V had vaguely approved the doctrine of conciliar supremacy. His successor, Eugene IV, had never favored the theory, and it was apparent from the outset that at Basel the pope and the council would be facing each other as adversaries.

During some two years of haggling between the papal-supremacist party and the conciliarists, who maintained that supreme ecclesiastical authority was vested in the general council, Nicholas quietly researched his major work of political theory, *De Concordantia Catholica* (Concerning Universal Harmony), which he submitted to the council shortly before Eugene IV agreed to its decrees. This overpowering, monumental volume was no mere polemical tract defending conciliarism against a papal monarchy. It was rather, as Paul E. Sigmund observes (see bibliography), the last great work of political theory before Machiavelli. The *Concordantia* is an outstanding example of the Renaissance humanistic mind at work, in the truest sense of that term. Nicholas brought an awesome, encyclopedic knowledge to bear on his overall theme, which was that everything created can be brought into a universal harmony if it is correctly understood and if it understands its own place in the universe. The work showed Nicholas's familiarity with all the major philosophical schools, from Plato and Aristotle through Christian Neoplatonism, scholasticism, and nominalism, and their variations in his own day. And running through this grand synthesis, which tried to show a God-given order in the universe, in society, and in the church, was the subtle thread of the history of conciliarism.

Strongly influenced by the Christian Neoplatonic writing, Nicholas envisioned a reform of the church based on the heavenly model found in the very nature of God, diversity in unity or triune unity. This triune unity is reflected in the makeup of the church: sacrament, priesthood, and the faithful. Since all men are by nature equally free, church law and civil law alike may demand their obedience only with their consent. It is in view of this consent that the bishop represents his diocese and the general council the entire church. Bishops and pope have essentially the same authority. The pope's primacy is that of an administrator. Supreme power in the church belongs to the general council, which in turn receives its power directly from Christ its founder. Hence the council is above the pope and if need be may depose or correct him. Harmony within the church and empire can come about only when each part is fulfilling its own function, or put another way, harmony results when all things conform to their celestial archetypes and assume their natural place in the universe. Weaknesses in Nicholas's grand synthesis were largely due to its unpolished Latin style and its repetitiousness, probably the result of haste, although Nicholas frankly admitted in the introduction: "We Germans must almost do violence to our nature to use Latin eloquently." On the other hand, some of

Nicholas's later writings have been long considered the work of no less a stylist than Petrarch himself.

Some time during the next three years, 1434–37, Nicholas completely reversed his position from moderate conciliarist to staunch supporter of the pope. Volumes have been written trying to discover Nicholas's reasoning. Contemporary detractors, among them Enea Silvio Piccolomini, who had a similar change of heart later on, viewed the change as a betrayal for the sake of convenience. Modern historians, while not ruling out opportunism, tend to see it as a genuine change of attitude, arising from Nicholas's sincere conviction that harmony within the church should only be guaranteed by accepting the pope as the supreme authority in matters of faith and morals. Nicholas's deep concern for unity within the church is further evidenced by his efforts to win back the Hussite heretics of Bohemia. This reform group, named after Jan Hus (1369?–1415) had split from Rome because of several reform demands, among others, their insistence that laymen be allowed to receive the Eucharist under both species, both bread *and* wine. It was largely through Nicholas's efforts that the council was persuaded to grant this privilege to the laity of Bohemia.

Immediately after the breakup of the council he went as envoy to the Greek emperor and the patriarch of Constantinople in an effort to effect a reconciliation with the Greek church, returning with the two of them to Italy for discussions with the pope—a major diplomatic success. On this trip Nicholas found time to purchase a number of Greek manuscripts dealing with the seventh-century church councils of Constantinople. Letters of Italian humanists testify that more than once they took advantage of Nicholas's good command of Greek in their own work of translating.

Now firmly established as the leading German papal diplomat, Nicholas spent the next ten years working tirelessly for Pope Eugene IV in meetings with the German emperors and princes. In recognition of his great services, Eugene's successor, the humanist Pope Nicholas V, made his namesake bishop of Bresserone in the Tyrol and, shortly thereafter, cardinal.

Sometime during the early years of these diplomatic negotiations between Rome and the German princes, Nicholas found time to write his first major work on the philosophy of God, *De Docta Ignorantia* (On Learned Ignorance). Presupposing the Judeo-Christian tradition of a personal God, Nicholas investigated God's being in itself and man's ability to know God. The originality of the work is to be found in Nicholas's synthesis of well-known philosophical approaches to the problem, particularly as taught by the Neoplatonic school, the German mystic Meister Eckhardt, and the medieval philosopher Pseudo-Dionysius, who stressed the negative approach to the knowledge of God: by understanding what God is not, we can come to some shadowy understanding of what he is.

The title of Nicholas's work expresses the principle that true learnedness admits the limits of human reason. Nicholas began with the concept of God as absolute maximum, which is infinite. Since the human mind learns by comparing the known with the unknown, and since there can be no relationship of comparison between the finite and the infinite, human reason alone cannot comprehend God's true nature. Without attempting to summarize the elusive thought of this paradoxical and often opaque work, one other philosophical principle might be mentioned, the "coincidence of opposites." According to this principle, all things are united in God, even those that appear to be opposed. Since the absolute maximum contains all things in itself, the universe is nothing else than the unfolding of God's nature. Because of such writing Nicholas was accused of pantheism, the same charge brought against Meister Eckhardt a century earlier. Nicholas's tireless work for church unity and reform, however, soon laid such suspicions to rest.

By the time Nicholas wrote the thumbnail sketch of his life in 1449, all earlier brooding over his middle-class origins was a thing of the past. His contributions to classical scholarship, legal history, and philosophy, together with striking successes in the field of diplomacy, had made him the logical choice to lead a church reform mission in Germany and the Low Countries.

It falls outside the scope of this essay to detail the religious

spirit of the northern European countries at the middle of the
fifteenth century. Studies in this area agree that among lay people interest in religious practices was very intense, almost a matter of urgency. The two organized heretical movements, the
Hussites and Waldensians, were fast losing their fire. The frantic
collecting of relics, the inflation of indulgences, and the multipli-
cation of miracles were visible signs of the judgment Nicholas
would make a few years later (1453) in his work *Visio Dei* (The
Vision of God): "Much of the Christian religion has degenerated
to an appearance." These phenomena were also anxious gestures
of distressed Christians reaching out for help. Such help should
have come from a clergy intellectually and morally equipped for
the task. Although the situation at the mid-fifteenth century
mark was not yet catastrophic, evidence points to a steady deteri-
oration in the ranks of the clergy. Less than one-half of the parish
priests had studied theology at the university, and preaching
standards were astonishingly low, judged by extant sermon out-
lines. Accustomed as they were to consider themselves a social
class above the laity, too many of the clergy were more concerned
with church revenues than with the care of souls.

As though he sensed the explosiveness of the situation,
Nicholas asked the pope for a mandate in December, 1450, to
work for a revitalization of doctrine and morals among his fellow
countrymen. Records of his eighteen-month journey describe
the great receptions he received as a German cardinal and the
enthusiasm of the laity for his solid, reassuring preaching, in
which he emphasized faith and the presence of Christ in the
Eucharist as the mediator of man's salvation. The clergy, on the
other hand, greeted Nicholas's vigorous reform measures with
opposition, particularly when he denounced superstitious practices that increased their revenues. In the Brandenburg village of
Walsnach, for example, Nicholas lashed out against the local
clergy who encouraged the faithful to worship "miraculously
bleeding hosts," actually altar breads that had turned somewhat
red in the baking process. In his report to Rome the cardinal
wrote: "The faithful take the red color of the hosts for the blood
of Christ, and the priests do not merely tolerate but actually
encourage the belief because of the revenue it brings."

Nicholas deposed abbots who had bought their positions, and published notices in the town against clergymen living with mistresses, practices that did not endear him to the erring local churchmen. Never before in the history of northern Europe had the reform efforts of one man produced such lasting results as in the localities Nicholas visited. In many monasteries, the Cusanian decrees remained in effect until secularization by Napoleon at the beginning of the nineteenth century. As the historian Will Durant wrote, if there had been more reformers with the determination of Nicholas of Cusa, the Reformation some fifty years later would have been unnecessary.

The success of his reform efforts, so evident in the north, was denied Nicholas in his own Tyrolean diocese of Bressanone, where he arrived in 1453. Inflexible in his determination to make his diocese a model for the church, Nicholas met with strong opposition from a clergy long entrenched in a life of ease and questionable morals. In addition, he was forced into a long conflict with Archduke Sigmund over episcopal revenues and land jurisdiction. After suffering imprisonment and threats against his life, Nicholas in 1460 left the diocese for Rome where he served the newly elected Pope Pius II, the former Renaissance scholar Enea Silvio Piccolomini, and with conspicuous distinction until his death in 1464.

The seven years Nicholas spent in his own diocese can be considered very lean or quite productive, depending on one's viewpoint. As an administrator and reformer, Nicholas was a failure. But these troubled years did yield a rich harvest for scholars in a field to which Nicholas had not previously turned his full attention: the area of the exact sciences. Nicholas never considered himself a scientist, but, as a true Renaissance man, his penetrating mind was interested in all areas where he sensed an imminent breakthrough. Nicholas never made an original scientific discovery, but by rejecting ancient suppositions and by suggesting new directions and modes of experimentation, he directly influenced such world figures as Leonardo da Vinci, Giordano Bruno, Copernicus, and Kepler.

From his mathematical speculations Nicholas concluded that only through mathematics could the mind reach absolute certitude, but he floundered on the impossible task of squaring the circle. A more important contribution was his challenge to the classical conception of a closed, hierarchical universe. Nicholas rejected the view that the celestial spheres revolve around the earth as their center. His universe had "its center everywhere and its circumference nowhere." Nicholas's unlimited universe finally became the infinite universe of modern thought when the idea was taken up by Bruno, although neither of them anticipated the solar system of Copernicus. When it came to explaining the continuous rotation of the earth on its axis, however, Copernicus returned to Nicholas's theory that because the earth was a perfect sphere, it needed only an initial impetus for it to remain in motion, and this initial impetus was given it by God at the Creation.

Nicholas's theorizing in quantitative physics, judged by modern standards, was also simplistic. Much of his writing in this area focused on the study of nature based on weights and related qualities. Measuring experiments indicating variations in the weight of a piece of cloth should show the relative humidity in the air. Nicholas suggested that air itself could be weighed by measuring the difference in weight of an inflated and deflated balloon. Despite some naïve procedures, his basic ideas were often proved basically sound by later Renaissance scientists.

The establishment of the Cusanus Commission in Germany in the 1920s to study and edit Nicholas's numerous works, and of The Cusanus Society, which publishes articles dealing with various aspects of his thought, would indicate that the impact of this fifteenth-century humanist on later generations is finally being recognized. Cultural historians have suggested several reasons for this late recognition. Nicholas's contemplative, almost mystical approach to philosophy ran counter to the firmly established Aristotelian scholasticism of Aquinas, with its "proof mechanism of logical subtleties," so uncongenial to Nicholas's way of viewing reality. Nor did the problems confronting the German intellectual in the mid-fifteenth century fire the imagination of Europe as did the rediscovery of classical literature by the Italian humanists. And, great as Nicholas's reform work was, it was soon overshadowed by the Reformation.

Lastly, part of the reason may be found in the man himself. Nicholas was possessed by a tremendous urge to achieve, matched only by his capacity for work, as though driven to explore all fields of knowledge. In the intellectual history of Europe Nicholas is usually ranked with the philosophers and legal historians, but none of the later northern humanists, outside of Erasmus, contributed so much to so many areas of scholarship as did Cardinal Nicholas of Cues. He was indeed the precursor of northern humanism.

Selected Bibliography

PRIMARY SOURCES

Nicholai de Cusa. *Opera Omnia*. Leipzig-Hamburg, 1932–59.
Cusanus-Texte, issued in the Sitzungsberichte der Heidelberger Akademie der Wissenschaften, Philosophisch-historische Klasse:
    Briefwechsel des Nikolaus von Kues, part iv, 1. Josef Koch, ed. Heidelberg, 1944.
    Briefwechsel des Nikolaus von Kues, part IV,2: *Das Brixener Briefbuch des Cardinals Nikolaus von Kues*. Friedrich Hausmann, ed. Heidelberg, 1952.
    Briefwechsel des Nikolaus von Kues, part IV,4: *Nikolaus von Kues und der Deutsche Orden*. Erich Maschke, ed. Heidelberg, 1956.
    Brixener Dokumente, part V,1: *Akten zur Reform des Bistmus Brixen*. Heinz Hürten, ed. Heidelberg, 1960.
Nicholas of Cusa. *The Idiot*. London, 1650. Transl. with introd. by W. R. Dennes. San Francisco, 1940.
———. *Of Learned Ignorance*. Transl. by Germain Heron, O.F.M., with introd. by D. J. B. Hawkins, D.D. New Haven, 1954.
———. *Unity and Reform: Selected Writings of Nicholas de Cusa*. Transl. and ed., with introd., by John Patrick Dolan. Notre Dame, Indiana, 1962.
———. *The Vision of God*. Transl. by E. Gurney Salter, with introd. by Evelyn Underhill. London, 1928, rpt. New York, 1960.

SECONDARY SOURCES

A. Books

Andreas, Willy. *Deutschland vor der Reformation*. Stuttgart, 1959.

Bett, Henry. *Nicholas of Cusa*. London, 1932.

Burckhardt, Jacob C. *The Civilization of the Renaissance in Italy*. H. Holborn, ed., transl. by S. G. Middlemore. New York, 1954.

Cheyney, Edward P. *The Dawn of a New Era, 1250–1453*. New York, 1962.

Crombie, A. C. *Medieval and Early Modern Science*. 2 vols. Cambridge, Mass., 1967.

Dolan, John P. *History of the Reformation*. New York, 1964.

Ferguson, W. K. *The Renaissance in Historical Thought*. Boston, 1948.

Gilmore, M. P. *The World of Humanism, 1453–1517*. New York, 1952.

Haskins, Charles Homer. *Studies in the History of Medieval Science*. Cambridge, Mass., 1927, rpt. New York, 1958.

Huizinga, J. *The Waning of the Middle Ages*. London, 1924.

Humanitatis. Ernesto Grassi zum 70. Geburtstag. E. Hora and E. Kessler, München, 1973, 89–101.

Hyma, A. *The Christian Renaissance*. Grand Rapids, 1924.

Koyre, Alexandre. *From the Closed World to the Infinite Universe*. New York, 1958.

Kristeller, Paul O. *The Classics and Renaissance Thought*. Cambridge, Mass, 1955.

Marx, J. *Verzeichnis der Handschriften-Sammlung des Hospitals zu Cues*. Trier, 1905.

Meuthen, Erich. *Nikolaus von Kues, 1401–1464*. Buchreihe der Cusanus-Gesellschaft, Münster, 1964.

Müller, Günther. *Deutsche Dichtung von der Renaissance bis zum Ausgang des Barock*. Darmstadt, 1957.

The New Cambridge Modern History. Vol. I, *The Renaissance 1493–1520*. Cambridge, 1957.

Ramsay, William. *The Mostellaria of Plautus*. London, 1869.

Rashdall, Hastings. *The Universities of Europe in the Middle Ages*. 3 vols. 2nd ed. rev. by F. M. Powicke and A. B. Emden. Oxford, 1936.

Robb, N. A. *Neoplatonism of the Italian Renaissance*. London, 1935.

Sigmund, Paul E. *Nicholas of Cusa and Medieval Political Thought*. Cambridge, Mass., 1963.

Spitz, Lewis W. *The Religious Renaissance of the German Humanists*. Cambridge, Mass., 1963.

Stammler, Wolfgang and Karl Langosch, eds. *Die Deutsche Literatur des Mittelalters.* In *Verfasserlexikon.* 5 vols. Berlin, 1943.

Taton, René. *History of Science: The Beginnings of Modern Science from 1450–1800.* Transl. by A. J. Pomerans. New York, 1964.

Thorndike, Lyon. *Science and Thought in the Fifteenth Century.* New York, 1929.

Vansteenberghe, Edmond. *Le Cardinal Nicolas de Cues.* Paris, 1920. Rpt. Frankfurt am Main, 1963.

Watanabe, Morimichi. *The Political Ideas of Nicholas of Cusa with Special Reference to His "De Concordantia Catholica,"* Genève, 1963.

B.   *Articles*

Cranz, F. Edward. "St. Augustine and Nicholas of Cusa in the Tradition of Western Christian Thought." *Speculum* 28 (April 1953), 297–315.

Jacob, E. F. "Nicholas of Cusa." In *Social and Political Ideas of Some Great Thinkers of the Renaissance and Reformation.* F. J. C. Hearnshaw, ed. London, 1925, 32–60.

Joachimsen, Paul. "Humanism and the Development of the German Mind," transl. from "Der Humanismus und die Entwicklung des deutschen Geistes," *Deutsche Vierteljahrsschrift für Literaturwissenschaft und Geistesgeschichte,* 8, (1930), 419–80. Rpt. in *Pre-Reformation Germany,* Gerald Strauss, ed. New York, 1972.

Meister, Aloys. "Die humanistischen Anfänge des Nikolaus von Cues," *Annalen des Historischen Vereins für den Niederrhein,* 63 (1896), 1–21.

Moeller, Bernd. "Religious Life in Germany on the Eve of the Reformation." In *Pre-Reformation Germany,* Gerald Strauss, ed. New York, 1972, 12–42.

Randall, John Herman, Jr. "The Development of Scientific Method in the School of Padua." *Journal of the History of Ideas,* 1 (1940), 177–206.

Rice, Eugene. "Nicholas of Cusa's Idea of Wisdom." *Traditio,* 12 (1957), 345–368.

Sigmund, Paul E. "The Influence of Marsilius of Padua on XVth Century Conciliarism." *Journal of the History of Ideas,* 23 (1962), 392–402.

Ullmann, B. L. "Manuscripts of Nicolas of Cues." *Speculum,* 13 (1938), 194–197.

4

The Pagan Influence of the Italian Renaissance on German Life and Letters, 1450-1520

Gerhart Hoffmeister

The Italian Renaissance is an exceedingly complex cultural and artistic phenomenon, with many facets. It seems advisable, therefore, not to attempt a comprehensive new definition of the era but rather to single out a particular aspect—the surge of individualism, worldliness, and sensuality—and to trace its impact on transalpine Germany in the period of early humanism. This aspect of the Renaissance is linked to its etymological meaning: "rebirth" of the arts and culture of antiquity, a return to the ancient masters in ideals and style. Going back to the sources, with the ensuing cult of pagan Latinity, led in turn to a fresh interest at the end of the Middle Ages in man and his world. A new secular culture came into being, one that was emancipated from the restrictive values and norms of medieval church-controlled life. Following the example of ancient models, a zest for the things of this world developed, replacing the earlier emphasis on eternal life. Artists and authors alike wanted to learn and to live, to experience sensory delights, to express their visionary and imaginative impulses. They took pride in their worldly achievements and in the creative power and dignity of man.

In Italy the arts and sciences flourished in the city-states of Florence, Venice, Mantua, and Ferrera during the fifteenth century, the quattrocento. During the High Renaissance, Rome replaced Florence as Italy's leading cultural center, attracting artistic geniuses such as Michelangelo, Raphael, and Leonardo. Machiavelli and Castiglione were outstanding among men of letters. Students and artists flocked to Italy, and upon their return to their homelands spread Renaissance ideas to most of Europe. But the Renaissance peaked at different times in different countries and fields. After its beginnings in the fine arts in quattrocento Italy, it climaxed in Northern Europe with the Reformation and in England with Elizabethan drama and Shakespeare.

How did it happen that the Renaissance originated in Italy, the cradle of medieval Catholicism? One likely reason is the early rise of powerful city-states, which grew more and more independent of Pope and Emperor after the twelfth century. The feudal-vassal system was gradually replaced by that of the condottieri who ignored every moral restraint. Commerce and banking in the cities enabled leading members of the middle class to rise to a position equal to that of the nobility and to establish themselves as patrons of the arts. Another contributing factor was the conquest of Constantinople by the Turks in 1453, after which many Greek scholars fled to Italy with piles of ancient manuscripts, thus promoting the return to a study of the classic world. And, paradoxically enough, during the fifteenth century Italy was a country where firm religious convictions and traditions were being questioned, although the religious roots of the Renaissance and the constant struggle between the divine and the profane, the joy of living and the penitent mood must not be overlooked (e.g., Rienzi, Petrarch, Savonarola). The Renaissance remained above all a fundamentally Christian era with increasingly non-religious interests in life, letters, and the arts (*see* Kristeller, "Paganism and Christianity").

While the Renaissance in Italy embraced the entire spectrum of life, culture, and politics, in Germany it was identified with humanism and remained by and large a scholarly affair. Humanism is a modern term derived from the Ciceronian phrase *studia humanitatis* (humanistic studies, i.e., the liberal arts), rediscovered during the Renaissance and used, as Cicero did, to designate the formation of character and of civil behavior—civilization as opposed to barbarism. Essentially, the humanists were those students of antiquity who, in the fifteenth and sixteenth centuries, turned away from late medieval theological studies to the joys of examining the world scientifically and perusing ancient manuscripts.

In Renaissance humanism there were fundamental differences between the Italian active, socio-political orientation (as exemplified in Machiavelli and Castiglione) and the German contemplative-religious approach; in Italy humanism was a secular ideal of education, whereas in Germany scholars looked to ancient writers primarily for advice on how to lead a pious life. Italian civic humanism had only to revive its classical Republican past; German humanism remained largely a matter of school and university in-fighting between the still intact medieval scholastic tradition and the new thinking.

These basic distinctions should not obscure the fact that the early German humanists underwent a long period of learning from Italian models until they came of age, when the arch humanist Conrad Celtis (see below) could assert what even conceited and arrogant Italians had to admit: not only had the Holy Roman Empire migrated to the North but also fine literary education. How did this come about?

In spite of essential differences both the South and the North agreed in one respect: humanism is based on a classical education. The Swiss humanist Niklas von Wyle quite clearly underscored the significance of these studies: "Everything has been prefigured in the ancient works, recognized and visualized in them." Not only was the style of the ancients to be imitated, but through their style their spirit was to come into its own. Cicero's essays on the moral life of man served as guides for those seeking to become harmonious, humane persons. Following in the footsteps of Lorenzo Valla, some German humanists demanded, moreover, a free secular science based not on such authorities as Aristotle and the Bible but on experience and knowledge of the universe. German mathematicians and astrologers (such as Regiomontan and Georg Peuerbach, Viennese court astronomer) were to develop the means for the discovery of the New World. The elitist character of German humanism becomes apparent, however, when we learn of the humanist's password: Are you a "poet"? This greeting not only implies a distance from the common people but also, since poet and prophet were considered identical, the humanist claim to literary nobility.

Although the Italians in general made no particular effort to transmit their ideas to their northern colleagues, their influence on Germany was quite strong during the fifteenth century. This is true not only with regard to economic relations (Nuremberg-Venice) and the impact of the Council of Basel (1431–49) on religious life, but also in the literary realm and the style of life of many early German humanists. The reception of "paganism" into life and letters was an important factor. Jacob Burckhardt, in his famous book *The Civilization of the Renaissance in Italy* (1860), claimed that the great leaders of the age were pagan individuals—tyrant princes, condottieri, courtiers. Though this tenet has come under attack by Toffanin (see bibliography) as being too extreme, it can be validated by the frequent charges, during the period, of private and public immorality and by the superficiality of faith and the lack of a sense of duty in many Renaissance figures. The meaning of paganism clearly goes beyond its religious reference to non-Christian or non-Jewish moral attitudes. In our context it signifies a scholarly orientation toward the pre-Christian pagan era of Greece and Rome; with this developed the desire of Renaissance men to lead a life in keeping with the classical ideal of natural reason and the golden mean. Humanists were never seriously interested in "reviving ancient pagan cults" (Kristeller), but they were devoted to creative and scholarly endeavors independent of religious doctrine. In the arts an aesthetic approach prevailed, while "the ideal, cheerful, sensuous, pagan life" (Matthew Arnold) opened new horizons. After the discovery of the individual and of the physical world, men were drawn to a more refined enjoyment of life and of sensual Epicurean pleasure, which in turn led to the substitution of Venus for *Minne* and the theoretical rehabilitation of women in Florence, although in everyday life women were still treated as sexual prey. In sum, man as the new standard of all things on earth grew in importance, because man believed in divine forces in nature and in himself. Paganism thus essentially stands for a nonreligious, amoral, secular interpretation of life and art—all within the framework of a rather tolerant church.

Attracted by the new learning, many Germans came to Italy. Among them were such famous figures as Rudolf Agricola, who, after spending some years in Ferrara and Rome, developed into the German equivalent of *un uomo universale*. What Agricola was for Heidelberg, Mutianus Rufus exemplified in Erfurt, a university town where pagan humanism dominated the scene and, where, ironically enough, Luther was to study. Both men had received their training in Roman law in Italy. Willibald Pirckheimer also studied law in Padua before settling in Nuremberg, which he turned—along with his friend, the artist Albrecht Dürer—into a German version of Florence. The great scholar Erasmus received his doctorate in theology from the University in Turin. Like Agricola and Pirckheimer, he was celebrated by the Italians as a leading transalpine humanist. These learned men leaned, from all we know about them, toward the more serious contemplative or moralistic side of humanism. There were also German scholars who went to Italy and then spread the new ideas in various German university towns without ever settling in any particular place for long. Men like Samuel Karoch, a wandering humanist who taught at Leipzig and Heidelberg, Peter Luder, Conrad Celtis, and Jakob Locher, translator into Latin of Brant's *Ship of Fools*, belong to the first generation of German humanists to introduce humanistic studies on their native soil. In contrast to the former group, they aggressively defended their Renaissance ideals against scholasticism.

Just returned from Padua, Peter Luder addresses the entire University of Heidelberg on the 15th of July, 1456, in these words: "A youthful restlessness led me to visit foreign places. I traveled beyond my homeland across treacherous rivers and the

extremely rough summits of the Alps, finally reaching Rome."
Luder went on to speak of visits to Venice and Greece looking for
an ideal field of study and finding it in the humanities: "In order
not to commit myself to one (discipline) alone while neglecting
the others, and in order to establish a true and infallible founda-
tion for all fields, I applied myself with all my heart to humanistic
studies, to the historians, rhetoricians, and poets." According to
Luder, historians provide guidelines and examples for virtuous
behavior, rhetoric distinguishes man from animals, and poets
combine usefulness with pleasure. Luder argues that the schoolmen are not the only ones endowed with judgment in religious
matters: "poet" stands for prophet (as in Vergil). These new
studies make men not only virtuous but immortal in worldly
fame as well.

Luder concludes his lecture with a rousing appeal to his
students, which has a certain familiar ring to it, reminding us
that the liberal arts program of today is a product of humanism
and is still fighting for survival in a profit-oriented society. He
says: "Let us begin now! Gather all your strength now and concentrate all your energies, work, and industry on humanistic
studies! I beseech you to apply yourselves to the poets, rhetoricians, and historians, reading them with me, for through these
readings . . . you will bring forth, finally, perpetual growth of
honor and benefit to yourselves, personal distinction, and indelible fame to your country."*

With Luder's arrival on the one-hundred- to two-hundred-
student campus in Heidelberg, a fresh wind suddenly blew from
the south. Luder's teachings were revolutionary: in contrast to
the schoolmen's Aristotle, he discussed Cicero, Terence, Seneca,
quite worldly authors in the eyes of the church, but less so than
Ovid, whose *Art of Love* he interpreted with personal involvement. Luder felt very much at ease among the young student
radicals of those days who wanted a change in ways of living and
loving. Humanism became a mode of life in Heidelberg, and
from that time on its reputation as a romantic town of love,

* Translated from the Latin by Frank Baron. (Luder based his
speech, by the way, on a number of lectures by Guarino of Verona.)

wine, and student freedom was established. Nevertheless, for all his appeal to students, Luder's character and "liederlicher Lebenswandel" (disorderly conduct) made it impossible for him to find a place in the system, and ultimately he had to leave Heidelberg.

The German arch humanist Celtis, or, to use his bourgeois name, Conrad Pickel zu Wipfeld, far surpasses Luder in stature and achievement. Celtis grew up in a Franconian vineyard. After finishing his studies in Heidelberg he traveled all over Europe; between 1487 and 1489 he frequented Ficino's neo-Platonic circle in Florence and Guarini's lectures in Ferrara. Inspired by Plato and the Italians, he established humanistic societies wherever he stayed for a few years, e.g., in Vienna and Heidelberg. He had himself crowned as a poet laureate, taking Petrarch as his precedent, and started a personal calendar for himself from that day on. His studies of Greek and Hebrew were of prime importance, as were his editions of Latin authors and of the German poetess Roswitha von Gandersheim, his theater productions of Roman comedies, and his own festive masques. In his famous inaugural lecture in Ingolstadt in 1492, Celtis went along with Luder's plan for curriculum reform with an emphasis on rhetoric, because he doubted that learning was of any particular use if one could not talk about it eloquently and elegantly. But as a professor he did not live up to his ideal of eloquence: students complained about his poor readings, which were hardly understandable and were interspersed with rude descriptions of the students as barbarians, fools, and savages. In disgust he sometimes left for a drinking spree right in the middle of his lecture. In many respects he lived like Bacchus, and he died as one of the earliest famous victims of syphilis. But Celtis was much more than a mere pleasure-seeking humanist. As an all-round Renaissance man he felt the urge to investigate everything under the heavens; he was a prototype of Dr. Faustus, possessing high self-esteem and pride in German achievements in the face of Italian arrogance. With his church criticism, he was a precursor of the Reformation.

A word about the biographical background of Celtis's masterwork, his "Four Books of Love" (*Quattuor libri amorum*, 1502). An erotic novel in four lyrical cycles, it was based partly on Strozzi's *Erotica*, partly on his own ten-year experience as a wanderer. The subject is Celtis's sensual love of four temperamentally different women in four cities at various stages of his life. There is some evidence that the first woman, Hasilina (Book I), actually existed and was a married Polish lady. A letter in her hand has come down to us, addressed to Celtis of Vienna, complaining about a Master of Arts recently returned to Cracow from Vienna who read from Celtis's poems during a party; she mentions that her very name came up in the poems several times without anybody's noticing an immediate link between her and the poet's beloved, but one can imagine that the evening must have seemed like a year to her. Hasilina further complains that Celtis had not kept his promise to remain faithful to her, and had jeopardized her reputation by singing her praises on fiddle and lute. She concludes quite succinctly: "Stop this, stop this, doctor, and consider what you owe me. Given in Krakau Anno saeculari 1500." One of the poems Hasilina might have in mind is the famous "De nocte et osculo Hasilinae, erotice."

Transforming his life experience into sensual poetry, Celtis at times came surprisingly close to Catullus and the revival of erotic lyrics in the Italian Renaissance. For Germany his poem constitutes one of the highlights of humanism, and an important breakthrough in that Christian ethics was pushed aside by an aesthetic, amoral approach.

Although many leading German humanists who had traveled to Italy and returned imbued with new ideas joined in the rising plea for more liberal attitudes in private and public affairs, they generally failed to persuade their countrymen to follow suit. Luther's Reformation, in this light, can be considered a backlash against the liberated individual's desire to lead a richer, more joyful life. Let us go one step further and examine the impact of erotic Renaissance literature on Germany more closely. The Italians created two new genres: the novella and the sonnet, both forms that lend themselves readily to the expression of ideas about love and life.

Professor J. H. Tisch (see bibliography) has established that courtly patrons sponsored mainly "German translations from humanist Latin of the gems of Renaissance literature—above all renditions of novella." The courts availed themselves of learned men "from the upper bourgeois strata" who were trained in several languages. These translators addressed themselves to the patricians and the nobility, among whom women played a prominent part. The first literary appearance in German of a Renaissance tale was in 1432, with the Griselda story detailing female humility and faithfulness. Around 1460 additional novellas were rendered into German, among them Enea Silvio's *De duobus amantibus historia, Eurialus et Lucretia* (1444).

Silvio played a significant role as an intermediary between the Italian and German humanists. He came to Germany as a bishop's secretary for the Council of Basel (1432–42) and quickly found admirers of his elegant Latin. Designated poet laureate by Frederick III at the Imperial Diet in Frankfurt in 1442, he was hired as an imperial secretary for the chancellery in Vienna, where he met Chancellor Kaspar Schlick, later his employer, and stayed for several years before embarking on his episcopal career. Everybody of consequence was fascinated by his Latin prose and classical learning; they were impressed not only by his intellectual abilities, but also by his way of life. He early declined the honor of being consecrated a priest in order to continue indulging in pleasures not officially permitted to the clergy. Only in 1446, at 46 years of age, did he take orders as a subdeacon, "forsaking Venus for Bacchus" as he put it. To us today it does not appear to be the true conversion of a penitent mind, since in his letters we find these remarks: "I am a subdeacon, something I once thoroughly abhorred to be. Levity has left me. . . . I own to you, dearest brother, I am satiated, surfeited; I have grown disgusted with Venus. . . . Venus even shuns me more than I abominate her" (March 6 and 8, 1446).* Silvio achieved his greatest fame not as the pope he later became, Pius

* As quoted in "Pius II," *The New Schaff-Herzog Encyclopedia of Religious Knowledge.* 2nd ed. Vol. IX (Grand Rapids, Michigan: Baker, 1959), pp. 76–78.

II, who took the cross and died of fever at Ancona (1464), but as the author of *Eurialus et Lucretia*, fashioned in the vein of Ovid and Boccaccio. This love novella with letters interspersed went to twenty-seven printings in half a century and was quickly translated into the major European languages.

Eurialus, a fictitious name for Chancellor Kaspar Schlick, falls in love with Lucretia, a married lady from Siena. Their passion for each other leads them to rebel secretly against the conventional mores of the time. When the emperor, whom Eurialus serves as a knight, is ready to depart from Siena, a tragic conflict arises between the two lovers: Lucretia wants to accompany her lover lest she die of grief and sorrow. Eurialus, however, tells her straightforwardly that her reputation would be at stake and that he could not yield to her pleas, since he would thereby jeopardize his position in the emperor's retinue. So she pines away like Isolde, while he lives on to marry—after a short period of grief—a woman picked for him by the emperor. This novella, with its biographical details and early psychological analysis of human desires and frailties, was to serve as a model for the budding sentimental novel in Spain, France, and Germany, in which the protagonist usually suffers the deadly consequences of an unrestrained and absolute love.

In 1462 the Swiss humanist Niklas von Wyle, a typical man of the Renaissance, who had been educated in Italy and was a friend of Enea Silvio, translated *Eurialus et Lucretia* into German. Wyle was a writer, teacher, statesman, and administrator. After serving as a city clerk in various German towns, he became chancellor for the Count of Württemberg in Stuttgart. As an envoy on diplomatic missions he twice went to the Gonzaga court in Mantua and to Milan, and as a humanist he dominated the circle around Countess Mechthild's court at Rottenburg on the Neckar. Between 1461 and 1478 Wyle published his *Translatzen oder Tütschungen*, a collection of eighteen translations from the Latin and Italian. The work was inspired by Enea Silvio and included his novella and Boccaccio's *Guiscardo and Ghismonda* (*Decameron* IV, 1). What interested Wyle was not only the Latin elegance, which he attempted to convey into German by strictly observing the rules of Latin grammar, but also the subject matter of the novellas and speeches, which revealed a different attitude toward life.

Comparing Wyle's translation with the Spanish version of 1495 and the English rendition of 1596, one must come to the conclusion that the English version falls far behind. It is completely lacking in any erotic appeal, which comes through unexpurgated in both other versions. Wyle did not hesitate to translate faithfully the erotic scenes as well as the mythological embellishments, features of love literature at the period that are present in Celtis's Hasilina poem as well. The effect in both cases is as if you had just gazed at one of the famous Venus paintings of the period. The function of mythology goes beyond mere embellishment: it raises the individual to godlike stature.

In examining how Neo-Latin literature was introduced to Germany, we must make some mention as well of the vernacular. Boccaccio, as a friend of Petrarch, is, of course, a transitional figure between the Middle Ages and the Renaissance, but there are already strong indications of the dawning of a new era in his *Decameron*. This masterpiece is a product of a rising middle class with its utilitarian thinking. Boccaccio succeeds in depicting this social milieu with virtuosity in his mother tongue, keeping at a humorous distance from his subject matter. Though the apparent purpose of the novella-cycle is the description of the vanity of all human endeavor and strife in the face of higher powers—as the moralizing framework suggests—the narrator's attitude toward the stories gives him away as an early representative of the subjective amorality of the free Renaissance artist. The new ideal is the educated courtier—an expert in polite conversation and an example of moral behavior.

In 1472 Heinrich Schlüsselfelder of Nuremberg published his translation of the *Decameron*. Lacking Boccaccio's courtly polish, the rendition was at first a failure. Nevertheless, shortly after the Reformation its popularity rose immensely: it became one of the most widely read books next to Luther's Bible and Pauli's collection of anecdotes (*Schimpf und Ernst*; Fun and Earnestness, 1522). Eight printings appeared between 1535 and

1575 alone. What is the reason behind this sudden popularity?
The Reformation, with its school reform, had created a large new
group of readers with an indiscriminate hunger for sheer enter-
tainment in the vein of the popular joke and travel books of the
period. And this they found in Schlüsselfelder's translation.
Proof is found in the fact that about forty out of the one hundred novellas were gradually and freely adapted to German
tastes, appearing in popular joke books without any regard to
their original form. The favorite material was drawn from the
eighth day of lovemaking and then from the witty tales of the
seventh day. Adaptations for the stage were even carried out by
Hans Sachs (see *Tragedi, dess Fürsten Concreti und Gismunda,*
1545; *Comedi Griselda,* 1546).

A typical adaptation was from a Boccaccio tale in the German anecdote book *Schimpf und Ernst* by Johannes Pauli (No.
228, 1522). The original Boccaccio novella of the eighth day tells
how "Nastagio degli Onesti, falling in love with a lady of the
Traversari family, spendeth his substance without being beloved
in return, and betaking himself, at the instance of his kindsfolk,
to Chiassi, he there seeth a horseman give chase to a damsel and
slay her and cause her to be devoured of two hogs. Therewithal
he biddeth his kindsfolk and the lady whom he loveth to dinner,
where his mistress seeth the same damsel—it befell every Friday
—torn in pieces and fearing a like fate, taketh Nastagio to husband" (argument). Certainly we may consider this an exemplary
account of cruelty of beloved ladies, which is punishable from an
exclusively male perspective; for not loving, the female is treated
like a wild beast, her so-called cruelty appears as a social crime
and even as a sin in the eyes of God. "All the ladies of Ravenna
became so fearful by reason thereof, that ever after they were
much more amenable than they had been before to the desires of
the men." A cruel lesson is being taught, but the offense is
treated not in terms of dogmatic Christian ethics but rather as
something undesirable within relationships, thus shedding a re-
vealing light on the plight of women in the fourteenth century.

Pauli cuts Boccaccio's tale to about an eighth of its original
length, and in addition makes significant changes as to plot and

message: first he introduces a count, who has nothing at all to do with the gruesome event; then he transforms the motif of unrequited love to one of mutual adultery. This entails a complete change in interpretation. Instead of an amoral novella reproving cruel women, we end up with a moral example in the strictest sense of church dogma. Definitely the Reformation—with its popular-democratic tendencies and its school reform after 1525— had some beneficial effects on the literary scene, but we understand now that it completely changed the climate. The Boccaccio adaptations of the period are sufficient proof of the German tendency to prefer a crude, realistic approach to the subject matter, with strong moralizing overtones, rather than novellas written in a polished courtly style. With the Reformation an ever increasing coarseness (*Grobianismus*) pervaded the literary realm, and any attempts by individual humanists to continue an independent "pagan" life were crushed. Dr. Faustus, as a full-fledged Renaissance man, was condemned to hell. Paganism, after a brief interlude, failed to take root in German literature, and the religious strain of the Renaissance won the day.

Yet taking a final look beyond the realm of literature, we discover to our surprise that a pagan delight in this world's beauty, particularly the Epicurean enjoyment of nude figures, was by no means suppressed by the Reformation. A case in point is Lucas Cranach the Elder, who, as a friend of Luther, worked at the very beginning of the Reformation as a court painter to the elector of Saxony at Wittenberg. From 1508 until approximately 1540 Cranach not only portrayed the reformers and illustrated the Bible; he also painted a long series of mythological pictures, ranging from the *Judgment of Paris, Venus,* and *The River Nymph* (1518, modeled on Giorgione) to *Lucrecia, The Graces, Eve*. Paintings like *Eve* (1537), *The Three Graces* (1531), and *Venus with Amor as a Honey Thief* (1531) stand out for their portrayal of seductively posing female nudes, totally untouched by Reformation moralizing. These pictures in particular seem to have been in high demand, inasmuch as many variations of the same motifs have come down to us. But how can we explain Cranach's continued exhibition of pagan interests while didactic-reformatory works prevailed in literature? It is not only the tradition of painting mythological scenes, an established practice since Dürer, but primarily Cranach's strong position in Wittenberg (he was mayor twice) that must be taken into consideration. All of his works were commissioned, and he chose a racy style to meet the expectations of courtly taste. Apparently the court at Wittenberg had been compelled to discontinue its patronage of literary "pagan" humanism, whose works were mass-produced by means of the new printing process, and it then switched to a more exclusive medium to maintain their pagan interests. "The pagan point of view is aristocratic rather than democratic" (Henry C. Hatfield). Only through the growing political and cultural strength of the princely courts, during the second half of the sixteenth century, was a gradual return to more liberal attitudes in literature made possible. By 1600 *Grobianismus* was gradually replaced by a belated revival of humanism in its more sensual and courtly vein.

Selected Bibliography

GENERAL WORKS

Allen, D. C. *Mysteriously Meant: The Rediscovery of Pagan Symbolism and Allegorical Interpretation in the Renaissance.* Baltimore, 1970.
Baeumer, Max L. "Voluptas und frühbürgerliche Revolution. Neue Sichtweisen der Literatur des 15. und 16. Jahrhunderts." *Monatshefte,* 65 (1973), 393–415.
Buck, August. "L'Italia e gli albori dell'umanésimo tedesco." *Rivista di letteratura moderne e comparate,* 14 (1961), 20–23.
Burger, Heinz O. *Renaissance Humanismus Reformation. Deutsche Literatur im europäischen Kontext.* Bad Homburg, Berlin, Zürich, 1969.
Ellinger, Georg. *Italien und der deutsche Humanismus in der neulateinischen Lyrik.* In *Geschichte der neulateinischen Lyrik Deutschlands im 16. Jahrhundert,* 1. Berlin, Leipzig, 1929.
Hatfield, Henry C. *Aesthetic Paganism in German Literature, from Winckelmann to the Death of Goethe.* Cambridge, Mass., 1964.

Hoffmeister, Gerhart. *Petrarkistische Lyrik*. Sammlung Metzler, 119. Stuttgart, 1973.

Karstien, C. "Beiträge zur Einführung des Humanismus in die deutsche Literatur (E. Sylvio, Wyle, Eyb)," *Germanisch-Romanische Monatsschrift*, 11 (1923), 217–25, 278–88.

Kristeller, Paul O. "Paganism and Christianity." In *Renaissance Thought: The Classic, Scholastic, and Humanistic Strains*. New York, Evanston, London, 1961, 70–91.

Newald, Richard. *Probleme und Gestalten des deutschen Humanismus*. Berlin, 1963.

Petriconi, Hellmuth and Walter Pabst. "Die Einwirkung der italienischen Literatur auf die deutsche." In *Deutsche Philologie im Aufriß*, 3. W. Stammler, ed. 2nd edition, Berlin, 1962, 107–146.

Ristow, Brigitte. "Humanismus," in *Reallexikon der deutschen Literaturgeschichte*, 1. Werner Kohlschmidt und Wolfgang Mohr, eds. Berlin, 1958, 693–727.

Rupprich, Hans. *Vom späten Mittelalter bis zum Barock*. In *Geschichte der deutschen Literatur*, 4. München, 1970 (De Boor-Newald).

Seznec, Jean. *The Survival of the Pagan Gods; The Mythological Tradition*. New York, 1953.

Spriewald, Ingeborg. "Reformation und deutsche Literatur. Kennzeichen der literarischen Situation nach Luthers Thesenanschlag." *Weimarer Beiträge*, 1967, 687–98.

Stammler, Wolfgang. *Von der Mystik zum Barock*. Stuttgart, 2nd edition, 1950.

Toffanin, Giuseppe. *Storia dell'umanesimo*. Bologna, 2nd edition, 1964. 4 vols. (English transl. *History of Humanism* by E. Gianturco. New York, 1954).

INDIVIDUAL HUMANISTS

Peter Luder

Baron, Frank E. "The Beginning of German Humanism: The Life and Works of the Wandering Humanist Peter Luder." Dissertation, Berkeley, 1966.

————. "Peter Luder." In *Neue Deutsche Biographie*. Ed. Historische Kommission der Bayrische Akademie der Wissenschaften. Berlin, 1964 ff.

Wattenbach, W. "Peter Luder, der erste humanistische Lehrer in Heidelberg." *Zeitschrift der Geschichte des Oberrheins*, 22 (1869), 33–127. (Appendix contains Luder's letters and speeches.)

Celtis

Bezold, Friedrich von. *Konrad Celtis, der deutsche Erzhumanist*. München, 1883; rpt. Darmstadt, 1959.

Celtis, Conrad. *Quattuor libri Amorum*. F. Pindter, ed. Leipzig, 1934.

Preiss, Kurt L. "Konrad Celtis und der italienische Humanismus." Dissertation Wien 1951.

Schnur, Harry C., ed. *Lateinische Gedichte deutscher Humanisten*. Stuttgart: Reclam 8739–45, 1967.

Spitz, Lewis M. *Conrad Celtis: The German Arch-Humanist*. Cambridge, Mass, 1957.

Enea Silvio

Lhotsky, Alphons. "Aeneas Silvius und Österreich." Basel, 1965 (Lecture)

Silvio Piccolomini, Enea. *Opera omnia*. Basel 1551; reprinted Hildesheim, 1965.

———. *Selected Letters of Aeneas Silvius Piccolomini*. Albert R. Baca, transl. Northridge, Cal., 1969.

———. *The Most Excellent Historie of Euryalus and Lucresia*. London, 1596.

———. *The Tale of the Two Lovers*. Flora Grierson, transl. London, 1929.

———. *Historia muy verdadera de dos amantes, Euralio, franco, y Lucrecia, senesa*. Sevilla, 2nd edition, 1512; rpt. Madrid, 1952.

———. *Der Briefwechsel des Eneas Silvius Piccolomini*. Rudolf Wolkan, ed. Fontes rerum Austriacarum II, 61. Wien., 1909 (with Latin version of the novella).

———. *Briefe, Dichtungen*. Transl. and ed. by Max Mell and Ursula Abel. Die Fundgrube, 16. München, 1966 (includes the novella in German).

———. *Enea Silvio Piccolomini, Papst Pius II. Ausgewählte Texte aus seinen Schriften*. Berthe Widmer, ed. Basel, 1960 (Latin).

———. *Enea Silvio Piccolomini. Papst und Humanist*. Kurt Adel, ed. Stiasny Bücherei, 111. Graz, Wien, 1962 (pocketbook, with Mell's novella translation).

Weiss, Anton. *Aeneas Sylvius Piccolomini als Papst Pius II. Sein Leben und sein Einfluß auf die literarische Cultur Deutschlands*. Graz, 1897.

Niklas von Wyle

Strauß, Bruno. *Der Übersetzer Niclas von Wyle.* Berlin, 1912.

Tisch, J. H. "Fifteenth-Century German Courts and Renaissance Literature." Hobart: University of Tasmania, 1971. (Lecture)

——. "The Rise of the Novella in German Early Humanism: The Translator Niclas von Wyle (1410–1478)." *Australasian Universities. Language and Literature Association: Proceedings and Papers of the 12th Congress held at the University of Western Australia, February 1969.* Sydney, 1970, 477–99.

Wyle, Niklas von, *Translationen.* Adelbert von Keller, ed. Bibliothek des Litterarischen Vereins Stuttgart, 57. 1861; rpt. Hildesheim, 1967.

Boccaccio

Boccaccio. *Decameron.* Transl. by John Payne. New York, 1931.

——. *Das deutsche Decameron.* Adelbert von Keller, ed. Bibliothek des Litterarischen Vereins Stuttgart, 51. 1860.

Leube, Eberhard. "Boccaccio und die europäische Novellendichtung." In *Neues Handbuch der Literaturwissenschaft.* A. Buck und H. Baader, eds., Frankfurt, 1972. IX, 128–61.

Monostory, Denes. *Der Decamerone und die deutsche Prosa des 16. Jahrhunderts.* Den Haag, 1971.

Pauli, Johann. *Schimpf und Ernst.* H. Oesterley, ed. Bibliothek des Litterarischen Vereins Stuttgart, 85. 1866.

Schwaderer, R. "Boccaccios deutsche Verwandlungen. Übersetzungsliteratur und Publikum im deutschen Frühhumanismus." *Arcadia,* 10 (1975), 113–28.

Wetzel, K. "Zur Überlieferung der ersten deutschen Übersetzung von Boccaccios Decamerone." *Leuvense Bijdragen,* 54 (1965), 53–62.

Lucas Cranach

Glaser, Curt. *Lukas Cranach.* Leipzig, 1923.

5

Sebastian Brant:
The Ship of Fools

Gerhard Dünnhaupt

No other work of German literature before Goethe can match the resounding popular success and lasting influence both at home and abroad of Sebastian Brant's *The Ship of Fools*—or, to give it its original name, *Das Narrenschiff*. The phenomenal speed with which this book became known and popular throughout Renaissance Europe is as astonishing as the variety of genres in which its influence may be felt to this day.

As early as 1494, the year of the first Basel printing, pirated versions of the High German original of *The Ship of Fools* appeared in Nürnberg, Reutlingen, Strassburg, and Augsburg. No less than five authorized editions were published in Basel within the first fifteen years, not counting further pirated printings. Several Low German and Latin translations began to make their appearance from 1497 onward. The Latin version by the humanist Jacob Locher—personally supervised by Brant—received high praise, quickly became a European best seller, and was subsequently reprinted and translated all over Western Europe. For the first time in history German letters had entered the mainstream of world literature. The earliest English adaptations, by Alexander Barclay (1508) and Henry Watson (1509), in turn sparked many further imitations and derivations that left their mark throughout English and American literature, the most recent being Katherine Anne Porter's novel and the film of the same title. Counting both German and foreign printings, the number of editions of *The Ship of Fools* works out to an average of one every six years over the past 480 years!

In Germany an entirely new literary genre evolved out of Brant's original concept: the "Narrenliteratur," i.e., the personification of human follies. Many prominent authors of the age— from Geiler von Kaisersberg, Thomas Murner, Johannes Fischart, Erasmus of Rotterdam, and Hans Sachs in the Renaissance to Moscherosch, Weise, and Grimmelshausen in the Baroque—were profoundly influenced by it. Indeed, the theme of human folly formed the very basis of many satirical publications produced during the century of religious strife and political upheaval that was to follow the Reformation. The Franciscan monk Thomas Murner wrote a widely read, vicious satirical attack on Martin Luther, entitled *Of the Great Lutheran Fool* (1522), in which Murner himself appears as an oversize tomcat ("Murr-Narr") exorcising the follies of a gargantuan Luther figure. By way of the same author's earlier *Narrenbeschwörung* (Fools' Exorcism) —a book that incorporates sixty-nine of Brant's original wood-cuts—the concept of the fool gradually gave way to personifications of human shortcomings as "devils." Thus another new genre, "devils' literature," came into being, in which formerly harmless follies, such as love of hunting or fashion, were personified and denounced as "hunting devil," "fashion devil," etc. Even a single chapter of *The Ship of Fools* (number 72), for which Brant had humorously invented a "Saint Grobian" (Saint Ruffian), started a minor literary genre all on its own: "grobianic literature," a satirical approach to the teaching of social graces and table manners by means of negative examples.

Sebastian Brant himself laid no claim to originality. Far from it; standing, as he did, on the very threshold of the Middle Ages and the Renaissance, he proudly pointed out the many

sources upon which he relied for his numerous exempla: the Old
and New Testaments of the Bible; classical poets like Ovid, Vergil, and Juvenal; medieval proverbial wisdom; as well as his own
legal specialty: canon law. The collecting of moral exempla for
didactical purposes was a long-standing medieval custom, but to
bring them together under the unifying theme of folly—through
personification in individual fools—gave his work an epochal
new character. To Brant's contemporaries *The Ship of Fools*
represented a mirror of the world with all its errors and shortcomings, a total inventory of human follies. To the modern
reader it affords a unique insight into the daily life, customs,
manners, morals, and superstitions of central Europe in the early
Renaissance.

As the first seventy-three chapters of *The Ship of Fools* uniformly number either thirty-four or ninety-four verses, they were
once believed to have been written for publication as individual
broadsheets similar to others Brant had produced in his youth.
No evidence has ever been uncovered, however, to support such a
theory. It is more likely that each poem was planned to fit exactly
on two or four pages of the large-letter first edition. This plan,
too, must have been abandoned after chapter 73, for at this point
poems of varying length are introduced. Despite all efforts to
prove the contrary, there appears to be no recognizable grouping
of follies according to categories, nor are we able to detect any
sequence or progression from relatively harmless transgressions to
the seven mortal sins. No doubt Brant felt that such pedantry
would have yielded tiresome results, for variety is what he sought
to achieve, and the superb woodcuts assisted him in this aim.
Usually they tend to illustrate one or several aspects of the particular folly under discussion. Often they refer to specific passages
in the main poem, while the function of the motto verses is
clearly to help the reader recognize the connection between picture and poem. The tripartite division of each chapter—woodcut,
motto, poem—prefigures the basic concept of "emblematic poetry," a genre that was to become immensely popular during
the century following the publication of *The Ship of Fools*. In
emblematics, however, the woodcut does not merely illustrate the

poem or parts thereof, but often conveys a message of its own, so that all three parts are needed by the reader to comprehend and interpret the whole. Brant's poems, on the other hand, can easily stand on their own.

The work is introduced by the frame motif of the fools' ship, a symbol for the uncertainty of human endeavors, tossed about like a nutshell by the stormy seas of fate. After the introduction, however, the ship motif does not recur until chapter 48. Later on it is briefly mentioned a few more times, but not until the very end of the book (in chapters 103, 108, and 109) do we encounter the ship motif again. Brant's concept of human life as a voyage across uncharted seas could hardly have come at a more appropriate time, for those were the days of the great discoveries. Christopher Columbus had just returned from his first great overseas voyage, and none other than Sebastian Brant, together with his printer Bergmann von Olpe—who also collaborated with him on *The Ship of Fools*—had edited the famous Columbus letter to acquaint his countrymen with the earliest report of the newly discovered lands. An allusion in chapter 66,

> They've found in Portugal since then
> And in Hispania naked men,
> And sparkling gold and islands too
> Whereof no mortal ever knew.
>   *(66, 53–56)**

appears to be a direct reference to these new discoveries. Only eleven years after the first edition of Brant's book, in 1507, Martin Waldseemüller of Strassburg named the new continent "America." And before another decade had passed, Martin Luther posted his ninety-five theses on the castle church of Wittenberg. The sum total of knowledge that had been uncritically accepted for centuries was suddenly thrown open to question.

---

* Translated by Edwin H. Zeydel, in an edition published 1944 by Columbia University Press (see bibliography). Quotations in this article are from that edition.

Sebastian Brant stood in the mainstream of this exciting intellectual development, and was able to count men like the artist Albrecht Dürer, Paracelsus, the famous physician-alchemist, and Erasmus among his personal friends. There were tremendous achievements in almost every field of the arts, the sciences, and the humanities. Brant's fools' ship omitted none of these disciplines, for he attacked folly wherever he found it. Hence it was not contradictory when he denounced the clergy for their immorality and greed while simultaneously urging his countrymen to cease their religious strife and return to the church. Nor did he hesitate to attack pseudoscholars, shoddy printers, and quacks, though he was of course not opposed to learning, publishing, or medicine per se. Brant condemned not the activity as such— merely its excess or abuse.

Several chapters of *The Ship of Fools* follow medieval tradition by providing exempla for the biblical commandments and the seven mortal sins. But it is predominately in the chapters dealing with lesser transgressions that we are able to gain an insight into the everyday world of Renaissance life and its customs, mores, and superstitions. We learn of corrupt priests selling fake relics to unsuspecting believers, of silly fashions for both men and women, of the nuisance created by nightly serenaders wooing their loved ones in the streets, and of profit-hungry advocates endlessly stretching out their court cases until both parties are bled dry. A colorful parade of whores and pimps, hypochondriacs and quacks, merchants, witches, and beggar-monks passes before our eyes, and we become curious to learn more of the contemporary educational, financial, and marital problems, about the games people played and the kind of food they ate, even the manner in which they consumed it. The variety of everyday situations satirized by Brant never ceases to surprise us—yet his *Ship of Fools* appears to have room for all of them.

Aside from the ship symbol there is a second motif that signifies the transience and ultimate futility of all earthly endeavor: the wheel of fortune. It is introduced in chapter 37, repeated in chapter 56, and frequently alluded to in other chapters as well. Similar to the ship, the wheel suggests uncertainty,

but it also serves as a warning against attaching too much importance to one's worldly possessions and achievements, for the next
turn of the wheel is bound to cause death and destruction. Here
Brant's fools' parade closely approaches the medieval concept of
the "dance of death." In fact, Brant reserved the entire chapter
85 for the topic of death. We quickly realize that Brant's concept
of death offers considerably less consolation than the accepted
teachings of the Christian church:

> To die and flow away we're bound
> As water flows into the ground.
> *(85, 9–10)*

Death is praised not as the glorious moment of entry into the
Kingdom of Heaven but merely as the cessation of all sorrows
and bitter experiences of earthly existence:

> For many death has been a gain,
> Since thus they're rid of grief and pain.
> *(85, 73–74)*

Thus the hour of dying is dreaded, for it inevitably brings the
horror of the final judgment:

> Death is like a judge who hears no plea
> Of any man for clemency.
> *(85, 83–84)*

In this respect Brant's view of death almost coincides with that of
the *Plowman of Bohemia* by Johannes of Teplá (1401),* who also
sees it in all its finality rather than as a new beginning.

Despite Brant's somewhat unorthodox treatment of religious
matters, he was a strict Roman Catholic who displayed no
sympathy for the various reform movements that sprang up during his own lifetime. Nowhere is his ultraconservative attitude
better illustrated than in the visionary, almost apocalyptic chap-

---

* Translated by Alexander and Elizabeth Henderson, Ungar, 1966,
under the name Johannes von Saaz.

ter 103, whose verses betray Brant's real fear of an ultimate vic-
ory for the Antichrist:

> We're now approaching total night,
> Such things have never happened yet,
> The vessel sways, it may upset.
>   (*103, 149–51*)

Over and over he exhorted his readers not to listen to the temp-
tors but to adhere firmly to the traditional ways. In view of the
fact that Brant tended to side with the state in its conflicts of
authority with the church, and considering his frequent reproofs
of the clergy, one cannot help wondering whether his criticism
did not further rather than impede the development of reform
movements.

It thus appears that Brant tended to favor the maintenance
of the status quo, for he warned his contemporaries of too rapid
progress and looked toward the future with considerable appre-
hension. Did this make him a pessimist? Was it not indicative of
a forward-looking Renaissance spirit to trust—as Brant did—in
the power of education, to believe optimistically that man can be
improved, and to employ recently invented printing techniques
to convince his contemporaries? Why then the gloomy picture?
The answer lies in Brant's didactic principle: to present his
reader with a series of negative examples, to hold up a mirror to
him so that he may recognize himself and mend his ways. Self-
recognition, after all, is the first step toward improvement. Hence
Brant felt obliged to dramatize the alternatives in order to emphasize the need for change. In this respect *The Ship of Fools* is
at once conservative and progressive; although based on traditional medieval principles, it is nevertheless forward-looking
and optimistic in spirit. Standing at the end of a dying world, it
ushered in a new era. Only when we fully comprehend this fact
can we begin to understand the enormous impact this work had
upon Europe at the dawn of the northern Renaissance.

Notwithstanding the fact that *The Ship of Fools* was written
in the vernacular, Brant's learned contemporaries were quick to

recognize that it owed its satirical spirit to the classical tradition, to the great Roman examples of Lucilius, Horace, Persius, and Juvenal, who are frequently quoted in the text. The Basel humanist Jacob Locher, author of the Latin version *Stultifera navis* (1497), made a strong point of aligning Brant's work with the classical tradition of his satire. Another contemporary, the great educator Jacob Wimpheling, lauded the work as the first German satire and demanded that it be made required reading in German schools. The learned Abbot Trithemius, author of the first German literary history, lavishly praised it as a "Divine Satire," a fitting counterpart to Dante's "Divine Comedy." Erasmus of Rotterdam, the greatest of all humanists, was profoundly influenced by this work. His own satirical *Praise of Folly* (1509) includes no fewer than twenty topics corresponding to chapters of Brant's book, and even some of its woodcuts—by the renowned Hans Holbein—are strongly reminiscent of *The Ship of Fools*. It has been argued that Brant's work lacks the unity of *The Praise of Folly*, but the inner unity of a satire does not rely on outward form as much as on the critical attitude of the satirist. Whether he chooses to deal with each exemplum in an individual poem, or to combine various exempla in a continuous prose piece, is merely a matter of artistic preference. The humanist Jodocus Badius, in his *Stultiferae naviculae, seu scaphae, fatuarum mulierum (Ship of Foolish Women*, Paris, 1500) characterized Brant's satirical manner as teaching the foolish, who are initially attracted by his humorous tone without realizing that they themselves are the butts of his satire—almost exactly the same characterization that the Roman poet Persius used for the satires of Horace. Brant's poetry thus stands as much in the Roman satirical tradition as does the prose of Erasmus. If the creation of works of art in the manner of the classics is the criterion by which we recognize a Renaissance artist, then Brant must be seen as a true humanist, like Erasmus. The difference in the satirical approach of the two writers is purely technical: while Brant exposed the foolishness of his characters by letting them utter their respective follies individually, Erasmus preferred to personify Folly—perhaps in analogy to Brant's personification of Wisdom in chapter 22—and ironically let her praise herself.

There is little doubt that the magnificent woodcuts contributed in large measure to the success of *The Ship of Fools*. This is strikingly demonstrated by the fact that even the foreign translations invariably used either the original woodcuts or faithful imitations of them. Moreover, books by other authors on similar topics, such as Thomas Murner's *Fools' Exorcism*, which were strongly inspired by Brant, also made use of many of his woodcuts, for no copyrights existed then to protect artists and writers. Although our information concerning the creation of the original woodcuts is somewhat scanty, it appears that Brant himself was directly involved in their planning and execution in the Basel workshop of his friend Bergmann von Olpe. From the textual evidence available it appears that specific instructions were issued by the poet to the artists, for in some cases the woodcuts illustrate scenes merely alluded to but not explicitly described in the text. Without direct supervision by the poet, no artist working independently could possibly have gained such insight from a mere reading of the poem. Though we do not know their identities, it is quite evident that artists of varying talents collaborated in the production of *The Ship of Fools*. Without difficulty we are able to recognize the hand of the so-called "Master of the Bergmann Shop" in many woodcuts of superior quality, while another group appears to have come from the hands of less skilled craftsmen. The superior woodcuts are almost invariably distinguished by finer lines, a great number of individual details, as well as a vastly improved sense of perspective. Often they are enhanced by a portion of background landscape: a castle on a hill, a village in the distance, or a glimpse into the town from an open window.

Who was the artist that created these masterly woodcuts? Various theories have been advanced to lift the veil hiding his identity. As there is evidence that young Albrecht Dürer served his apprenticeship in Basel between 1492 and 1494, strong arguments speak in his favor, and according to more recent comparative analyses of Dürer's work, his participation in *The Ship of Fools* may now be considered almost certain.

Sebastian Brant was the first German poet to achieve truly international renown and to leave a profound impression on the literature of other countries. Born in Strassburg in 1458, the son of a prosperous innkeeper and city alderman, he studied law at Basel, at that time one of Germany's most important universities and a major center of northern humanism. Here he received his doctorate in 1489, but continued to serve the university in various teaching capacities—including that of Dean of Law—for another decade. Aside from writing numerous legal treatises during those years, he also made a name for himself as a Latin poet and translator. Of more immediate consequence, as forerunners of *The Ship of Fools*, are his numerous pamphlets and broadsheets on a wide variety of subjects, bearing titles such as "Of the Thunderbolt Fallen in 1492 near Ensissheim," "Of the Curious Sow at Landser in the Sundgau," "Of the Two-headed Goose at Guggenheim," or dealing with comets, floods, plagues, and similar unusual events. Since newspapers were not to appear until the next century, such broadsheets were the only available source of news. Like the chapters in *The Ship of Fools*, each consisted of three parts: a woodcut, an extended headline (in place of the later motto), and the actual news story in prose. Popular, too, were Brant's instruction manuals on social graces, as well as his collections of proverbs from the classics, all of which probably contributed indirectly to the shaping of *The Ship of Fools*.

Throughout his life, Brant remained a staunch supporter and fervent admirer of the German emperor Maximilian I. Thus, in 1499, when his adopted city of Basel decided to leave the empire to join the Swiss confederation, Brant immediately returned to his native Strassburg where he continued his legal career, to be rewarded subsequently for his loyalty with the post of Imperial Councillor. By now he was famous both as the poet of *The Ship of Fools* and as a legal authority, and his far-flung correspondence connected him with most of the great humanists of his day. After the death of his beloved hero Maximilian I in 1520, it was none other than Sebastian Brant who stood at the head of Strassburg's citizenry to pay homage to the old emperor's grandson, young Charles V. Only one year later, on May 10, 1521, Brant died in Strassburg. Though he had witnessed the beginnings of the Lutheran Reformation, he did not survive long enough to realize its full impact: the dreaded change of the old order that he unwittingly may have helped to bring about.

Selected Bibliography

PRIMARY SOURCES

A. In German

Brant, Sebastian. *Das Narrenschyff*. Basel: Bergmann von Olpe, 1494; facsimile Franz Schulz, ed. Strassburg: Gesellschaft für elsässische Literatur, 1913. (First edition in any language.)

Sebastian Brants Narrenschiff. Friedrich Zarncke, ed. Leipzig, 1854; rpt. Hildesheim: Olms; and Darmstadt: Wissenschaftliche Buchgesellschaft, 1964. (The best annotated edition, without the woodcuts.)

Brant, Sebastian. *Das Narrenschiff*. Manfred Lemmer, ed. Neudrucke deutscher Literaturwerke, N.F. 5. Tübingen: Niemeyer, 1962. (Latest edition of Brant's original text.)

Brant, Sebastian. *Das Narrenschiff*. Transl. and ed. by H. A. Junghans. Stuttgart: Reclam, 1964. (The best annotated translation into modern German, with all woodcuts. Paperback.)

B. In English

Barclay, Alexander. *The Shyp of folys of the worlde . . . translated out of Laten, Frenche, and Doche into Englysse tonge*. London: Richard Pynson, 1508; rpt. Edinburgh and London, 1874; with introduction by T. H. Jamieson.

Brant, Sebastian. *The Ship of Fools*. Transl. and ed. by Edwin H. Zeydel. New York: Columbia University Press, 1944; rpt. New York: Dover Publications, 1962. (The best annotated English translation, with all woodcuts. Paperback.)

Watson, Henry. *The Shyppe of Fooles*. London: Wynkyn de Worde, 1509.

SECONDARY SOURCES

Böckmann, Paul. "Die Narrensatire als Weg der menschlichen Selbster-
kenntnis bei Sebastian Brant." In Böckmann, *Formgeschichte der
deutschen Dichtung*, Hamburg, 1949, 227–239.

Bond, E. Warwick. "Brant's 'Das Narrenschiff,' " in Bond, *Studia Otiosa,
Some Attempts in Criticism*. London, 1938, 18–42.

Burckhardt, Daniel. *Dürers Aufenthalt in Basel 1492–1494*. München,
1892.

Claus, P. *Rhythmik und Metrik in Sebastian Brants Narrenschiff*. Quellen und Forschungen, 112. Strassburg, 1911.

Eberth, Hans Heinrich. *Die Sprichwörter in Sebastian Brants* Narrenschiff. Greifswalder Forschungen, 3. Dissertation Greifswald, 1933.

Fischer, C. B. "Several Allusions in Brant's *Narrenschiff*," *Modern Language Notes*, 68 (1953), 395 ff.

Fraustadt, Fedor. *Über das Verhältnis von Barclays Ship of Fools zur
lateinischen, französischen und deutschen Quelle*. Dissertation,
Breslau, 1894.

Gaier, Ulrich. *Studien zu Sebastian Brants* Narrenschiff. Tübingen, 1966.

———. "Sebastian Brant's *Narrenschiff* and the Humanists." *PMLA*, 83
(1968), 266–270.

Genschmer, F. *The Treatment of the Social Classes in the Satires of
Brant, Murner, and Fischart*. Dissertation, Urbana, Ill., 1934.

Gilbert, William. "Sebastian Brant: Conservative Humanist," *Archiv
für Reformationsgeschichte*, 46 (1955), 145–167.

Gruenter, Rainer. "Die 'Narrheit' in Sebastian Brant's *Narrenschiff*,"
Neophilologus, 43 (1953), 207 ff.

Herford, Charles H. *Studies in the Literary Relations of England and
Germany in the Sixteenth Century*. Cambridge, 1886.

Könneker, Barbara. *Sebastian Brant: Das Narrenschiff*. Interpretationen
zum Deutschunterricht. München, 1966.

Learned, Henry Dexter. *The Syntax of Brant's* Narrenschiff. Philadelphia, 1917.

O'Connor, D. "Notes on the Influence of Brant's *Narrenschiff* outside
Germany." *Modern Language Review*, 20 (1925) 64 ff.

Ohse, Bernhard. *Die Teufelliteratur zwischen Brant und Luther*. Dissertation, Berlin, 1961.

Pompen, F. Aurelius. *The English Versions of* The Ship of Fools. London, 1925.

Schönfeld, Hermann. "Die kirchliche Satire und religiöse Weltanschauung in Brant's *Narrenschiff* und Erasmus' *Narrenlob*." *Modern Language Notes*, 7 (1892), 78–92, 137–149, 345.

Sobel, E. "Sebastian Brant, Ovid, and Classical Allusions in the *Narrenschiff*." *University of California Publications in Modern Philology*, 36 (1952), 429 ff.

Weisbach, Werner. *Der Meister der Bergmannschen Offizin und Albrecht Dürers Beziehungen zur Baseler Buchillustration*. In *Studien zur deutschen Kunstgeschichte*, 6. Strassburg, 1896.

———. *Die Baseler Buchillustration des XV. Jahrhunderts*. In *Studien zur deutschen Kunstgeschichte*, 8. Strassburg, 1896.

Winkler, F. *Dürer und die Illustrationen zum* Narrenschiff. In *Forschungen zur deutschen Kunstgeschichte*, 36. Berlin, 1951.

Wuttke, Dieter. "Sebastian Brants Verhältnis zu Wunderdeutung und Astrologie." In *Festschrift für Hugo Moser*, W. Besch et al., eds. Berlin, 1974, 272–286.

Zeydel, Edwin H. "Notes on Sebastian Brant's *Narrenschiff*." *Modern Language Notes*, 58 (1943), 340–46.

———. "Sebastian Brant and the Discovery of America." *Journal of English and Germanic Philology*, 42 (1943), 410–411.

———. "Some Literary Aspects of Sebastian Brant's *Narrenschiff*." *Studies in Philology*, 42 (1945), 21 ff.

———. *Sebastian Brant*. Twayne's World Authors Series, 13. New York, 1967.

6

Desiderius Erasmus:
Cosmopolitan Christian Humanism

Wayne A. Rebhorn

"O Erasmus roterodamus, wo willst du bleiben?" (O Erasmus of Rotterdam, where will you settle down?). With these words Erasmus's friend, the great painter Albrecht Dürer, voiced the complaint in his journal that friends and foes alike directed at the famous Dutch humanist. All were baffled and frustrated by the constantly changing attitudes and intellectual positions, the kaleidoscopic array of personality images that Erasmus assumed. For instance, although sympathetic to many reforms desired by the Protestants, he refused to be either totally for or totally against Luther and his decision to break with the Roman Catholic church. The quintessential ironist, he always saw any issue from several perspectives, consistent only in refusing the blandishments and avoiding the threats designed to make him adhere to one doctrinaire camp in matters literary, philosophical, or religious.

Erasmus's character seems built out of contradictions. Hostile to crude superstitions and the selling of indulgences and relics, Erasmus sometimes appears a sixteenth-century Voltaire;

yet, at the same time, he consistently defends a simple, direct, emotional Christianity accessible to peasant as well as scholar. He shares Protestant desires for a purification of Christianity and a return to its supposedly "original" form, but he refuses to break with the church and carefully affirms basic dogmas.

A fervent partisan of the New Learning and its leading representative in northern Europe during the first third of the sixteenth century, Erasmus nevertheless rejects the excessive adulation of antiquity of contemporary Ciceronianism and uses his ironic masterpiece, *The Praise of Folly*, to satirize scholars and humanists like himself and his friends. There is the Erasmus who constantly complains of being unable to settle down anywhere, to find a permanent home, and there is, finally, the other Erasmus, who just as constantly refuses to accept the offers of permanent residence made him by countless monarchs, cities, and states and who places his freedom to wander as he desires above any concern for a fixed abode. All this contradictory information raises the unavoidable questions: just who was this Desiderius Erasmus? what did he really stand for in intellectual, moral, artistic, and religious terms? and is there any consistency at all in the character he displays to contemporaries and posterity alike?

The vital center of Erasmus's life was the fervent pietistic Christianity that he absorbed during his childhood and adolescence in Holland. The illegitimate son of a priest and a nun, he was born in Rotterdam in either 1466 or 1469. He was educated first at Gouda and was then sent to the school at Deventer (1475–1484) run by the Brethren of the Common Life, who are alternately called the Devotio moderna. The Brethren, who enjoyed a fairly widespread following in the Low Countries during the fifteenth century, were a late medieval, pietistic, lay religious movement whose aim was to return Christianity to the sincerity, simplicity, and cheerful industry which they felt marked its earliest phases. Not at all a contemplative order, they directed their adherents toward action in this world, toward lives of preaching, evangelical piety, chastity and, especially, teaching. Reacting against the merely mechanical observance of ritual and dogma,

they insisted upon the interiorization of religion—personal involvement, introspection, meditation, and prayer—and urged
their followers to model their lives entirely upon those of Christ
and his disciples. Fittingly, the movement's most enduring
monuments have been *The Imitation of Christ* by Thomas à
Kempis and, of course, the life and works of Erasmus.

Having imbibed the spirit of the Devotio moderna during
his stay at Deventer, Erasmus took monastic vows at Steyn in
1488, a decision he regretted throughout his life. Nevertheless, it
is certain that Erasmus would have been a deeply committed
Christian even if he had remained a layman. His association with
the Brethren helps explain some of the seemingly contradictory
elements that appear in his writings and in the positions he took
in intellectual and religious debates. Like the Brethren, Erasmus
conceived of Christianity mainly as a matter of life and morals,
not of dogma and theological distinctions. In the preface he
wrote for his edition of the Greek New Testament, he proclaimed his credo as he defined what he meant by the philosophy
of Christ—a "pure and simple faith" that he wanted to have
restored everywhere "not in ceremonies only and in syllogisms,
but in the heart itself and the entirety of life."

Hence, it is completely understandable that Erasmus would
attack unthinking superstition, religious charlatans and huck-
sters who sold the easy salvation of indulgences, and the for-
mulaic character of contemporary worship. He struck out at these
not because he was an atheist or a Voltairean type of rationalist
but because he rejected any form of Christianity that relied on
external, mechanical devices rather than being anchored in the
sincere, inward experience of the believer. At the same time,
because his approach to Christianity was ethical in the broadest
sense, more than dogmatic or intellectual, he could easily admire
the upright lives of pagans as well as Christians. A character from
his colloquy *The Godly Feast* (*Convivium religiosum*) expressed
his admiration with the most audacious parody, "Saint Socrates,
pray for us!" and proclaimed the Erasmian doctrine that the true
spirit of Christ obviously extends well beyond the confines of
Christendom's spatial and temporal domains.

Finally, the emphasis on Christian living, the emphasis on the heart more than the head, also appears in Erasmus's praise for the Christian fool at the end of *The Praise of Folly*. In that passage, pious women, simple children, and holy madmen are ironically praised as fools who will enter the kingdom of heaven long before the wise and powerful who direct the affairs, both religious and secular, of this world.

Although a man of great learning and sophistication, widely traveled and with knowledge of many cultures, Erasmus remained faithful to a simple Christianity, one that he felt did not necessarily deny his intellectual activities, but that certainly came before them in his system of values. It was a religion that bound the Latin-speaking humanist as firmly to peasants as to popes and princes, and that prompted him to urge the translation of the Bible into every vernacular tongue from Irish to Turkish, so that farmers at the plow and weavers at the shuttle might sing psalms while they worked and fill their daily conversation with matter derived from the Gospels.

If his stay at Deventer shaped Erasmus's religious philosophy, it also helped make him into a humanist. Toward the end of his education there he had the opportunity to hear lectures by the famous German scholar Rudolph Agricola, who had studied in Italy and played an important intermediary role in bringing Italian humanists' philological methods and enthusiasm for classical antiquity north of the Alps. Erasmus was inspired by the new philology and by Agricola's enthusiasm for Greek, and in the years after he entered the monastery at Steyn—at the time also a center of classical learning—he intensified his study of Greek as well as continuing his development as a Latin stylist. By 1495, when he left Steyn for Paris, Erasmus was well on the way to completing the training that would eventually make him the leading humanist in northern Europe.

In one sense, of course, there were no humanists at all during the Renaissance. The *umanisti* at the Renaissance university were simply the teachers of the humanities, the *studia humanitatis*, and comprised a much larger and more heterogenous group than those scholars and teachers—men like Agricola and Eras-

mus, Thomas More, the English author of *Utopia*, and Juan Luis
Vives, the Spanish educator and editor of St. Augustine—whom
nineteenth- and twentieth-century scholars refer to as humanists
and discuss as representatives of what has been called humanism.
For modern historians, the humanists included authors and scholars, artists and political figures, as well as some *umanisti*, from
Petrarch in the fourteenth century, through Italian writers and
teachers like Petrus Paulus Vergerius, Battista Guarino, and
Enea Silvio (Pius II) in the fifteenth, down to Erasmus and
More. All of them shared at least one central concern—the development of an educational program based on the detailed study
of Greek and Latin authors from antiquity and the early Christian period.

All the humanists, though in varying degrees, also shared an
antipathy to the Latin style of late medieval writers and to what
they felt were the arid philsophical speculations of men like
Thomas Aquinas and like Duns Scotus, whose name they un-
fairly but characteristically transformed into "dunce." Instead,
the humanists admired the prose style of Cicero, the philosophical dialogues of Plato, and the theology of early church fathers
like Jerome and Augustine. With one voice they cried out "Ad
fontes!"—return to the sources of classical culture and the Christian tradition—and if the humanists never breathed the word
"Renaissance," it is clear that all nevertheless believed themselves assisting in the colossal rebirth of the ancient world in
their own time.

Implicit in the pronouncements and programs of these men
are several assumptions with rather far-reaching consequences.
First, all the humanists—including Erasmus—conceived of the
past as composed of distinct ages, each with its own special cultural
characteristics, systems of values, and essential styles. They came
to this awareness because all were, first and foremost, philologists
trained to distinguish between what they detested as the corrupt
style of the late Middle Ages and the more desirable style of
Latin antiquity that they attempted to emulate in their own
writings. Through this awareness of linguistic and stylistic difference came a broader, if imperfect, awareness of cultural differ-

ence, sharpened by their realization that antiquity was, after all, pagan and thus quite distinct both from the Middle Ages and their own epoch. Consequently, they realized the possibility of remodeling their own culture on the model of antiquity, and at the same time they knew that it had to be Christian and hence profoundly new and different. In other words, the humanists' philology led to cultural revolution; it filled them with the hope that by altering the basic institutions, the educational processes, the language that men spoke in their world, they could create a new society based on an elevated, Christianized vision of antiquity.

For some humanists, like More and Vives, the transformation of society depended primarily upon the alteration of basic social institutions. For most, however, including Erasmus, the education of the individual offered the best possibility for a general cultural rebirth. Their faith in education depended upon the assumption that men are malleable creatures at birth who could be shaped more or less as the educator desired.

Characteristically, in his treatise on the education of children (*De pueris statim ac liberaliter instituendis*), Erasmus proclaims that men are not born, but made, and that when it produces a child, Nature brings forth a crude mass, an unformed creature whose mind is a blank slate ("tabula complanata") on which the educator can write at will. At birth, man is merely potentially human, having within him both the capacity to become a truly rational creature and the equal capacity to degenerate to the level of the beasts. Like the Italian humanists before him, Erasmus believed in education as the crucial means by which man's potential for rationality could be actualized and his bestial proclivities avoided, and in his countless treatises, letters, and polemics, he sounded the optimistic note that most, if not all, men could be formed into true human beings with ease, if only the right educators, companions, tutors, servants—in short, the right sort of environment—surrounded them from the very start.

While Erasmus shared the general enthusiasm and many of the particular aims of preceding Italian thinkers, the fervent

Christianity at the center of his being did affect his educational program and its underlying conception of man in two important ways. First, the Christian doctrine of Original Sin and man's corrupt and fallen nature served as an explanation for Erasmus for all of man's wayward tendencies and effectively checked an unbridled optimism about human potential. Thus, while Erasmus might ultimately conclude that most men could still be educated into rationality, he also realized that the process required great care and that the resulting achievement remained a fragile one. The old earthly Adam, he says in his *Handbook of the Christian Knight (Enchiridion militis christiani)*, dwells within us, and even the best-trained individual must continually keep a sharp look-out for diabolically inspired misdirections. Secondly, Erasmus' Christianty led him to distance himself from the paganizing tendencies he felt he discerned in the works and lives of some Italian humanists.

Not only did Erasmus object to the doctrinaire Ciceronianism of some Latin stylists that would lead them to refer to the saints not as "sancti," but as "patres conscripti," an orthodox Ciceronian phrase for the members of the Roman Senate, but more profoundly, he objected to the practice of establishing as role-models for the child such pagan figures as Alexander the Great and the Roman hero Scipio Africanus. Instead, he urged the educator to set before the child the glowing example of Christ and His saints and apostles. The ultimate goal of education in Erasmus's opinion was not primarily to produce a learned philologist or a competent statesman, but a fervently moral Christian, and if necessary, Erasmus was ready to sacrifice other educational ends, both physical and intellectual, to achieve this all-important one.

Erasmus's Christian Humanist mission—to transform the world by making individual men into model Christians also trained as classical humanists—did not come to him immediately. After leaving the monastery of Steyn in 1492, he worked as a teacher and secretary and continued his studies until the fateful summer of 1499 when he accepted an invitation to visit England that had been offered to him by one of his pupils in Paris.

Erasmus arrived there a superb philologian and classically oriented humanist who was concerned with literature above other matters, and he left a year later with a sure sense that his task in life was to employ his substantial gifts as scholar, thinker, and elegant Latin stylist in the service of a renewed Christianity.

This change came about through the influence of John Colet and Thomas More and the circle of English humanists around them. Colet was deeply immersed in both classical and biblical studies and was currently lecturing on the New Testament and the Pauline Epistles at Oxford when Erasmus arrived. The classically trained More, who quickly became Erasmus's lifelong friend, was an equally devout Christian who had spent several years in a Carthusian monastery in London before deciding on a secular career as a lawyer. Both men demonstrated to Erasmus how zeal for classical scholarship could be combined with zeal for Christian reform and education and how the skills and knowledge acquired in the study of pagan antiquity could be used to study the Bible and the early church fathers.

Specifically, Colet urged Erasmus to put his philological training to use in lectures on the New Testament, a task for which Erasmus did not yet find himself suitably prepared, and both men enlisted Erasmus's help on later visits to England in designing an educational program for the school at St. Paul's cathedral, which they were organizing along Christian humanist lines. Erasmus left them in 1500 to return to the continent, determined to acquire the skill and knowledge necessary—and particularly the extensive acquaintance with Greek that he realized was needed—in order to complete the tasks he now saw as his life's work.

From 1500 to his death in 1536, Erasmus produced an astounding amount and variety of material concerned with the reform and improvement of Christendom. There were satires of social and religious abuses such as *The Praise of Folly* and the *Colloquies*, and works of classical scholarship such as the *Adagia*, a collection of sayings and proverbs culled from Erasmus's extensive readings in classical and Christian authors that served generations of European writers and intellectuals as a treasury of quotable material. He produced numerous treatises on subjects ranging from letter writing and good manners to education and marriage, as well as hundreds of letters that he had collected and published during his life and that performed a somewhat journalistic role in disseminating Christian humanist ideas to a wide European audience.

While Erasmus may survive primarily through his satirical writings, the bulk of all his work was directed at the instruction and reformation of European society. Moreover, he thought of himself not as a social critic or a literary person, but primarily as a theologian, and he considered his religious writings and his editions of works by men like Jerome the most important achievements of his life. From this perspective, the climax of Erasmus's career must be seen as occurring in 1516 with his publication of a new edition and translation of the New Testament, the first reediting of the Greek text since antiquity that revealed the many substantial errors contained in the Vulgate. If Erasmus had achieved a European reputation by publishing the *Adagia* in 1500, his fame reached its heights with this appearance of the New Testament. He was courted by monarchs and churchmen, attracted swarms of pupils and followers and patrons, and scholars throughout Europe began referring to themselves with the flattering title of "Erasmiani."

What Erasmus and his disciples, whose number included not only scholars like the Spaniard Juan Luis Vives, but literary geniuses like François Rabelais, stood for was a combination of the New Learning with a sincere Christianity and a concern for a renewed society. Just as they argued for a return to the pure Latinity of Cicero and Vergil, they advocated a purification of the church and a reformation of society in keeping with Christian morality. They opposed contemporary injustices and inhumanities, ranging from excessive corporal punishment in the schools, through political tyranny and the oppression of the poor, to the shameless pursuit of war, even when it was directed against supposed infidels under the rubric of a holy "crusade." They believed, optimistically and a bit naïvely, that through increased knowledge and educational reform alone society could be made a better, more Christian place, and that since the truth would supposedly triumph in any reasonable discussion among reasonable men, toleration of dissent was preferable to its brutal suppression. While Erasmus and his friends and followers consistently defended this program, however, the emergence of Luther on the European scene in 1517 exposed the desperately "utopian" quality of all their hopes.

Luther and other leaders of the Reformation repeatedly called upon Erasmus to join sides with them in their attack on Catholic orthodoxy, and there was much in Erasmus that might have led him to ally himself with the Protestant cause. His satire of superstition and the mechanical repetition of dogma and ceremony, his dislike of reliance on intercessors instead of directly praying to Christ Himself, and his critical attitude toward received texts and dogmas, all led men like Luther, Melanchthon, and Ulrich von Hutten to see in him a Protestant in embryo. Badgered by them on one side, Erasmus was also exposed increasingly to the pressure of orthodox authorities on the other, urging him to break out of his silence and denounce the heretics.

Erasmus and those like him vainly sought a *tertium quid*, a third way between the two camps—a reformed Catholicism that preserved fundamental tenets and institutions and avoided the extreme Protestant denials of sacraments, papal authority, and the like. They urged conversation, rather than confrontation, with the heretics in the desperate hope that differences could be reconciled. Unfortunately, both camps launched attacks on Erasmus and his followers, denouncing their open-mindedness and calls for toleration as mere temporizing. Finally, in 1524, Erasmus could no longer keep silent, and in a short treatise entitled *On the Free Will* (*De libero arbitrio*) he took on the most formidable adversary among the Protestants, Luther himself.

Erasmus's treatise did not concern a doctrine of little importance for the sixteenth century; the debate over free will was repeatedly the testing ground for Protestants and Catholics, and its repercussions were felt in many domains outside theology proper. In his work, Erasmus affirmed the traditional Catholic position: man's faculties may have been impaired by the Fall, but he was not totally depraved and could cooperate in his own salvation by performing good acts through his free will. Ultimately, his free will made it possible for man to shape himself into a truly Christian being, provided, of course, that God's grace seconded his efforts. Luther replied to Erasmus quite characteristically in a treatise entitled *On the Enslaved Will* (*De servo arbitrio*), affirming the fundamental tenet shared by many Protestant groups that man's will was absolutely impaired by the Fall, that he could not perform good actions by his own choice, and that he had to depend on divine grace even for the ability to will Christian faith, not to speak of Christian activity.

Although many contemporary scholars feel Luther's work is the better argued of the two, Erasmus's defense of human freedom seems in retrospect the more appealing position. It was also essential to his Christian humanist optimism, since only a man free to shape his activities by himself could possess the potential for education and true culture with which the humanists were concerned. In spite of the horrific events that shook Europe and must have tormented him during the last years of his life—religious wars in Germany, persecutions, tortures, and executions in every country, and the death of Thomas More on the scaffold in 1535—Erasmus maintained a dogged hope for cultural and human rebirth. It should be added that his stand against Luther did not completely mollify the church either; it remained totally ambivalent toward him to the end, at one point offering him a cardinal's hat, which he refused, and ultimately placing his works on the notorious Index Purgatorius.

Erasmus's exclusion from both Protestant and orthodox Catholic camps symptomizes the outsider's position he occupied throughout his life with regard to many basic social, political, and religious institutions in Europe. Although filled with a deep affection for his native Holland, for instance, he did not live there after his youth and never wrote a word in Dutch. In fact, he consistently refused to attach himself permanently to any city or state, to serve any monarch, and he even obtained papal permission to dispense with wearing the monk's habit he disliked. Instead, Erasmus wandered from city to city, traveling to Italy to work at the Aldine Press in Venice, visiting England on three separate occasions, and spending many months in France. He lived in Paris and London, Venice and Louvain, but seemed to prefer the relatively greater freedom of Swiss cities like Basel where he resided for as much as eight years at a stretch. Partly, Erasmus kept moving because governments and rulers were notoriously undependable, and there were always the dangers of political tyranny and religious persecution. But more profoundly, he refused to settle down anywhere because he refused to define himself as the citizen of just one city, the subject of any particular monarch.

Although some have objected to Erasmus's peregrinations as a reprehensible lack of patriotism or an immature *Wanderlust,* they might be more positively evaluated: Erasmus felt himself part of a pan-European culture, a universalist's world of scholars and theologians and educated laymen whose roots were buried in the universal culture of Greek and Latin antiquity, who spoke the universal language of classical Latin, and who adhered to the credos of an undivided, universal church. In a profound way, Erasmus was out of step with the times, which were increasingly dominated by incipient forms of nationalism, the rise of the vernaculars, and religious sectarianism that led to intolerance and brutal slaughter. Placed against this scene, Erasmus stands out as a true cosmopolitan in a world of petty nationalists, a courageous defender of tolerance and humanity in an age of savage tyranny and repression, a spokesman for true Christian charity at a time when most Christians manifested conspicuously little love for their fellows.

Living in a world from which the Christian humanist could experience only alienation, Erasmus remained in it, but not of it, moving within an international circle of like-minded friends and patrons. His journeys took him from the homes of bosom companions like More, through houses he rented and turned into scholarly retreats, to the printing establishments of men like Johannes Froben who at that time were scholars and editors as well as printers and whose houses were thronged with scholars and translators. From these refuges of security in a world gone

mad, Erasmus launched his verbal attacks, his satires and treatises and letters, in an ultimately futile attempt to bring men to
their senses, to reform a society already plunged into the chaos
and violence of religious and national disputes.

Understandably, Erasmus longed for a reformed Europe he
scarcely imagined he would see in his lifetime, and he just as
understandably turned to his writing to depict the ideal life he
desired for everyone and that he modeled on the sort of life he
must have enjoyed, however imperfectly and incompletely, with
his friends and fellow laborers. Repeatedly, he displays this
idealized world in the settings he uses for his dialogues, the
homes and gardens of rational men who could converse, even
dispute, with civilized restraint, toleration, and Christian love.
This characteristic setting, based in part on the symposia of classical writers like Plato and Xenophon and the country settings of
Cicero's works, nevertheless represents more than mere homage
to antiquity; it was the kind of world, idealized to be sure, in
which Erasmus lived, the only home he really recognized. His
continual wanderings offer eloquent proof that it was a home he
never found permanently established in the Europe of his day.

The most memorable and engaging representation of the
cosmopolitan Christian humanist's ideal environment occurs in a
short colloquy Erasmus wrote entitled *The Godly Feast* (*Convivium religiosum*). The central action of this brief symposium
involves a kind of secular communion engaged in by a group of
nine laymen who dine together at a villa one of them owns. All
of them are devout Christians, speak an elegant classical Latin
together, and spend their dinner hour discussing religious and
ethical questions and analyzing passages of Scripture. The villa
where they meet is a most striking product of Erasmus's imagination: they dine in a garden that is planted to grow all the food
the house needs and in which a stream is carefully utilized to
provide fresh drinking water and carry out wastes. The walls of
the garden are painted with pictures representing every conceiv-
able species of animal and plant as well as geographical and
historical curiosities; there are statues and pictures of Christ and
His apostles; the house is well provided with an ample library;

and the whole structure is protected by walls whose doors remain generously open to the neighborhood but can be closed when danger threatens from outside.

This garden and house constitute the cosmopolitan Christian humanist's dream of an ideal environment; it is a place of continuing education that teaches with pictures as well as books and avoids the potential dangers involved in real experience. The ideal garden is self-sustaining, separate, and protected from the implicitly corrupt, disorderly, and dangerous world around it.

Significantly, at the colloquy's end, the master of the house invites his friends to stay on as long as they like, while he himself rides out on missions of mercy to bring comfort to a dying man and to help settle a quarrel. Unmistakably, the master is an idealized vision of Erasmus himself, the Christian knight sallying forth with his books of satire, morality, and religion, bringing aid to the weary and peace to the quarrelsome, and returning at night to the secure and abiding haven where the good fellowship of like-minded men awaits him.

If never perfectly in his life, then at least in his art Erasmus could realize his Christian-humanist dream and transmit it to later ages as one of the most enchanting visions of the European Renaissance.

Selected Bibliography

PRIMARY SOURCES IN LATIN

Opera Omnia. Johannes Clericus, ed., 10 vols. Leyden, 1703–1706.

Opus epistolarum. P. S. Allen, H. M. Allen, and H. W. Garrod, eds., 12 vols. Oxford, 1906–1958.

Ausgewählte Schriften. Werner Welzig, ed., 8 vols. Darmstadt, from 1967. (This edition is equipped with facing German translations and includes most of the important writings of Erasmus. At this writing, only vols. 1, 3, 4, 5, 6, and 7 have appeared.)

PRIMARY SOURCES IN ENGLISH

NOTE: All of the texts cited below are available in paperback editions, except where otherwise noted.

Christian Humanism and the Reformation: Selected Writings of Desiderius Erasmus. Transl. and ed. by John C. Olin. New York, 1965. (Contents include the preface to the New Testament and letters concerning More, Luther, *The Praise of Folly.*)
The Education of a Christian Prince. Transl. by Lester K. Born. New York, 1936. (Not available in paperback.)
Erasmus on His Times: A Shortened Version of The Adages of Erasmus. Ed. and transl. by Margaret M. Phillips. Cambridge, 1967.
Erasmus-Luther. *Discourse on Free Will.* Transl. by Ernst Winter. New York, 1961.
The Essential Erasmus. Transl. by John P. Dolan. New York, 1964. (Contents include: *The Handbook of the Militant Christian,* abridged; *The Praise of Folly; The Complaint of Peace; An Inquiry Concerning Faith.*)
The Praise of Folly. Transl. by Hoyt Hudson. Princeton, 1941.
Ten Colloquies of Erasmus. Transl. by Craig R. Thompson. New York, 1937.
Desiderius Erasmus Concerning the Aim and Method of Education. Transl. and ed. by W. H. Woodward. Cambridge, 1904. (Contains translations of several treatises.)

SECONDARY SOURCES

Adams, Robert P. *The Better Part of Valor.* Seattle, 1962.
Bainton, Roland H. *Erasmus of Christendom.* New York, 1969.
Huizinga, Johan. *Erasmus and the Age of Reformation.* Transl. by F. Hopman. New York, 1957. (Also contains a selection of letters; available in paperback.)
Hyma, Albert. *The Youth of Erasmus.* Ann Arbor, 1930.
Phillips, Margaret M. *Erasmus and the Northern Renaissance.* London, 1949. (Available in paperback.)

For a more complete bibliography, see the work of Roland H. Bainton cited above, and J. K. Sowards, *Erasmus.* TWAS, 353. New York, 1975.

7

Erasmus: *The Praise of Folly*

James Hardin

Moriae Encomium, The Praise of Folly, is Erasmus's best-known and probably most enduring work. The polished, sophisticated form, the subtle wit and the no less subtle play of ideas in this relatively short Latin declamation have charmed readers throughout five centuries. The ironic eulogy—one of the first written by a humanist—is one of the most significant works of the Northern Renaissance, and one of the most influential. Montaigne, Rabelais, Cervantes, and probably Shakespeare are all indebted to Erasmus.

When he wrote *The Praise of Folly*, Erasmus had just completed a reworking of his *Adagia*, an ever-growing collection of adages of classical antiquity. All he had absorbed from the literature of Greece and Rome was fresh in his mind as he wrote the *Moriae Encomium* (1509) in England at the home of his close

Note: The author acknowledges the generous assistance of the Alexander von Humboldt-Stiftung for the academic year 1974–75, when this article was written.

friend, the humanist Thomas More. The title is a pun on the name of Erasmus's friend, meaning "Praise of More" as well as "Praise of Folly." The work was probably conceived at first as a light, ironic jest written in the manner of the Greek satirist Lucian (ca. A.D. 125–182), several of whose works, which mocked religious superstitions of late antiquity, Erasmus and More had translated into Latin three years earlier. Both the manner and the matter of Lucian were well suited to Erasmus's satiric intentions. But the jest became a mordant attack on the intellectual establishment of the time, the theologians, Scholastics, bishops and popes.

The first version of the work circulated for over a year among friends and was published in October 1511 in Paris, where the author saw it through the press. It proved to be immensely popular: six editions appeared in thirteen months, and at least forty-two Latin editions existed by the time of Erasmus's death at fifty-nine in 1536. The edition printed in the famous Froben publishing house (Basel, 1515) warrants special mention since it included an erudite and lengthy commentary by Gerhard Lijster, a student of medicine and classical languages who worked for Froben. The commentary assumes unusual significance in that Erasmus himself apparently collaborated in its preparation. It served as the basis for most later commentaries on the *Moriae Encomium*.

The book's fame was durable. In the seventeenth century it went through at least thirty-eight dated editions, and in the eighteenth century at least sixty editions are recorded. The number of printings declined in the nineteenth century, but scholarly interest remained high, as is exemplified in the critical edition of J.-B. Kan (The Hague, 1898).

Translations into the European vernaculars began appearing quite early, the first French translation coming in 1520, followed by at least a dozen others in the next four hundred years. Franck's German translation in 1534 was again the first of many, as was Sir Thomas Chaloner's English *The Praise of Folie* in 1549. Italian interest in *The Praise of Folly* has been keen ever since the first Italian rendering appeared in 1539, and there are, fittingly, several Dutch translations. A Spanish version could finally be printed in the nineteenth century.

Moriae Encomium stands in the satirical tradition of fool literature; it is one of those works that enumerated and satirized various classes of fools. One of the most popular was Sebastian Brant's *Das Narrenschiff* (The Ship of Fools) of 1494 (translated into Latin in 1497), which catalogued 112 kinds of fools according to their sins and grimly illustrated the consequences of folly. This work is memorable for its stark picture of the late medieval world and for its fine woodprints, and some commentators have seen in the two works a stylistic and philosophical contrast between the Middle Ages and the Renaissance. Indeed, while Erasmus's work betrays his knowledge of medieval thought, it is chiefly a work of the Renaissance: its elegant classical Latin, its sympathetic understanding of classical antiquity as embodied in its mythology and in some of its most illustrious literary figures (such as Homer, Vergil, Seneca, Horace, and Ovid) represent literally a "rebirth." Erasmus's blending of classical and Christian thought is truly remarkable. Folly herself is something of a cross between a late medieval jester and a goddess of classical antiquity.

Erasmus's ingenious scheme was to establish an ironic situation allowing him to distance himself from a caustic satire that often borders on the heretical: he let Folly (Moria) praise *herself* —in itself a surprising twist—and her followers, who are legion. This imaginative stroke, characteristic of the sophistication of the work as a whole, has the effect of rendering key passages ambiguous, since Dame Folly is not consistent and slips, sometimes unexpectedly, sometimes imperceptibly, from one posture to another—from brilliant satire to unanticipated earnestness. To plumb the meaning of this superficially frivolous work one must weigh Folly's words carefully to determine, from passage to passage, the extent to which she speaks for Erasmus. One may not, naïvely, simply turn Folly's words around, as even her irony contains much wisdom. The ambiguity of her attitude was rendered with intent; it obscured Erasmus's relationship to a work that, even today, has been termed "explosive" and "revolutionary," and this ambiguity accounts for widely divergent interpretations of *The Praise of Folly* to the present time.

The *Moriae Encomium* is usually prefaced by a letter of Erasmus to Thomas More, to whom the work is dedicated. It indicates that Erasmus clearly recognized that the satire would not escape criticism, for he argues, somewhat lamely, that the satire is harmless because it mentions none of the followers of Folly by name, and that vices, not individuals, are censured; the satire is to amuse, not to give offense. Yet, when Erasmus attacked abuses in the state and church, he had specific individuals in mind who surely would be recognized by informed readers; his war-mongering pope, for instance, is clearly Pope Julius II, whose armies Erasmus had seen at first hand in Italy. He argues, with tongue in cheek, that those who feel they have been criticized should remember that Folly, not he, is the speaker, and that there is merit in being attacked *by her*.

Folly's thesis is simply that she is the source of all gaiety and happiness in life, the bestower of all good things; her declamation quite properly praises the benefits of Folly. In her speech she follows classical, especially Greek, rhetorical practices, by describing herself, her origin, manner of birth, companions, powers, followers—all according to long-established models. The epilogue treats the "Christian Fool."

Folly is the daughter of Plutus and Youthfulness, the offspring of riches and youth. Her attendants are Self-Love, Flattery, Forgetfulness, Idleness, Pleasure, Madness, Voluptuousness, Sound Sleep, Revelry; these hold sway over the entire world, so that even great rulers serve Folly. She is the source of life itself, for who would consent to the responsibilities and sorrows of marriage if it were not for her attendant, Madness? All of life's pleasures come from her, she claims, although the Stoic philosophers will not admit it; and those who serve Folly most assiduously are the happiest of mortals. "Now whence comes the charm of youth if not from me? I've seen to it that youth has so little wisdom and hence so few vexations. It's a fact that as soon as the young grow up and develop the sort of mature sense which comes through experience and education, the bloom of youthful beauty begins to fade at once, enthusiasm wanes, gaiety cools down and energy slackens. The further anyone withdraws from me the less and less he's alive. . . ." (chapter 13, p. 78).*

Folly assuages the cares of the aged by blessing them with a second youth, so that "the nearer people approach old age the closer they return to a semblance of childhood, until the time comes for them to depart this life, again like children, neither tired of living nor aware of death" (chapter 13, p. 80).

Even this early in the declamation one is aware of its ambiguity: what Folly says is, of course, playful exaggeration, jest, parody; her view of old age is hardly realistic. But one perceives also a most serious undertone that suggests, not without bitterness, that Folly's interpretation of human affairs is unfortunately not a completely false one. Much of what she says, from the very beginning, is marked not only by stylistic virtuosity, but also by sagacity. One must therefore be careful to distinguish between Folly, the narrator, who is seldom "foolish," and her followers.

Shifting from an ironic to a quite serious attitude and back again without warning, Folly claims that she is the source of friendship and love, for it is she who provides that self-deception necessary to foster and perpetuate human relationships. It is thanks to her that the cuckolded husband overlooks the sins of his wife and lives on contentedly in his delusion. One cannot love others, be self-confident and productive without self-love, one of Folly's most prized bounties, "this salt of life" (chapter 22, p. 94).

Now in these statements there is much psychological truth. But sarcasm predominates again when Folly praises war, the source of all glory: "When the mail-clad ranks confront each other . . . what use . . . are those wise men who are worn out with their studies. . . ? The need is for stout and sturdy fellows with

* Translation by Betty Radice, *The Praise of Folly and Letter to Martin Dorp 1515*, with introduction and notes by A. H. T. Levi, Penguin Books, 1971. Copyright © 1971 by Betty Radice. This translation is used throughout the article by permission of the publisher.

all the daring possible and the minimum of brain. . . . Besides, it's the spongers, pimps, robbers, murderers, peasants, morons . . . who provide the glories of war, not the philosophers and their midnight oil" (chapter 23, p. 96).

Here, Erasmus's message is clear and as relevant now as ever, while his relationship to the narrator remains unambiguous. Later passages, dealing with the nature of wisdom and wise men, cut in two directions. The reader is not sure whether the satire is directed more against "wise men"—i.e., true humanists, not Scholastics, who of course are an object of Erasmus' satire—or against the rest of society in general; on the one side there is Erasmus's self-parody, on the other, elitism. "Ask a wise man to dinner and he'll upset everyone by his gloomy silence or tiresome questions. . . . It's quite impossible for him to be of any use to himself, his country or his family because he's ignorant of ordinary matters. . . . And so inevitably he is also disliked, doubtless because of the vast discrepancy between ordinary life and minds like his. For nothing happens in this world which isn't full of folly, performed by fools amongst fools" (chapter 25, p. 99).

In the context of the entire work this quotation is not quite as cynical as it sounds in isolation, and yet it represents many similarly unclear passages which take up the fate and role of the philosopher or scholar in society. One other passage is particularly striking: "Imagine some paragon of wisdom . . . , a man who has frittered away all his boyhood and youth in acquiring learning, has lost the happiest part of his life in endless wakeful nights, toil and care, and never tastes a drop of pleasure even in what's left to him. He's always thrifty, impoverished, miserable, grumpy, harsh and unjust to himself, disagreeable and unpopular with his fellows, pale and thin, sickly and blear-eyed, prematurely white-haired and senile, worn-out and dying before his time" (chapter 37, p. 119). There is an autobiographical tone here, one of self-pity, although Erasmus's own life was not so ascetic as the passage might suggest. At the same time, he is poking fun at himself and at the scholar in general.

Folly no longer Folly, but the healthy, affirmative, vital force in worldly affairs: that is the theme Erasmus develops ever more strikingly. We have seen already that Folly creates an illusion that permits us to play out our "roles": "Now, what else is the whole life of man but a sort of play? Actors come on wearing their different masks and all play their parts until the producer orders them off the stage. . . . It's all a sort of pretence, but it's the only way to act out this farce. . . . It's a true sign of prudence not to want wisdom which extends beyond your share as an ordinary mortal, to be willing to . . . wear your illusions with a good grace" (chapter 29, p. 104f).

But the stoic model of the wise man has been stripped of all illusions and emotions. He is not fooled by worldly trappings, that is, by Folly. But he is as cold as a marble statue; what state would elect such a man to office, what woman marry him, Folly asks. A common, ordinary fool would be preferable, a man who "would be pleasant to his wife and agreeable to his friends, a congenial guest for a meal and good company for a drink, a man in fact who thinks every human interest is his concern. The wise man's a bore . . ." (chapter 30, p. 107).

Up to this point Folly has developed the thesis that, paradoxically, she is the source of those instinctual, irrational forces that hold together and propel society. The work thus far, it can be argued, is less a satire than a witty, penetrating examination of the human condition. In later chapters of *Moriae Encomium*, however, Folly directs her scorn against specific abuses, especially religious attitudes and practices, such as the idolatry of saints, and against the abuses of evil or heedless princes. Here Erasmus allows Folly to step out of her ironic role and to address herself to controversial issues that concerned Erasmus as a churchman and reformer. She attacks sycophantic, mercenary friars, profiteering merchants who "handle the meanest sort of business by the meanest methods" (chapter 48, p. 142), sadistic schoolmasters, pettifogging lawyers, self-important philosophers "who insist that they alone have wisdom and all other mortals are but fleeting shadows" who "know nothing at all, yet . . . claim to know everything" (chapter 52, p. 151), and then theologians, "a remarkably supercilious and touchy lot" who might denounce Folly as a heretic since "this is the bolt they always loose on anyone to whom they take a dislike" (chapter 53, pp. 152–53).

Folly, speaking unmistakably for Erasmus, denounces the cold logic-chopping of late medieval Scholasticism, which still held sway in the universities and was naturally hostile to humanism with its fervor for Greek, for neglected philosophers of classical antiquity, especially Plato, and for reevaluation and translation of basic Christian writings, such as the Bible. Rather, according to Folly, Scholasticism concerned itself not only with significant religious issues, but also with such questions as "Could God have taken on the form of a woman, a devil, a donkey, a gourd or a flintstone? If so, how could a gourd have preached sermons, performed miracles, and been nailed to the cross?" (chapter 53, p. 154).

Folly has sharp criticism for secular princes as well; most of these men know nothing of law, care little for the welfare of their subjects and are dedicated only to their own interests; they are voluptuaries, hostile to learning and freedom. They are given to "dice, draughts, fortune-telling, clowns, fools, whores . . ." (chapter 56, p. 176). What is worse, "such practices of princes have long been zealously adopted by supreme pontiffs, cardinals and bishops, and indeed, have almost been surpassed" (chapter 57, p. 177). Erasmus emphasizes the ethical aspect of Christianity: if the popes, who are the vicars of Christ, "made an attempt to imitate his life of poverty and toil, his teaching, cross, and contempt for life, . . . what creature on earth would be so cast down? . . . they believe they do quite enough for Christ if they play their part as overseer by means of every kind of ritual, near-theatrical ceremonial and display. . ." (chapter 59, pp. 178–79).

Erasmus comes back to his attack on the Scholastics and links their reliance on logic and the tools of deductive reasoning with the last and most paradoxical ideas of the *Moriae Encomium*. "The apostles consecrated the Eucharist with due piety, but had they been questioned about the *terminus a quo* and the *terminus ad quem*, about transsubstantiation, and how the same body can be in different places . . . they wouldn't, in my opinion, have shown the same subtlety in their reply as the Scotists do in their dissertations and definitions" (chapter 53, p. 157). Folly (Erasmus) mentions especially Paul with admiration and contrasts his example with the mendicant monks who beg for their living and make a public nuisance of themselves.

The pomp, wealth, display, and worldly wisdom of the popes and princes, and the logical subtleties of Scholasticism, as Erasmus has excoriated them over a goodly number of pages, are, by an unexpected turn in Folly's declamation, brought into sharp contrast with the Christian "folly" and simplicity of St. Paul, who said: "We are fools for Christ's sake" (1 Cor:4) and "Whoever among you thinks himself wise must become a fool to be truly wise" (1 Cor:3).

This "wise folly," this unlearned, childlike faith was exemplified by Jesus, as Folly explains in a passage which is as daring as it is central to the meaning of the entire work: "All mortals are fools, even the pious. Christ too, though he is the wisdom of the Father, was made something of a fool himself in order to help the folly of mankind, when he assumed the nature of man and was seen in man's form; just as he was made sin so that he could redeem sinners. Nor did he wish them to be redeemed in any other way save by the folly of the cross and through his simple, ignorant apostles, to whom he unfailingly preached folly. He taught them to shun wisdom, and made his appeal through the example of children, lilies . . . and humble sparrows, . . . which live their lives by natural instinct alone, free from care or purpose" (chapter 65, pp. 198–99).

Erasmus is performing a delicate balancing act here; he, the learned humanist and scholar, is apparently glorifying the simple creed of the apostles and early Christianity. Folly says: "It is quite clear that the Christian religion has a kind of kinship with folly in some form. . . . You can see how the first great founders of the faith were great lovers of simplicity and bitter enemies of learning. . . . The biggest fools of all appear to be those who have once been wholly possessed by zeal for Christian piety. They squander their possessions, ignore insults, submit to being cheated, make no distinction between friends and enemies, shun pleasure . . . and desire only death" (chapter 66, p. 201).

After this speech, the full complexity of Erasmus's work emerges; it consists of three primary idea-complexes, which are, first, folly as an instinctual force, as life-illusion; second, need for reform in church and state; and third, Christian "folly." These complexes interact significantly, for instance in the contrast between the corruption of Christianity in the time of Erasmus and the faith of Paul. While one cannot doubt the sincerity of Erasmus's admiration for fundamentalist Christianity, it does not necessarily follow that he regarded it as a model for all men or that it was his personal attitude toward Christianity. The last lines of Folly's speech above—which describe a blend of asceticism and Stoicism—belie Erasmus's own, more harmonious attitude toward life.

There are several possible explanations for the glorification of simple piety. It is likely that the passage reflects the influence of Erasmus's education in Deventer and Herzogenbusch, schools connected with the Brethren of the Common Life, a religious society that stressed simple Christianity and good works. Or one could say that Erasmus is looking back, in *Moriae Encomium*, on innocent, cherished, but youthful beliefs; or that he is using this high ideal as a foil to the religious abuses he wished to censure, and that the ideal is "utopistic," to be found nowhere; or that his praise of Folly, which here really means praise of the spiritual and neglect of bodily things—a happy madness in contemplation of the eternal and linked by Erasmus with Platonic ideas—is more than a playful idea, an exercise in eloquence and wit, and represents views sincerely held by Erasmus at the writing of the work. Erasmus is clearly suggesting the danger of extremes, whether those of asceticism or of the instinctual. The two poles in his work—folly, in the conventional sense, and Stoicism, the repression of emotion—may well have been intended to represent the timeless philosophical question of the relationship of nature and spirit.

After her words of praise for Christian "folly," where she has totally departed from her role, Folly reassumes her former ironic attitude to say farewell to her many followers, but only after she has remarked: "At the same time, don't forget the Greek proverb 'Often a fool speaks a word in season.' "

Selected Bibliography

PRIMARY SOURCES

Opera Omnia. John Le Clerc, ed., 10 vols. Leyden, 1703–1706; facsimile, London: Gregg Press, 1962.
Opus Epistolarum. P. S. and H. M. Allen, eds., 12 vols. Oxford: Clarendon Press, 1906–1958.
Stultitiae Laus. J.-B. Kan, ed., The Hague, 1898.

TRANSLATIONS (German and English)

The Essential Erasmus. Transl. by John P. Dolan. New York: New American Library, 1964.
Das Lob der Torheit. Transl. and ed. by Anton J. Gail. Stuttgart: Reclam, 1969.
The Praise of Folie. Transl. by Sir Thomas Chaloner. London, 1549.
———. C. J. Miller, ed. London: Oxford University Press, 1965.
The Praise of Folly. Introd. and transl. by L. F. Dean. Chicago: Packard and Co., 1946.
The Praise of Folly. Transl. by H. H. Hudson. Princeton: Princeton University Press, 1941.
The Praise of Folly. Transl. by John Wilson. London, 1668.
———. "With expurgations and an introduction by Mrs. P. S. Allen." Oxford: Clarendon Press, 1913 ff.
Praise of Folly and Letter to Martin Dorp 1515. Transl. by Betty Radice with an introduction and notes by A. H. T. Levi. Copyright 1971. Harmondsworth, Middlesex: Penguin Books, 1971.

SECONDARY SOURCES

Allen, P. S. *The Age of Erasmus: Lectures Delivered in the Universities of Oxford and London.* Oxford: Clarendon Press, 1914.
Bainton, Roland H. *Erasmus of Christendom.* New York: Charles Scribner's Sons, 1969.
Bush, D. "Erasmus in England," *Dublin Review,* 1942, 36–49.
Campbell, W. E. *Erasmus, Tyndale and More.* London: Eyre, 1949.
Eckert, Willehad P. *Erasmus von Rotterdam I.* Köln: Wienand, 1967.
Faludy, George. *Erasmus of Rotterdam.* London: Eyre and Spottiswoode, 1970.
Gail, Anton J. *Erasmus.* Reinbek bei Hamburg: Rowohlt Bildmonographie, 1974.

Hauffen, Adolf. "Zur Literatur der ironischen Enkomien." *Vierteljahrs-schrift für Literaturgeschichte*, 6 (1893), 161 ff.

Hudson, H. H. "Current English Translations of the *Praise of Folly*." *Philological Quarterly*, 20 (1941), 250–65.

Huizinga, Johan. *Erasmus*. New York, London: Charles Scribner's Sons, 1924.

Kaiser, Walter J. *Praisers of Folly: Erasmus, Rabelais, Shakespeare*. Cambridge: Harvard University Press, 1964.

Könneker, Barbara. *Wesen und Wandlung der Narrenidee im Zeitalter des Humanismus: Brant—Murner—Erasmus*. Wiesbaden: Franz Steiner, 1966.

Meissinger, Karl A. *Erasmus von Rotterdam*. Vienna, 1942. 2nd ed. Berlin: A. Nauck, 1948.

Miller, Clarence H. "Current English Translations of *The Praise of Folly*: Some Corrections." *Philological Quarterly*, 45 (1966), 718–32.

————. "Some Medieval Elements and Structural Unity in Erasmus' *The Praise of Folly*."*Renaissance Quarterly*, 27 (1974), 499–511.

Newald, Richard. *Erasmus Roterodamus*. Freiburg im Breisgau: Verlag Erwin Burda, 1947.

Nigg, Walter. *Der christliche Narr*. Zürich, Stuttgart: Artemis, 1956.

Saxl, F. "Holbein's illustrations to the *Praise of Folly* by Erasmus." *Burlington Magazine*, 83 (1944), 275–79.

Schoenfeld, Hermann. "Die Beziehung der Satire Rabelais' zu Erasmus' *Encomium moriae* und *Colloquia*," *PMLA*, 8 (1893), 1–76.

Smith, Preserved. *Erasmus: A Study of his Life, Ideals, and Place in History*, 1923; rpt. New York: F. Ungar, 1962.

8

Ulrich von Hutten: Representative of Patriotic Humanism

Sam Wheelis

The best introduction to Ulrich von Hutten (1488–1523) is found in his great German poem *Ein neu Lied* (A New Song), his most accessible and familiar work to students of German literature. Written in 1521, at the outset of the feud Hutten declared on the clerical orders in Germany, the poem is both a self-justification and a challenge to his enemies. Even if we know little of its background, the poem reveals much about its author. In fact, in the long period of German literature between the death of Walther von der Vogelweide and the emergence of the young Goethe, there is scarcely a single poem that can offer a more vivid and telling picture of its author and his concerns. Even a prose rendering into English conveys a measure of its force.

> I dared it as I planned it and I still do not regret it, and though I may gain nothing from it, still you must grant my steadfastness. I did it, if you want to know, not for myself but for the country, although people simply call me anticlerical.
> Let them all lie and speak what they will; had I not disclosed

the truth, I would have had supporters enough. But now I've spoken out and I've been banished. This I lament to all worthy men, although I'm not going to flee farther, indeed I may come back.

I will not ask for mercy, because I am without guilt. I would have submitted myself to the law, had not impatience been so obstinate as to deny me my ancient rights to a hearing. Perhaps God wills it, perhaps fate forces it, that they have acted this way.

Now this sort of thing has also happened before, that one of the mighty has wagered and lost. A large flame has often grown from a small spark. Who knows, if I can avenge myself? Things are already in motion, and I'm part of it, do or die.

Incidentally, my conscience is good, for none of the evil ones can damage my honor, or say that I have ever by any means acted other than honorably. I started this affair in the right.

If you won't tell this country to rid itself of its ruin, as I have warned, then I'm sorry. I will cut and shuffle the cards better. I am undismayed, I dared to do it, and look forward to the result.

And though the wiles of the courtiers are plotting against me, a heart that knows it's right is not hurt. I know that many others want to join the game as well, even if it costs them their lives. Arise, ye yeomen and ye chivalry. Do not let Hutten perish.

Hutten's contemporaries would have been quick to recognize the first line, "ich habs gewagt," as a translation of Caesar's "jacta est alea," i.e., "the die is cast," as Hutten's own repeatedly expressed motto, and as the signature he invariably put on his works. Many editors have gone so far as to substitute "The Die Is Cast" for the proper title of the poem. Indeed, at the time of this poem's publication, Hutten had crossed his own Rubicon, and even to this day the poem emits the light of the burning bridge he left behind.

Defying excommunication and risking far worse, Hutten was the first to invoke the cause of freedom by raising arms against the property and might of the Roman church itself. This action alienated him from the good will of most of his erstwhile supporters, including Martin Luther. While Luther and Hutten were perceived for a time as equal threats by Rome, Luther had stood for caution, and in his tract *On the Freedom of a Christian*

Man he had accordingly severely limited his definition of freedom to his followers. It was perhaps to Hutten, more than anyone else, that Luther addressed this warning. But Hutten ignored the warning of the reformer.

Hutten's poem expresses the character of a restless and reckless spirit, of an earnest gambler in a game for high stakes. Here
we meet a man entirely convinced of the rectitude of his position,
a man righteously free of any troubling shadow of personal
doubt. The character that stands revealed in this poem is one of
profound personal ideals—loyalty, selflessness, truth, justice,
honor, conscience, and righteous confidence—ideals that derive
more from chivalry than from humanism, to be sure, and to
which Hutten characteristically added one further element, the
ideal of nationhood, of patriotism. Hutten's humanism was dominated more by his poetry than by his scholarship, and less by
detachment than by engagement. Of his time, Hutten was, without equal, *l'homme de lettres engagé*.

Hutten has been called a muddle-headed thinker by the
prominent historian Johan Huizinga. It appears to this observer
that if anything muddled Hutten's mind it was his chivalry. Yet
the call for political union and spiritual freedom that Hutten
sounded in this poem and in his other works has echoed through
the years of German history. That he made the call with both
pen and sword in hand makes Hutten a significant mover and
shaker in Western history.

The spectre of Hutten's activism haunted his enemies for
generations. Here Hutten may appear in a negative light, for the
harshness of the later Counter Reformation derived in part from
fears such as those Hutten kindled. Even a cursory reading of his
works reveals that Hutten identified humanism and patriotism
(and ultimately the nascent movement that came to be called
Protestantism) as a single cause. He was not unique in this, but
his exceptional energies and talents as a publicist marked him as
the most important proponent of German national interest in his
time; indeed, it is to Hutten that one must turn if one seeks to
locate the beginnings of modern national feeling in Germany.
The idea that nationalism traces its roots to the very heart of the

humanist movement may be startling, but it is supported by the
weight of historical evidence offered by Hutten's short, but brilliant, controversial, and often violent life.

That northern humanism is generally viewed as cosmopolitan is the legacy of Erasmus of Rotterdam, Hutten's sometime
friend and mentor, with whom Hutten entered his final and
perhaps bitterest conflict, an inevitable conflict, that continued
even after Hutten's death and embittered the declining years of
the aging Erasmus to an extraordinary degree. That in the popular view European humanism as a whole continued to be seen as
a cosmopolitan, supranational movement hostile to any sort of
nationalism is also largely due to Erasmus's dominance. Yet this
view ignores the strongly local character of the beginnings of
Italian humanism. Humanism was a movement characterized by
a return to the past for a sanction of the canons of taste, beauty,
style, and truth, and in Italy the sources to which the humanists
returned were local and Italian. In a real sense, the Italian humanists were but rediscovering their own lost *national* tradition.
This gave Italian humanism a distinctly different flavor from
that of its northern counterpart.

The northern humanists, having no direct claim as heirs of
the classical Roman tradition, tended toward views generally
more cosmopolitan than those of their southern predecessors and
contemporaries. But when other German humanists—although a
minority, including Celtis, Wimpheling, Vadianus, and Bebel—
began to explore the German past with a zeal that matched that
with which the Italians had explored their own past, it became
clear that Hutten was not alone in his interests. Beyond their
delight in the flattering picture of barbarian Germany found in
the newly rediscovered writings of the Roman historian Tacitus,
the German humanists were pleased with the discovery of something resembling greatness in the Carolingian and Ottonian
periods of their own empire. Celtis's discovery of the Ottonian
Hrotswitha von Gandersheim's Latin plays (derived from Terence) charmed the German humanists, who had had to live with
their barbarian heritage in the face of Italy's previous (and continuing) grandeur. The empire was, in fact, the Renaissance

German's soundest claim to antique credibility, for the Holy Roman Empire was the legitimate, historically validated heir to the Augustan Empire. Yet even this claim was flawed, and long before Voltaire remarked that the Holy Roman Empire was neither holy, nor Roman, nor, in fact, an empire, Hutten came to recognize that the empire was an empire in name only. It was the aim of Hutten's reform to make the empire live up to its lofty name.

In equating patriotism with humanism, Hutten merely carried to an extreme a tendency already rather well established within the framework of the general European humanistic movement. Thus this equation had the all-important sanction of the past, so necessary to the humanist mentality. What set Hutten apart from the school of Erasmus was Hutten's belief that beyond its generally ennobling effects, humanistic learning was something to be put to overt political use; it was to be consequential.

While Hutten expressed understanding for the detached, scholarly quietude of an Erasmus, his own temper was overactive and he spent his life exhorting people to act for the cause of truth as he saw it. Hutten's activism contrasts vividly with Erasmus's tolerant, apolitical cosmopolitanism. Hutten invoked the German imperial tradition against the tradition of papal supremacy. While this imperial tradition was not entirely an historical fiction, its continuity was in Hutten's time certainly not unbroken, and the pulse of its vitality was decidedly weak. Hutten wanted to renew the struggle of the Hohenstaufen emperors of the High Middle Ages. The cornerstone of his political thought and the basis for his activities both scholarly and political was Hutten's belief in the empire's superiority in all temporal and some ecclesiastical affairs.

Prior to the Reformation, the empire had lagged far behind France and England in the governance of local church affairs and the accompanying control of fiscal matters. Rome exacted heavy tithes of assorted annates and tributes to the papacy from Germany, which both England and France had long ceased to pay. The disunity of Germany, whose emperor nominally presided over an independent collection of often jealous and conflicting principalities, made it easy for the papacy to exploit the empire. It is an apparent paradox that this political disunity could foster a successful religious reform, yet leave the political structure of Germany unchanged. The seven powerful elector princes had no interest in *political* reform; they were unwilling to cede to the emperor anything that might diminish their own position.

Yet from Hutten's point of view the time doubtless seemed ripe for reform. There were in Hutten's own lifetime a larger number of Reichstag meetings than at any prior (or, as it turned out, later) period in the history of the empire. Reform was in the air, but it was hampered by the intransigence of the territorial princes. It is easy to see why the later Hapsburg princes turned their efforts toward building a dynasty outside the empire, in Spain, where their control was more direct, their power more secure. Where Hutten gambled and lost was in staking his faith on the ability, or the inclination, of either Maximilian, or his successor Charles, or his fellow humanists and Protestants to interpret the imperial role as he did. Hutten's political failure seems in retrospect to have been foredoomed, because, for all his talents, his political and social views seem scarcely to have extended beyond the limits and prejudices of the aristocratic class into which he was born.

Ulrich von Hutten was born on April 21, 1488 at his family estate of Steckelberg, near Fulda. His noble birth made him the true child of the late medieval chivalric tradition, whose ideals and style of life he ever maintained. He was proud of his birth and his name, and, significantly, unlike many of his humanist contemporaries, he did not choose to Latinize it. His family was large, with several branches, and though not particularly prosperous, was rather prominent in civil and religious affairs. Hutten saw himself first and foremost as a knight. In humanism he saw the hope of reviving the feudal aristocracy as a modern cultural elite. The sense of responsibility with which his knighthood endowed him was a source of great strength and, however one interprets the rightness or wrongness of his later ventures, one has to concede at the very least that Hutten was a man of uncommon, indeed dazzling courage.

Yet Hutten's aristocratic background served to hinder both his intellectual and his political judgment. For this very class, which Hutten would endow with a new claim to old authority, was essentially moribund. We can now see clearly that the feuding robber barons of the late Middle Ages, from whom Hutten was himself scarcely one generation removed, were being pushed off the historical stage by forces beyond their control or their understanding. Feuding had been outlawed in Hutten's youth, though Hutten and Franz von Sickingen were later to ignore this legal nicety outrageously *in the name of honor*. Indeed, both came to be counted as nothing more than outlawed robber barons themselves prior to Sickingen's death during a successful, and portentously unchivalric, artillery siege against him.

While Hutten became humanist enough to give something more than a passing nod to the idea of an aristocracy of merit (most notably in his famous letter of October, 1518 to the Nürnberg partician, Willibald Pirckheimer), and while many of his closest friends (Eobanus Hessus, for one) were of humble origin, Hutten retained the aloofness of his class toward the prosperity and concomitant growing dominance of the mercantile-banking class, already quite evident in his time. A poor man himself, in spite of his knightly birth, Hutten believed that a society dominated by money was entirely repulsive. His visceral rejection of the corrupt market place is reflected in his antipapal pamphleteering. He saw Rome as ruled by gold, and the thrust of his criticism of the relationship between Rome and the empire tends to be economic.

In 1505 Hutten forsook monastic life against his parents' wishes. He was to spend the next dozen years in penurious wandering and scholarly errantry. Hutten, unlike Luther, never spoke ill of his six years in the cloister. During his years of wandering, Hutten perfected his skills as a poet, gaining a fluid and graceful Latin style. He received a baccalaureate at Frankfurt on the Oder in 1506. And it is during this time that he fell prey to the syphilis that eventually was to kill him.

Hutten later developed friendships with a number of prominent humanists, such as Crotus Rubianus, Eobanus Hessus, Rhagius Aesticampianus, and Mutianus Rufus. Of the Neoplatonic theism derived from the Italian humanists Marsilio Ficino and Pico della Mirandola, which Mutianus taught and fostered in Germany, there is, however, no trace in Hutten. He was no speculative thinker. What he did perhaps draw from Mutianus was rather a general skepticism concerning both the sacramental system and the Scholastics in general. Mutianus, who prudently chose not to publish his heresies, appears to have made the church almost superfluous in terms of human salvation. The implications for Hutten's own development are clear. Hutten moved in a bohemian, satirically oriented circle whose view of life approached the pagan. His schooling was, in a word, radical.

In the summer of 1510 Hutten published his first major poem, *Nemo* (Nobody), which he was later to amplify with extensive borrowings from Erasmus's *The Praise of Folly*. The work has a rather fetchingly elegant and clever wit. While Hutten was no prude, he seems to have shown more general discretion than was the rule in the letters of his time. There is in Hutten, with the exception of his later contributions to the *Letters of Obscure Men*, none of the pornography or scatology seen in other writers of the period.

Details of Hutten's days as a student are sketchy at best, yet even as a student Hutten began to betray character traits that remained evident throughout his life. Stung by the stinginess of his erstwhile benefactors in Rostock, Hutten published a tract against the Lötze family, vicious in tone, critical in content, personal in stimulus. Hutten *was* combative. The issues with which he concerned himself in his writing tended to be personal. This is seen in the anti-Lötze tract, in his polemics against the Duke of Württemberg (*Phalarismus*), in his essay on syphilis (which he called the French disease), and elsewhere.

Rejecting the suggestion of his family that he return to monastic life or take up the formal study of law, Hutten traveled to Vienna in 1511. While he was admitted into the Viennese humanist circle originated by Celtis, Hutten was forbidden to continue his illegally begun lectures at the University of Vienna. Thus his stay in the Austrian capital was short, albeit important. For it was here that Hutten began his political education and the concern for the German past that was to mark much of his further activity.

Hutten wrote a pamphlet exhorting Emperor Maximilian to continue his war against Venice and a poem in hexameters on "Why the Germans are not degenerate in comparison with former times." Evidence of contemporary German brilliance he saw in the inventions of gunpowder and the printing press, a brilliance that to him rivaled the glory of Germany's heroic (pagan) past. Hutten saw great promise for the political future of the empire in the coming generation. Actual events were to show this optimism as wishful thinking. Derived from Aesticampanius's lectures on Tacitus, Hutten's view of Germany is that of Tacitus, who in his *Germania* had held up a primitive, agrarian culture as preferable to the overripe culture of classical Rome. Hutten's class prejudice limited his understanding of his contemporary society, and he was at constant odds with the realities of the shopkeeping economy of his time—it was the perfidy of the Venetian shopkeepers that Hutten castigated in his exhortation to Maximilian.

After a rather stormy and difficult period in Italy as a student and soldier, Hutten returned to Germany in 1514 in financial distress. He managed to gain the support of the young Archbishop Albrecht von Brandenburg, to secure the friendship of Erasmus, and to involve himself in a feud with the tyrannical Duke Ulrich von Württemberg, who had murdered a member of Hutten's family. The contact with Albrecht was to result in a position at his court in 1517.

Hutten and Erasmus developed a mutual fondness, the younger man playing Alcibiades to the older man's Socrates. They corresponded regularly, and though in retrospect it appears that even at the time of their initial acquaintanceship their paths were going in different and conflicting directions, neither of them seems to have paid heed to this, and their relationship was to remain amicable for the next half-decade at least. Erasmus apparently recognized a powerful publicist in Hutten, while Hutten saw in Erasmus the restorer of primitive Christianity. In the conflict with Duke Ulrich, Hutten wrote a series of speeches patterned on Cicero's *Catalinian Orations*, but more importantly, he produced a dialogue of the dead in the style of Lucian, his *Phalarismus*. The dialogue became Hutten's favorite genre, and that it became the most popular literary form of the day as well is largely due to Hutten. The struggle against Duke Ulrich culminated in 1519 in a military action of the Swabian League that deposed the tyrant. Hutten took part in this effort and met Franz von Sickingen. At this time Hutten also adopted the Caesarian "jacta est alea" as his personal motto.

Again Hutten turned to Italy, a not all-too-willing student of Roman law. He seems to have shared with Wimpheling a feeling that the Roman law had no justifiable role in the affairs of the German empire, and he seems to have pursued his purely humanistic inclinations further at the expense of the study of law. Hutten turned up in humanist circles in Rome, Bologna, Ferrara, and Venice, driven from both Rome and Bologna in a rush of controversy. In Rome he killed a French soldier in a brawl and in Bologna played a leading role in a student revolt. His interest in the Reuchlin affair, already awakened in Germany, came to fruition in his contributions to the *Letters of Obscure Men*. Hutten may have received more credit than was his due for the composition of these letters, which hold both the literary and the life styles of the Scholastic opponents of Reuchlin up to bitter and telling scorn. Yet, though anonymous, these letters gained for Hutten a notoriety in the Western world and many enemies both in and outside the Roman curia.

Intellectually and politically Hutten was impressed with his reading of the *Annals* of Tacitus and with the picture of the great German hero, Arminius, that they portray. In *Arminius*, a dialogue of uncertain date, Hutten pictured his subject as the ideal German prince, the proper model for Emperor Maximilian. This dialogue started the Arminius cult in Germany. In Italy, too, Hutten came across Lorenzo Valla's previously unpublished essay that revealed the fraud of the *Constantine Donation*. This alleged "donation" was a chief document used by the papacy to justify the Holy See's claim to temporal power. Hutten edited and published this essay immediately on his return to Germany

in 1517, ironically dedicating it to the new Pope Leo X! The
significance of Hutten's publication of Valla's essay rests primarily on the profound effect it had on its most important reader,
Martin Luther. Stung by his rather unsuccessful debate with
Johann Eck, Luther seized upon this work like a godsend when it
came into his hands in 1520. To Luther it seemed clear, after
reading this document, that the Pope was the Antichrist. This
was not a point of view that lent itself to compromise.

We see that Hutten's humanism was by no means antiquarian in its orientation. Hutten's studies and efforts were all in
the direction of what is now popularly called relevance. Not
knowledge for its own sake, but knowledge for the sake of action
was always his guide. He might even be called an "applied"
humanist, though this would by no means imply that his humanism was actually practical in the real world of Renaissance politics and Reformation conflict. What impressed Hutten most in
Italy was not the local esthetic and antiquarian delights, but the
political machinations of the church apparatus, the abuses of
clerical power, the simony, bribery, immorality, licentiousness,
and general venality in human affairs. These he portrayed and
castigated in a series of epigrams, many of which reemerge later
in his antipapal, pro-Lutheran polemics. His dialogue *On The
Roman Trinity* (or, *Vadiscus*) of 1520 catalogues his perceptions
of Roman evil in excruciating detail.

Returning to Germany, Hutten found himself lionized, and
in July, 1517, Maxmilian crowned him poet laureate. He was
even in good favor, for a change, with his family; the poet's
laurel atoned in part for his failure to secure the desired law
degree. Hutten now entered the life of a courtier, composing a
work on court life (*Aula*) that he sent to Pirckheimer for criticism. It is Hutten's response to the Nürnberger's critique that we
find in his previously mentioned letter castigating the mercantile
class.

At this time Hutten also involved himself in political affairs.
Having entered the service of Archbishop Albrecht von Brandenburg, the powerful Imperial Elector, Hutten lent his talents to
propagandistic efforts to promote a Christian crusade against the

Turkish menace. Hutten, like Maximilian, saw in this an opportunity for the empire to prove its claim to leadership of Christendom as the military savior of Western values. What stamps Hutten's exhortation to the German princes with his own mark is his bitter criticism of both the selfishness of the territorial princes (such as Duke Ulrich) and the trickery of Rome. The Lutheran indulgence controversy was coming into full swing at this time, and Hutten turned his pen in two dialogues (*Fever, the First; Fever, the Second*) against Cardinal Cajetan, who had been sent to Germany to straighten out the entire Lutheran controversy. These works Hutten imbued with great invective and defamation, and in this he was the child of his time.

Hutten's diplomatic service to Albrecht included visits to the court of Francis I of France, to the Reichstag of Augsburg, and to Frankfurt for the imperial election following the death of Maximilian in 1519. In his letter to Pirckheimer, Hutten characteristically refused to admit a conflict between the demands of the active and the contemplative life. Yet he soon took leave of Albrecht's court, apparently despairing of further effectiveness in this environment. Hutten's activism now became even more overt. Having wielded the sword successfully against Duke Ulrich, Hutten offered his martial services in defense of a reluctant Reuchlin, allying himself with the powerful Franz von Sickingen, with whose fortunes Hutten's own life was now to be deeply bound up. Sickingen shared Hutten's knightly background, but had advanced as a *condottiere* to become the most powerful general in the empire and, doubtless, the most ambitious as well.

Hutten's humanism now came completely into the service of imperial reform. The shape this reform was to take remained something of a muddle, yet it was clear to Hutten that Rome's economic plundering of Germany, in which the sale of indulgences represented an important but not, for Hutten, overriding part, had to stop. Unlike Luther, the primary thrust of Hutten's reform was more political than religious, and the emperor was to have taken the lead in freeing the bonds shackling Germany. The monetary savings to the empire would serve to support a stronger standing army, which would in turn allow the emperor to play a more powerful role in world affairs. Hutten's reform would aim at restoring both the primitive piety of the early Christians and the primitive virtue of the early Germans. What Hutten had in mind was to reestablish the austerely moral, and independent, Germany pictured by Tacitus. Hutten's Germany would become an agrarian society ruled over by a benevolent and humanistically educated aristocracy. Men such as Hutten, of course, would play leading roles in public affairs.

While Luther used Hutten's support, he does not seem to have been attracted by Hutten's dream. The two men were, however, drawn together, and from 1520 both were closely identified by their enemies, and both were, from Rome's point of view, outlaws. They both needed and received the protection of the mighty. Hutten was threatened with delivery to Rome without a legal hearing, and he now came to identify his personal cause as the cause of all Germans. Hutten quickly penned a number of complaints addressed to the emperor, to the Elector of Saxony (Luther's protector), to Archbishop Albrecht, and to the estates of Germany demanding their defense of him as a matter of national interest. He turned the burning of Lutheran works in Mainz into the subject of another antipapal poem. And finally, in 1520 he wrote an indictment (*Anzoig*) against the papacy, in which he tried to show, by quite selective historical argumentation, that papal policy from the time of Otto I (d. 973) onward had meant only ruin for the empire.

Early in 1521 Hutten wrote furiously, hoping to influence public opinion both lay and clerical prior to the Diet at Worms. The four Latin dialogues resulting from this activity (*Bullicida* [The Bullkiller]; *Monitor I, Monitor II*, and *Praedones* [The Robbers]) show Hutten's gifts and limitations as a propagandist most clearly. Hutten himself appears in the dialogues, as do Luther, Sickingen, a personification of a papal Bull, the allegorical figure of German Freedom, cowardly papal supporters, indecisive Germans, and a merchant. The merchant appears in *The Robbers*, along with Hutten and Sickingen, a dialogue that shows how class-bound Hutten really was. The purpose of the dialogue was to convince the free German cities to support the knights in the upcoming conflict with the Church. But here again, Hutten expressed a contempt for mercantile wealth, and for the very merchant class whose support any rebellion would sorely need. Hutten's overt expression of class prejudice destroyed any possible chance of a positive response to his plea by the merchants of his time. And this dialogue appeared at the time when Hutten was at the very apex of his polemical career!

The Diet at Worms disappointed Hutten's hopes for a reform to be led by Emperor Charles. Hutten was in the service of the emperor at this time, and he and Sickingen had been assured by the imperial emissary, Clampion, that Charles supported reform. Yet when it became obvious that the imperial promises had been broken, when Luther was treated as an already adjudged heretic, Hutten let Charles know in no uncertain terms of the depth of his dismay at the Hapsburg duplicity—the emperor stood revealed as the tool of Rome. Luther appeared before the imperial body on April 17–18, 1521; by June, Hutten had terminated his imperial service. From this point Hutten's position, and Sickingen's, deteriorated rapidly. Hutten came to declare a feud against the entire priestly class. He meant to strike at the allies of those forces dominant in the Roman curia who were opposed to him, to Luther, to Reuchlin and to any and all forces of change in the empire. In October, 1521, Hutten drew on the support of Sickingen to demand 10,000 gulden from the Carthusian order in Strassburg.

While Erasmus had once demanded heroism from those who would fight the significant battles of Christian warfare, it is unlikely that he had in mind the flagrant sort of action Hutten was promoting. Yet Hutten was at war with all priests dependent upon Rome. He expected many of his fellow knights to follow his example. We note in stanza four of *Ein neu Lied* his confident assertion that great flames may grow from small sparks. The Carthusians of Strassburg were to be merely the first group attacked, the first sparks in a great conflagration. They were Romanists of the first order, prominent, wealthy, and vulnerable. There is reason to believe that the strategic choice was Sickingen's. Hutten contented himself with the payment of 2,000 gulden and counted the enterprise a success. Further success did not appear. By 1522 the church had gained the support of the cities, particularly Strassburg and Frankfurt, and the combined efforts of Sickingen and Hutten rapidly degenerated into what most people saw as highway robbery. A series of propagandistic pleas from Hutten to the cities of Germany for support came to nothing. Sickingen's campaign against the powerful Archbishop of Trier met a series of military defeats, culminating in Sickingen's death in his beleaguered Landstuhl in May, 1523. This also marked the end of Germany's Free Knights as a power in Germany.

Now Hutten was alone. He himself had less than six months to live. Rejected by Erasmus at Basel, Hutten turned on his erstwhile mentor and charged him with betraying Germany, Luther, Hutten, and the cause of reform. Erasmus responded in kind after Hutten's death, charging Hutten with betraying his humanistic calling. Expelled from Basel, Hutten turned to the only available refuge, Ulrich Zwingli. The Swiss reformer put Hutten, who was forced to conceal his name from the local population, on the Isle of Ufenau in the Zurichsee. By the end of the summer of 1523 Hutten was dead.

In two letters written in 1518 Hutten expressed most succinctly his attitude toward his enemies. "Let them hate us," he wrote, "as long as they fear us at the same time." Perhaps even more than his *Ein neu Lied*, these words illustrate the reckless, gambling nature of the man. The formula, which Hutten employed on other occasions as well—in his dialogue *Inspicientes* (The Onlookers) he put the words into the mouth of an opponent, Cardinal Cajetan (here the "us" was Rome, the "them" the Germans)—is a rather chilling statement. It was, in fact, not original with Hutten, for he had borrowed it from a classical source, the late-Greek tragedian Accius, who had given the line to Caligula. One suspects that those among Hutten's contemporaries whose erudition matched his own reacted with various and mixed degrees of amusement or embarrassment, pleasure or chagrin, when they realized Hutten's appropriation of the Roman tyrant's extraordinarily cruel formula. Hutten's repeated use of this let-them-hate-us statement suggests that it became a sort of magical formula for him, not unlike his famous motto, *"ich habs gewagt."* Apparently fearless himself, Hutten seems not to have understood the power of fear to move men to action. What he expressed as a defiant challenge became instead his own inadvertent curse. The fears that he set loose did not, as he had hoped, immobilize his enemies.

Yet for all Hutten's feelings, his hopes for a finer *humanitas* within a framework of natural unity and spiritual freedom remained a worthy inspiration to generations of German thinkers, even in our time. Hutten's role as a pivotal figure in the age that separated the medieval from the modern world is secure. Hutten's contemporaries, friend and foe alike, conceded him this position, and our judgment must follow theirs.

Selected Bibliography

PRIMARY SOURCES

   A. In original language

Ulrichi Hutteni Opera. Ed. Eduardus Böcking. Vol. I–V et Suppl. I–II. Leipzig, 1959–70; rpt. Aalen, 1963.

Ulrich von Hutten. *Deutsche Schriften*, Peter Ukena, ed. München, 1970. (Contains an afterword by Dietrich Kurze and a German translation of the 1518 letter to Pirckheimer.)

———. *Deutsche Schriften.* Selected and ed. by Heinz Mettke. Leipzig, 1972.

———. *Die deutschen Dichtungen.* DNL. Stuttgart, 1890/91; rpt. Darmstadt, 1974.

———. *Werke.* 2 vols. Berlin, Weimar, 1970. (An anthology of Hutten's writings, including selections from Martin Luther and Thomas Müntzer as well.)

———. *Gesprächbüchlein.* Strassburg, 1521. Richard Zoozmann, ed., Dresden, 1905.

   B. Hutten works in English translations

Epistolae obscurorum virorum. London, 1909. Latin and English translation by Francis Griffin Stokes. Rpt., London, 1925.

Donation of Constantine Treatyse of the donation or gyfte and endow-
    ment of possessions gyuen and graunted vnto Syluester pope of
    Rhome by Constantyne emperour of Rome . . . (London, T. God-
    fray, 1534.) Contains: The graunt and priuilege whiche is called
    the donation or gyfte of Constantyne, translated out of greke into
    laten/ by one Bartylmewe Picern.—A declamation of Laurence
    Valla . . . against the forsayd priuelege . . . with a preface of one
    ldalryk Hutten.
*Of the vvood called gvaicum, that heal(et)h the Fr(enc)c(kes), and also
    helpeth the goute in the feete.* London, 1536. Translation of *De
    morbo Gallico* by Thomas Paynell. Rpt. 1539, 1540.
Only one English translation of Hutten (by Stokes) is presently available
    to students in paperback. This is *On the Eve of the Reformation:
    Letters of Obscure Men.* New York, 1964.

SECONDARY SOURCES

Best, Thomas W. *The Humanist Ulrich von Hutten: A Reappraisal of
    His Humor.* Chapel Hill, 1969.
Flake, Otto. *Ulrich von Hutten.* Berlin, 1929. German.
Holborn, Hajo. *Ulrich von Hutten and the German Reformation,*
    transl. by Roland H. Bainton. New Haven, 1937. Probably the
    best study of Hutten to date.
Strauss, David Friedrich. *Ulrich von Hutten, His Life and Times.* Transl.
    by Mrs. G. Sturge, London, 1874.
Walser, Fritz. *Die politische Entwicklung Ulrich von Huttens während
    der Entscheidungsjahre der Reformation.* München und Berlin,
    1928.

9

Letters of Obscure Men

Peter Schäffer

Among the literary effusions of the Northern Renaissance the *Epistolae Obscurorum Virorum* (Letters of Obscure Men) occupies a singular position, since the letters address themselves not to the folly of the human situation in its totality, as Sebastian Brant and Erasmus [see pertinent articles in this volume] had done from their various vantage points, but to the crisis of a particular controversy. We are in a position to trace this development step by step from its beginnings; the appeal of the letters is to a sophisticated audience thoroughly initiated in the spheres of allusion from which their humor derives, and their effect results from an utter novelty nonetheless concocted out of thoroughly familiar ingredients.

In 1507 or 1508 a converted Jew called Pfefferkorn sought both to make a name for himself and to prove that he was now a thoroughly convinced Christian by calling for the confiscation and destruction of all Hebrew books in Jewish possession, in particular the Talmud, as being especially dangerous to his newly acquired faith. Somehow he succeeded in obtaining an imperial decree to implement this venture, whose execution, however, was impeded by the resistance of the archbishop of Mainz in his jurisdiction. Theological faculties of the universities and individual experts were consulted in the matter, and were for the most part acquiescent in Pfefferkorn's purpose, with the notable exception of Johannes Reuchlin.

That eminent jurist, philologist, and humanist had almost singlehandedly broken the ground for Hebrew studies in Germany as part of the larger program of returning to the undiluted sources of Scripture and of theology. Thereby Reuchlin, quite beyond his intention or desire, was drawn into the center of the dispute. Its scope had by this time widened from the specific question of the Hebrew books into one of principle between the old learning of the theological faculties, with their sterile scholasticism and their vested interest in ecclesiastical politics, and the new learning of the humanists, concerned with the study of classical languages and literatures as the way to a deeper understanding and an interior reformation of the Christian religion.

The closely knit humanist community throughout central Europe, none of them—to put it mildly—particularly concerned about the Jews and their books, and indifferent or even partial to Pfefferkorn up to this point, now began to realize that in the person of Reuchlin they were all exposed to censure and accordingly rallied to his support. While the case, more and more directed against the orthodoxy and the moral character of Reuchlin, went the cumbersome way of the ecclesiastical courts, and increasingly incendiary pamphlets emanated from both sides, a volume entitled *Clarorum Virorum Epistolae* (Letters of Famous Men) appeared in 1514. This was a collection of letters addressed over the years to Reuchlin, having little immediate bearing on the current controversy, but demonstrating that he enjoyed the esteem as well as the familiar confidence of Europe's most distinguished and doctrinally unexceptionable scholars.

As the title makes plain, this was the immediate literary predecessor to the present work, which appeared in the following year, anonymously, under the title of *Epistolae Obscurorum Virorum*. That an extraordinarily clever game was in the process of being played might appear to the astute reader from the first page. There is the fictive imprint of Aldus Minutius, which looks suspiciously but not quite like the name of Aldus Manutius, the famous Venetian printer, who, however, had died six months before. There is the curious designation *anno quo supra* (in the year mentioned above), meaningless because no year had been mentioned above, and there is the absence of any editor's name, of a dedication, of a preface—in a word, of all the hallmarks of a sixteenth-century publication. We have, however, indications that a few overly serious readers were taken in and accepted the letters at face value. The letters, which we shall presently examine more closely, constitute a fictitious correspondence addressed, with few exceptions, to Ortwin Gratius (one of the standard-bearers of the antihumanist camp and, incidentally, the only authentic person among the correspondents) by a motley collection of "obscure men." They were obscure, first of all, in the sense that nobody had ever heard of them, nor indeed could have, since their only existence was between the covers of the book. But within the rich meaning of the Latin *obscuri* they were also, by contrast with the *clari viri*, the bright luminaries who had written to Reuchlin, the votaries of darkness, or at least obscurantists and absurd nonentities. The original volume consisted of forty-one letters, the second edition was augmented by an appendix of seven more, while the following year a new second part appeared, consisting of sixty-two more letters. (Following the usual form of abbreviation, we shall refer to the first part, the appendix, and the second part, as EOV I, EOV I App, and EOV II, respectively, with the Arabic numeral after the abbreviation referring to the individual letters in each set.) All but three of the letters in EOV I are addressed to Ortwin Gratius, of which one (EOV I, 34) is a reply by Ortwin to his correspondent of the preceding letter, and two (EOV I, 31 and 35) are exchanges among pairs of obscure men.

The external form of the work is thus that of a collection of correspondence, in fact fictitious but presented as authentic. The humanist authors accordingly drew upon a form with which they were associated. They understood themselves as heirs to the epistolary art of Cicero, the younger Pliny and Seneca, but also to more recent masters such as Petrarch. Their letters were an integral part of their scholarly activity, serving to maintain communication within the academic world, to exchange views and articulate opinions, to express the appropriate congratulations on festive occasions and personal anniversaries, and, of course, to present their own accomplishment in the art of letter writing. The extensive correspondences that have been preserved and published from this period—that of Erasmus in the first place, and those of Celtis, Peutinger, Pirckheimer, Vadian, Beatus Rhenanus,* and others—attest to the refinement of this practice. A form so frequently used will soon develop its own stereotypes, and the salutation as well as the complimentary ending were the passages most readily given to such stylizations (some of which, incidentally, survive even into the conventions of letter writing in the present day). The obscure men were to make the most of these opportunities, as indeed they proceed to offer a parodistic mirror image of the entire humanistic epistolary practice.

Conspicuous even before they begin their letters are their outlandish names. The humanists had, with few exceptions, Latinized their names, either by simply adding a Latin ending to the vernacular form (thus Thomas More became Thomas Morus), or by translating the name itself into Latin (as Smith might become Faber), occasionally even into Greek (as Philipp Schwartzerdt did, to call himself Melanchthon). The obscure

* Conrad Celtis (1459–1508) instituted the study of literature at several European universities, especially Vienna; Conrad Peutinger (1465–1547), Augsburg patrician, promoted and contributed to the study of Germanic antiquities; Willibald Pirckheimer (1470–1530), jurist and historian, was a friend and patron of Albrecht Dürer; Joachim Vadian (1484–1551) was professor of literature at the University of Vienna before returning to his native St. Gallen in 1518 to devote himself to the city as physician, mayor, historian, and advocate of the Reformation; Beatus Rhenanus (1485–1547), Alsatian humanist, was editor of the classics, historian, and first biographer of Erasmus.

men for the most part prefer the first form, or rather their creator prefers it, because it brings about the most ridiculous possibilities. Even allowing for the fact that what may be a funny-sounding name in one language is not necessarily such in another, it is difficult to take with utter seriousness what appears in print under such preposterous appellations as Scherschleiferius, Daubengigelius, Schnarrholtzius, or Buntschumacherius, to name but a few. Their salutations range from simple greetings to countless greetings—greetings upon greetings—and such grotesque excrescences as greetings as copious as geese that devour grass (I, 37) or as the many bugs and fleas that are hatched every year (I, 39).

Similarly, the conclusions vary from subservient excuses for taking up the revered master's time (I, 6), or the coarseness of content (I, 21), to requesting news, counsel, or reassurance, commending the receiver to God's protection, or simply a childlike admission that the writer has nothing more to say.

But it is in the body of the letters—the subjects related, treated, or inquired about—that the obscure men are led to expose themselves and the real Ortwin Gratius, who sits at the hub of the correspondence and stands for many others like himself. As before, a few choice samples may serve to illustrate the tenor of their concerns. We should note at the outset that the affair of Pfefferkorn and the Hebrew books (or, in its briefest formulation, the Reuchlin matter), remains marginal throughout the EOV I. It is more commonly not even mentioned, or at most in passing through reflection upon some of its secondary aspects; in this lies the chief distinction of the first book and its literary superiority over the appendix and the second book. Here again we may note the author's technique as specifically different from that of Brant or Erasmus. Brant points the finger at each species of fool and remains present throughout the book as the relentless moralist. Erasmus has his Folly look down from above, as it were, at all the folly of mankind. She relates this with affection, good humor, and only rare outbursts of indignation, yet remains the sole speaker in this declamation of Praise. The fiction of the EOV is that the obscure men disclose their lives in their correspondence, are overheard by the author and, with him, by the reader, while they are totally unsuspecting óf any audience. The principle behind this indirect or mimic satire, as it has been called, is to let the obscure men write about anything in their lives they want, and sooner or later—more often it is very much sooner—they will give themselves away. There is no need, as indeed would hardly be likely, for them to discourse at great length on the Reuchlin affair. The author's purpose is sufficiently accomplished if they disclose what manner of men are the enemies of Reuchlin and the humanists so that with this disclosure the opposition may collapse of itself in the face of the reader's laughter.

Now for some of the subjects of their correspondence. In their own way these men are scholars, highly conscious of their magisterial dignity and particularly its external privileges, zealous for the solution of those excogitated problems which keep their cerebral mills grinding happily away. For example, is it a sin not to show proper reverence for a master who is not dressed to indicate his position? Or conversely, is it a sin to salute a Jew because by his dress he is mistakenly taken for a master at a distance? Or on less abstruse matters, and indeed, touching the personnel of the Reuchlin affair: what happens to a Jew like Pfefferkorn when he becomes a Christian; does he grow a new foreskin? There was a rumor to the effect that Pfefferkorn, who had a beautiful wife, secretly handed her around to the magistrates and the theologians to promote his cause. One of the obscure men guilelessly relates to Ortwin how he heard this rumor and how he replied to it. For one thing, he said, it was impossible because the magistrates had their own wives, and the theologians are celibates who have nothing to do with women. For another, it is commonly held that circumcised men please a woman more than the uncircumcised, and it is hardly likely that Frau Pfefferkorn, married to a Jew, would now take her pleasure from uncircumcised men. Or again, one of Ortwin's correspondents relates having met a coarse fellow who asserted that Ortwin was of spurious birth, that his mother was a whore and his father a priest, and this fellow insisted on spreading the calumny despite every admonition to desist. The correspondent regrets his inability to defend Ortwin directly, because unfortunately he never had the honor of knowing his parents, but hastens to add he is sure they were decently married people.

All these and countless other incidents—there are, after all, over a hundred letters—follow the Scholastic line of argumentation on disputed points, or what passes for it in caricature. The weightier assertions are supported by quotations, usually out of place and often out of context, from Scripture, Aristotle, the theological handbooks, or the codes of civil and canon law. Conclusions are demonstrated by fantastically wrought syllogisms; the rules of the craft are meticulously observed.

Not the least charm of these letters springs from the fact that they are written in Latin, a very peculiar kind of atrocious Latin, and that their humor derives in great measure from the language itself. For the obscure men are, on the one hand, steeped in the formulary of their illustrious sources from which, without any deeper understanding, they draw their "wisdom," and on the other conceive their thoughts in plain, everyday German, which they then transfer word by word and idiom by idiom into what they consider Latin. What they write is, in a word, plain German in Latin words. There is little heed for the proper forms, for grammar or sentence structure, for all the stylistic norms of classical or even the better varieties of ecclesiastical Latin. Their station in life and above all their unswerving orthodoxy were to offset all their linguistic blunders. This in particular was calculated to expose them to the ridicule of the humanists, for whom Ciceronian prose was the obligatory ideal and correct thinking was equated with a sovereign command of idiom. Under this aspect, of course, the EOV are untranslatable and in fact, until the last century, when the knowledge of Latin had grown something less than universal, at least in educated circles, no one had ever thought of translating them. But while this final refinement is even today accessible only to those conversant with Latin, there is enough of value beyond the humor of language in the letters to assure them a place in literature, and there have been, as the bibliography shows, translations made with varying success into both German and English as well as other modern languages.

Looking back over at least EOV I, we find emerging the little world of the obscure men. Besides common gossip and "scholarship" their lives consist of feasting, carousing, and variously sordid amatory adventures. We are offered descriptions to appeal vividly to the imagination, little genre pictures of the confined circles in which they move, of the almost idyllic existence which in their limitation they envision as the ideal of life. In their philosophy of life everything is certain, all problems have been conclusively solved, the pattern is given, and life rolls on mechanically according to its lines. They are obscure because they are backward, backward in their unimaginative orthodoxy, their complacency, and their unfelt limitation. It is this that makes them enemies of the humanists, not that they had the least understanding of humanistic concerns, but that humanism upset their convenient and conclusive little world. They felt threatened by whatever questioned their absolutes or could not be interpreted in terms of established norms.

The author of this eminently successful first part was most likely a man by the name of Crotus Rubeanus, and, apart from a few letters, this is his sole claim to literary renown. The appendix (especially the second part) reveals the heavier hand of Ulrich von Hutten, who is regarded as the author of most of these letters, with the possible addition of Hermann von dem Busche. Here the delicate balance of the indirect satire is upset; the obscure men are no longer shown in their little world oblivious to all that lies beyond it and especially to the fiction that they are being observed and overheard. They are now shown in confrontation with the humanists who appear in person or are at least mentioned by name, are generally victimized by them, and discuss the latest developments in the Reuchlin affair in almost tiresome detail. The subtlety of naïve self-exposure yields more and more to pointed satire and plain invective as the obscure men are made to reel under the blows received from the humanist camp and to report to their master for consolation and guidance.

Nevertheless, even these letters contain more than a few gems, of which one may be particularly worthy of mention because it depends for its effect on a clever allusion to the nearly contemporary *Ship of Fools* of Sebastian Brant. In EOV II, 52, one of the obscure men, Henricus Schluntz, sends to Ortwin the gift of a book, a copy of the famous *Rationale divinorum officiorum*, an analysis of the entire liturgy, by Gulielmus Durandus (1459), in return for Ortwin's having sent him Pfefferkorn's *Defensio*, his reply to the EOV I. We may note in passing that when the second volume appeared in 1517, the first had already become history. It is mentioned and acclaimed in EOV II, 1, since an obscure man obviously would not recognize that the joke was on him, and appears thematically in several other letters.

In itself this exchange of gifts was merely a gracious gesture, but Schluntz cannot let the matter rest there. For one thing, his Scholastic turn of mind drives him to accompany the simplest statement with the contrary objections and the replies to them. For another, he is beset by obscure anxiety about making a good impression. Thus he points out that he did not send Master Ortwin the book as if he thought Master Ortwin had not enough books already. He acted with the best of intentions, not in the least thinking lightly of him as one who possessed but a few books. On the contrary, he well recalls seeing Ortwin's library of numerous volumes in large and small format, some bound in boards, others in parchment, some in full leather of various colors, others in half-leather, and there Ortwin was sitting in the midst of them with a whisk in his hand to brush away the dust.

Falling all over himself to depict Ortwin as a bibliophile and hence a scholar, Schluntz has unwittingly conjured up the first woodcut of Brant's *Ship of Fools*, that of the "book fool," the collector of books useless to him because he never reads them but merely rests content in their possession, arguing in a fair syllogism that since books contain wisdom, one who possesses books also possesses wisdom. The apology for sending Ortwin yet another book leads into an encomium of Ortwin's scholarship, but intention and execution are now at total variance as a result of the graphic identification of Ortwin with the lead fool of the long parade in Brant's *Ship*.

Thus the literary sources that supplied motifs and techniques for the EOV reach into the present time of their composition, although there are other elements of older origin easily identified. There were the university satires (in academic Latin) in which the machinery of solemn Scholastic disputation was turned on trivial or salacious subjects for humorous effect, while the German vernacular supplied an unending carnival procession of stupid and grasping clergy, of bawdy monks trapped by irate husbands, of bookish learning bested by mother wit, all available for recasting. We have already mentioned the formal element of correspondence and the immediate antecedent of the *Letters of Famous Men* to Reuchlin. The artistic accomplishment of the authors of the EOV consisted in their ability to absorb all these derivative components into a new homogeneous whole: the collection of fictitious letters by which the writers expose, unmask, at times even demolish themselves.

The conjunction of the new work thus created with the Reuchlin affair was a powerful weapon of humanism against the fossilized, sterile, but still dangerously powerful theological establishment. Not only the current event serves to locate this end product of late medieval satire on the threshold of modern times. The publication of the EOV in utter anonymity, their reception in large parts of Europe within a few months, and the appearance of amplifications and replies within a few years, were possible only in the age of the printing press, the first of the modern mass media with their enormous capacity for moving the imaginations and influencing the minds of men.

The appearance of an appendix in the second printing of EOV I and of the even more extensive collection of the EOV II the following year attest to the success of this venture. Copies were in everyone's hands, and the acclaim on the humanist side was resounding and almost universal. Erasmus, however, though he had been amused by the EOV I, repudiated the EOV II, explaining in a letter that while he had also had his sport with the follies of men, he had never drawn blood, meaning, in particular, he had never mentioned anyone but himself by name. He resented his repeated mention in EOV II, even though the author had correctly apostrophized him as "his own man" (*Erasmus est homo pro se*—EOV II, 59), and he knew that adding such massive fuel to the flames of animosity was the last thing that was needed in this fateful year of 1517.

With the outbreak of the Reformation the Reuchlin affair—as indeed many of the concerns of the humanists—was swept into the background, and when the judgment finally went against the aged Reuchlin in 1520, there was no one to care very much, one way or the other. New questions were being asked and the fronts were differently drawn: obscure men continued to find their home on both sides, some in the old faith and some in the new. The humanists for the most part eschewed the Reformation, since they recognized its irrational and hence its antihumanist dimension. Although some flocked to Luther, others remained in the old church with Erasmus's reservation, "until he found a better one," and again like Erasmus or Beatus Rhenanus strove to keep aloof from the bitter feuding carried on in the name of religion.

But the popularity of the EOV, owing to its literary merit, far outlasted the specific occasion which gave it birth. In time a reply in the form of *Lamentations of Obscure Men* was issued by Ortwin, and eventually a third volume of EOV appeared, but these last fell far short of the achievement of the original with their interminable variations on the humor of language and situation. Not even the best of jokes can bear endless, let alone mindless, repetition. Yet the EOV continued to be reprinted, amplified and imitated well into the eighteenth century. Böcking (see bibliography) gives a listing of all the known editions, among which a large number of those in pocket size is conspicuous, evidently intended for travel or at least as a companion to be carried about from place to place. The prefaces to these later editions attest to a shift in the reception of the work over the years. Gradually the EOV took their place on the shelf of joke books and collections of anecdotes, became a negative style manual on how not to write Latin, and finally, in the enlightened eighteenth century, were looked upon as a document of cultural history to illustrate the waning of the Dark Ages.

Selected Bibliography

PRIMARY SOURCES

Briefe der Dunkelmänner. Transl. by Wilhelm Binder; rev., ed., with comments by Peter Amelung. München, 1964.

Briefe von Dunkelmännern. Transl. by Hans-Joachim Müller; introd. by Wolfgang Hecht. Berlin, 1964.

Epistolae Obscurorum Virorum. E. V. Böcking, ed. In: Ulrich von Hutten, *Opera*, Suppl. I & II. Leipzig, 1864–1869. (Critical edition of full text with contemporary documents, all in Latin.)

Epistolae Obscurorum Virorum. Aloys Bömer, ed. Vol. 1: Einführung; Vol. 2: Text. Heidelberg, 1924. (The first volume is an excellent introduction to all the critical problems.)

Epistolae Obscurorum Virorum: The Latin text with an English rendering, notes, and an historical introd. by Francis G. Stokes. London, 1909.

Letters of Obscure Men. Transl. by F. G. Stokes, introd. by Hajo Holborn. Philadelphia: U. of Penn. Press, 1972. (Reprint of the English portion of the preceding.)

SECONDARY SOURCE

Brecht, Walther. *Die Verfasser der Epistolae Obscurorum Virorum*. In *Quellen und Forschungen zur Sprach- und Culturgeschichte der germanischen Völker*, 93. Strassburg, 1904. (Offers a detailed analysis of style and literary techniques, still valuable in view of the paucity of recent secondary literature.)

10

Luther as Renaissance Writer

H. G. Haile

Unfortunately, the world of Luther studies, so long jarred by Protestant and Catholic, seems today filled with Christian and anti-Christian, and is graced with very few of that new race for whom Goethe found the happy term non-Christian. While non-Christians recoil from recondite theological dialogue (which continues to supply the bulk of Luther scholarship), an alternative— if such it be—is offered only by the Marxists and other zealots, to whom Luther is an outright hypocrite or a lackey for aristocratic and capitalist circles. As we gain a more balanced perception of European history, we must continue to appreciate Martin Luther's profoundly religious motivation, but if we retain the old charismatic image of him as an essentially religious figure, it will distort our otherwise secular understanding of history.

Note: Written originally for the present volume, this essay was subsequently adapted for publication in PMLA, October, 1976. It is included here by arrangement. Copyright © 1976 by Modern Language Association of America.

The Renaissance is understood as a phase in the expansion of modern experience in which a wealth of ancient literature was reborn, becoming available in modern languages to an immensely larger readership than ever before. For reasons not fully explained, the printed word took on unprecedented immediacy. Never before had the ancient Hebrew tales been received with such intense inner participation as in Luther's version of them for northern Europeans, three thousand years after their first telling.

Preoccupation with the Bible, and the debates that attended it, had a truly dynamic effect on the general literacy rate. "Literature" in the sense of the written word actually being read by a significant fraction of a populace was virtually brought into being by the young Wittenberg *Doctor in Biblia*. It seems ironical, therefore, that Luther's stature as a literary figure continues to be contingent on theological and even political considerations. The present essay will touch on four topics: 1. literacy rates around 1500; 2. Luther as popular songwriter and pamphleteer; 3. Luther the interpreter; 4. the relationship of Luther's "reformation" to the Renaissance.

LUTHER AND LITERACY

From a secular viewpoint the most far-reaching effect of Luther's writing was the radical increase in literacy rates in the early 1520s. It continued to be felt throughout Northern Europe during the rest of the century. In the Middle Ages reading had been an activity of professional scribes and scholars, while illiteracy remained widespread among the nobility and even among the clergy. The medieval poet Wolfram von Eschenbach is either being truthful or affecting a noble pose when he claims to be illiterate, but four hundred years later the baroque novelist Grimmelshausen is just telling an old, familar yarn when he lets his young hero come upon a hermit "conversing" with the pictures in his book. Literacy had increased gradually after Wolfram's day until the *Biblia pauperum* (which tells the familiar

stories in pictures) was at last replaced by the *Biblia deutsch.*
Luther's position in this long-range development is quite anala-
gous to his part in the gradual standardization of German, or to
his role in the long demanded reform of the church: Ongoing
processes merge in him, reinforce each other, and eventuate in
unprecedented change.

Mercantile activity and trade, technological developments
like the paper mill, copper engraving, woodcuts, and at last the
use of movable type had long been enhancing the availability of
reading materials. By 1500 about forty German imprints were
being produced annually, at issues of about five hundred each.
Compare that with 498 imprints in 1523, which averaged over
one thousand each. Luther was himself author of over one-third
of these. The flood of German works by no means reduced the
production of Latin books, which also continued to increase for
the next several generations. It appears that religious dispute was
transforming Germany into a literate nation in the modern
sense, and the same process was going on in other countries,
penurious Scotland being perhaps the best example. When dispute was submerged by Protestant orthodoxy toward the end of
the century, the demand for books in German began to level off,
and it actually declined during the Thirty-Years War, but by
then book production had increased tenfold during a period
(1470–1600) when population had only doubled.

Luther's sensational dispute and eventual break with the
church had been crucial in this popularization of literacy. The
common man, always curious, wanted to know what the fuss was
all about. Luther's radical new theology urged greater self-reliance on him, and he began to look into the sources for himself.
Luther not only played this key role in urging books into the
hands of the people; he produced a lion's share of the printings
themselves. Just as Luther expressly hoped (in the preface to his
Latin works), all these pamphlets would soon be forgotten, but
the new ability and eagerness to read was retained. The psychological power of the written word would continue to transform
the mentality of European man (to Luther's own surprise and
consternation) for another generation. Literacy had the effect of

general consciousness raising, as MacLuhan has convincingly shown, hence the tremendous impact of the vernacular Bible, an all-time classic in the German language. The admirable team-work that produced the Wittenberg Bible was to be duplicated elsewhere, notably by the scholars of King James's court in England.

In an achievement equal in importance to the popular success of the Bible, Luther formulated a theory of literature that for the first time enabled the people to understand the great works from ancient Hebrew as relevant to their own personal lives. This is the aspect of Luther's work that our own era, languishing in a new scholasticism, can most admire. Let us think of Luther as the consummate popular artist who democratized South European humanism. While the aristocratic Italian Renaissance tends to evoke visions of clear and balanced form, Northern Europe learned to take delight in the profusions of the poet and satirist Johann Fischart, and of Rabelais and Shakespeare with their endless combinations and bold juxtapositions. In this more boisterous sense, Luther is also a man of the Renaissance, who from long experience as professor and debater consciously played to the gallery.

THE POPULAR SONGWRITER

As a lyricist, Luther is kin to Scottish poet Robert Burns, our own Woody Guthrie, and others whose songs arose from the native strength of popular language, words and music coming as a coherent inspiration. Learned arguments, long and bravely fought, concerning the originality of Luther's melodies, quite miss the point that such artists as these scorn originality. When school children patriotically sing "This Land Is Your Land," when resolute Lutherans sing "Ein feste Burg," or when "Auld Lang Syne" unites Anglo-Saxons, they are not singing national hymns but modes that hark back to a common Indo-European background. He who places great store by originality must seek it in the craftsmanship with which these artists match lyric and melodic line. Any of Luther's songs might serve us as examples, but the very first one that has come down to us seems most naïve and appealing: "Ein neues Lied wir heben an" (We raise a new song).

The occasion was the public burning of two Antwerp Augustinians (July 1, 1523) at the beginning of the inquisition set up by Charles V in the Netherlands—the first martyrdom of the emerging sect. The song is a tendentious narrative which makes claim to art by its masterful recall of topoi (*sie sungen süss, sie sungen saur / die Knaben stunden wie ein Mauer,** etc.) The technique can yield touching beauty:

> *Der Sommer ist hart vor der Tür,*
> *Der Winter ist vergangen,*
> *Die zarten Blumen gehn herfür.*
> *Der das hat angefangen,*
> *Der wirt es wohl vollenden.*†

Use of these ancient motifs produces the same psychological effect as the melody: to unite the singers in consciousness of their common heritage. The narrative is strongly partisan, and the melody emphasizes conflict of good with wicked in melodramatic fashion, as is appropriate for the historical folk song.

Note how triumphantly the tale begins:

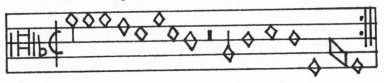

Ein neues lied wir heben an, Des walt Gott unser Herre.

* They sang sweetly, they sang bitterly, / those boys stood there like a wall.

† The summer just is at the gate / And the winter now is past, / The tender flower springs. / He who began these things / Will perfect them all at last.

Every strophe returns to words appropriate to the chant at F.
The refrain drops ominously down to A, with seven quarter
notes there before rising defiantly with the martyrs' names all the
way to the top of the scale. Singing or playing this song immediately conveys its propagandistic effectiveness. Luther has hewed
faithfully to the form of the historical folk song, widely cultivated from earliest times. In his day this genre was an important
and accepted vehicle for recording and disseminating news, just
as in our own era it can still be used to inform or shape public
opinion. "Jesse James" and "John Henry" of the last century, as
well as union workers' songs of this century are modern examples. Especially in the latter we hear the traditional techniques of
sarcasm and vitriolic attack, which Luther applied so well.

POPULAR POLEMIC

The craftsmanship that went into Luther's polemical pamphlets
is equally naïve. The most famous (and effective) example is his
Address to the Christian Nobility of the German Nation*
(1520). The body of the work takes its simple organization from
twenty-seven complaints familiar from their presentation at
numerous Imperial diets. Luther lets us know at the outset that
his will be an especially entertaining presentation of them, delivered by the universal favorite of the Renaissance, the fool. Who
could be better suited to play the fool, he asks, than a monk?
"No one need buy a cap or trim the coxcomb for me. We shall
see, however, who is to be belled." It is one of the most familiar
conceits of an age that delighted in puns and double entendre.
Equally familiar in popular culture with the fool was siege imag-
ery. Somewhat earlier Luther had complained that the papacy
"laid a bar across the door to guard its rascality." Now he develops his celebrated conceit of the three walls that, like the walls of
Jericho, shield the impious papists (Canon Law, ultimate authority in interpreting the Bible, and exclusive right to call a

---

* *An den christlichen Adel deutscher Nation* in the original.

council). The twenty-seven articles constituting Luther's treatise become in this frame a mere vessel for the many tricks of popular debate known to a practiced debater. Let us examine some of them in detail, as representative of Luther's numerous polemics.

At the lowest level, techniques may be simply invective and appeal to chauvinism and prejudice in harsh epithet of the sort which the sixteenth century loved. Luther likes crude neologisms. Among his many debater's tricks is the direct appeal to his audience, to his enemy the pope, or to Jesus Christ himself. He maintains a jovial tone by making fun of himself and ridiculing the pretensions of his opponents ("Why, it's just the same as if I called the keeper of the whorehouse: Madam Mayor."). From Luther's style we infer an audience that loved puns and had an endless tolerance of repetition. They obviously took delight in sheer prolixity. While Luther does shape his flood of words— most frequently with crescendo—we often feel that he is just venting his spleen in a tradition later to be taken up by Fischart and Abraham a Sancta Clara. He knows how to use the proverb in an argumentative, very convincing way: *O wie ein schlechter Schatz ist der Zoll am Rhein gegen dieses heilige Haus* (what a poor source of revenue a customs house on the Rhine is, compared with the church).

Proverbs are convincing because they distill the wisdom of the ages, with which one just does not quibble—but their use also certifies the native son, who can make a special claim on credence. In this connection, note that Luther imprints his slogans on our mind not with end rhyme (of Latin provenience) so often as with stave rhyme, a Germanic device. In *To the Christian Nobility* we have *Gewurm und Geschwurm* (vermin), *lügen und trügen* (deceive), *die Schrift zwingen und dringen* (distort Scripture), etc.; but uses of alliteration (stave rhyme) are much more numerous and inventive: *prachten und prangen* (extravagance), *Schätzerei und Schinderei* (gouging), *nur frisch mit füssen treten* (go ahead and kick it down), *irre laufen auf dem Land* (get lost in the wilds), of Hus's tormentors: *es hat sie der Teufel toll und töricht gemacht* (the devil drove them mad). Stave rhyme linkages reinforce the logic of an argument, as when

Luther says that we (not only) put up with (but even) praise God's shame: *solche Unehre Gottes leiden und loben*. He ties together greed and Canon Law: *der Geiz und das geistliche Recht*. It is fascinating to follow this highly associative mind as it seeks poetic release, now in fairy tale motif (*zehn Brüder, Königskinder, in eine Wüste gesetzt*), now into metaphor: to give a celibate monk a housekeeper is to put fire and straw together, and forbid them to burn. Luther knows how to turn his poetic gift to great harshness ("The pope gives you lead for gold, hide for meat, cord for purse, comb for honey, words for wares, letter for spirit, and if you ride toward heaven on his parchment and wax, your coach will soon break down and plunge you into hell"), or gently, especially when guided by his beloved Bible: *So doch allein die Schrift unser Weingarten ist* (For Scripture alone is our vineyard).

The untiring delight of medieval man in discovering his everyday life exemplified in the Bible puts forth its most stunning flower in Martin Luther. When he argues that we must apply the test of our own judgment to what we are told by the clergy, he recalls how "in olden times Abraham had to listen to Sarah, even though she was more subordinate to him than we are to anyone on earth—and Balaam's she-ass was cleverer than the prophet himself. If God could defy his prophet through a she-ass, why can't he defy the pope through a pious man?" The Bible becomes for Luther an immense storehouse in which the tiniest jewels are immediately accessible. On the subject of universities, he confesses his concern for young people that the professors are so unlearned: "Mine eyes do fail with tears and my bowels spill upon the ground . . ." Thus begins a lengthy recitation of Lamentations II—from memory no doubt—ten years before he translated it! Heinz Bluhm, who has compiled an index of Luther's Bible translations outside his Bible, comes to the conclusion that some of Luther's greatest successes occur in just such extempore quotations. Luther seems to have been a true artist in the sense that substance and beauty seemed one to him.

THE INTERPRETER

Not only did involvement in doctrinal dispute make Germans literate in the modern, democratic sense of the word, and soon other north Europeans as well. The Scriptures as doctrinal court of final appeal became the all-time literary classic of the West. Above all others, it seems to have been Luther who taught us to read these ancient songs and tales of the Near East in terms of immediate relevance to our own daily lives and thought.

In this, he became a shining example to all literature teachers. With the literary riches of an ancient, noble herdsman civilization of the south, he was able to transform superstitious tribesmen of the dark north European forest into an enlightened, even scholarly race—for a time. Numerous writers, each for his own parochial purposes, have addressed themselves to the topic of Luther's art of interpretation. The most important to our era is Karl Holl (see bibliography), who reduces the complex issue to two fundamental points: 1. Luther's insistence that the literal sense of Scripture is its sole and simple meaning (hence his rejection of the various symbolic approaches to the Bible that intellectuals had been urging on the congregation for many centuries), and 2. Luther's lively, imaginative, and sympathetic response to the text—as Holl put it, *Nacherleben des Inhalts.*

These qualities became apparent in Luther's very first lectures on Psalms in 1513, which a modern scholar still finds characterized by their "informal and strongly personal element" (Warren Quanbeck). Here, years before Luther became embroiled in doctrinal disputes, we find him using German in his lecture hall to make his meaning clear and immediate (Christian Thomasius is usually credited with being the first to conduct actual German lectures—in Leipzig, 1687). Luther's lectures are distinguished by their sensitivity to the poetic devices and poetic qualities of the Old Testament. He compares Moses with Vergil, stating that it is from Moses that all the other prophets learned to speak so eloquently. Other writers of poetry and history "depict various passions, are diffuse in the enlargement of things, and heap up words in large number. But Moses uses few words, repeating them so that the reader, thus admonished, reflects on the magnitude of the event. Thus the passion itself, not just one he has read about, rises up in him." Luther cannot cease to marvel at the terse pregnancy of old Hebrew style: "Scripture contains histories written most succinctly, but also most excellently: they pour out everything in one word. What Vergil says of Dido's love in many words, the Hebrew expresses most curtly: 'Amnon loved Thamar.' . . . In the same way, we are required to think David's thoughts as he killed the lion, or when he had to fight Goliath; 'What if I should die?—But I shall not, for my right hand is the right hand of God.' Then they call that *rhetorica.*"

Luther was an astoundingly close reader, sensitive to the broad range of ancient Hebrew literary devices. Impressed by the sorrow of Adam and Eve at the death of Abel, he notes how, after the terrible shock of the fratricide, the sequence of offspring reveals that the parents "refrained for a time from begetting." Naturally, he noted myriad discrepancies in the Biblical account and was more than once moved to an exclamation like that about Jonah: "Who would believe it and not think it a lie or a fairy tale if it were not in Scripture?" When in battles fought in Exodus the Israelites slay more men than are elsewhere reported to be in the entire opposing nation, Luther explains the numbers as symbolic for taking the enemy king. He wonders why the 600,000 strong Israelites should consider a victory over 60,000 Amorites as remarkable, calculates that a nation capable of raising 600,000 men would require six to seven days to march through the Red Sea even marching fifty abreast, and considers it a special miracle that the Israelites accomplished the passages in two hours. Karl Holl declares that Luther's close reading of the baptismal and resurrection stories would have—within fifty years of his death—effected his expulsion from the Lutheran church.

There seems to be no question that we do have with Luther some first beginnings of a view of the Bible as a literary document, i.e., a work that bears testimony to the limited time and place of its origins and undergoes its own history. This is espe-

cially apparent in his appreciation of specifically Hebrew devices
—"barbarisms of the Holy Ghost." Fragmentary features of the
prophetic books seem explicable to him now in terms of the
passions of the prophets themselves, or now because of faulty
transmission: "These sayings were not arranged by the prophet,
but excerpted by scribes." Bornkamm conjectures that one reason
motivating later publishers of Luther's Bible to drop his excellent prefaces may have been Luther's freely expressed doubts as
to authorship of books in the Bible. He repeatedly questions
Moses' authorship of the Pentateuch, and his outright rejection
of certain books of the New Testament is notorious (James,
Revelation).

LUTHER'S RENAISSANCE
OF ANCIENT LITERATURE

In calling attention to these things I am trying to map out a
broad common ground where Luther's approach to the Bible
resembles our own approach to great literature. The most striking difference between Luther and a reader such as myself may
be in Luther's confident assurance that the written word holds
high *practical* value for men of his day. As a professor, that was
the chief ax he had to grind. He was sure that interpretation as
practiced by his own contemporaries, whom he contemptuously
called "the Sophists," although it boasted a highly refined
method for extracting and expanding upon the so-called spiritual senses of the text, was oblivious to the real spiritual needs
of the congregation. It is probably true that scholastic inter-
preters had become more wrapped up in the fine art of distilling
various abstract meanings from the text than concerned with
its practical value. Luther seems to have felt that once this happens, once the process loses sight of the ends it serves, then interpretation itself degenerates. We have to concede that he was
stunningly successful in his own interpretation while at the same
time effecting unprecedented popularity of the text itself.

Is not a Renaissance in Luther's sense precisely what every

literature teacher longs for—a return to the sources as they are reborn in a new immediacy? "Renaissance" probably takes on its full meaning only in this religiously colored sense, which suffuses the sources in new affect and lends them relevance for and in the individual life.

With this in mind I offer this summing up of Luther's principles of interpretation from a literary point of view, as distinct from the more usual theological approach.

1. Surely the most striking feature of Luther's exegesis is that it does not aim at finality. On the contrary, the typical interpretation begins and ends with a statement that it is tentative, that it may be replaced tomorrow by a better one based on increased experience and understanding. As we grow, so does our appreciation—and the text helps us grow.

2. Luther insisted that the text was generally comprehensible, an elaborate interpretive technique unnecessary. "The Holy Ghost is the simplest of all scribes and counsellors in heaven and earth so that his words could not have more than one simplest sense, which we call the scriptural or literal sense." He readily allows for allegory . . . "as if I said: Emser is a crude ass, and a simpleton took me at my word and understood that Emser were a real ass with long ears and four legs—he would be deceived by the literal sense." But aside from allegory clearly intended by the author, Luther flatly refused to accept the time-hallowed manifold sense of Scripture. The humanists approved of allegorical interpretation and often could come to terms with the text in no other way. Luther, in lashing out at the *ludicri et lusores* who thus made a game of Scripture, enhanced respect for the Bible as a document that must be accepted on its own terms.

3. Luther's confidence in the simplicity of Biblical expression corresponds with his sure assumption of one simple, i.e., *uniform* sense or—as he put it with the Aristotelian term— *skopos* for the entire Bible: "All of Scripture would make us acquainted with Christ. This is the *skopos* of all Scripture." Rabbinical interpretation, for example, could never be correct, because it missed this simple, literal sense of the Old Testament. An interpreter must know the entire Bible intimately. The

meaning of the Old Testament will normally arise from the New Testament. Luther's own detailed acquaintance with the Bible was fantastic—he scorned users of concordances.

4. The text is its own best interpreter—in Luther's words: "Scripture itself is in itself most certain, simple, and apparent. It is its own interpreter, testing, judging, and illuminating all things." There are, to be sure, obscure and difficult passages aplenty. They must be illuminated by the clearer ones. This principle presupposes, of course, the simple, uniform sense of Scripture just discussed. Furthermore, both notions operate under the "analogy of faith" that the entire Bible is concerned with Christ and with His meaning for man and that hence no passage, when it is rightly construed, can contradict this fundamental article of belief.

5. So far, I have only listed principles that in one way or another are treated by theologically oriented Luther scholarship. I as student and teacher of literature find one more important principle arising almost everywhere Luther interprets a text. I will call it the *analogia experientiae*: analogy to shared experience. It is closely related to what Holl called *Nacherleben des Inhalts*. My emphasis, however, recognizes that Luther never interprets except that he is consciously interpreting for someone, be it in lectures to his students, introductions to books of his Bible translation, sermons and other kerygmatic writings, or in his tough polemics. He is always trying to communicate to others his special interpretation of the text. In doing so, his constant appeal is to the experience of his audience.

Of course this was not new with Luther, and it continues to be a most popular preacher's and teacher's device. It even embodies a whole philosophy of textual understanding. But Luther was highly adept at it, and I believe that his use of the analogy to experience must be regarded as a major characteristic of his entire attitude toward Scripture. Especially do I think that Luther's example here is likely to be useful to teachers of all texts in all societies. "No one," he declares, "can understand a text unless he experiences it."

Let me just conclude with a few examples. Luther's explanation as to how Christians should regard Mosaic Law is deservedly famous. He concedes that it is excellent, "Not that it should be imposed by force, but let the emperor take an example of a fine government from Moses, just as the Romans had fine laws, and just as the Germanic peoples had fine laws in the *Sachssenspiegel* [an early corpus of Germanic law], by which our land was governed. Gentiles don't have to obey Moses. Moses is the Jewish *Sachssenspiegel*"—by means of analogy, a brilliant demythologization of the Ten Commandments.

Rather than continue with numerous examples, I will conclude with what turned out to be Luther's last written words:

"Nobody can understand Vergil in his *Bucolics* and *Georgics* unless he has first been a shepherd or a farmer for five years.

"Nobody understands Cicero in his letters unless he has twenty years experience in important public office.

"Let no one think that he sufficiently savors Holy Scripture unless he has governed the churches with the prophets for a hundred years. Because the wonders are great, first of John Baptist, then of Christ, and third of the Apostles. Touch not this divine *Aeneid*, but bow down and adore his footsteps. *Wir sein pettler. Hoc est verum.*"

In short, Luther assumes—and often says explicitly—that the true medium of communication from soul to soul is shared passion and experience. Letters cannot be separated from life. The spirit must first bring meaning to the letter. A typical comment from his *scholia* on Psalms is: "Only passion and experience will reveal the meaning."

Selected Bibliography

PRIMARY SOURCES IN THE ORIGINAL GERMAN AND LATIN

Biblia. das ist die Gantze Heilige Schrift deutsch. Wittemberg, 1543. Facsimile, Leipzig, 1934.

Biblia pauperum—Faksimile Ausgabe des vierzigblättrigen Armenbibel-

Blockbuches. Hanau, 1967. (Also other facsimiles of this block Bible.)

Luthers Werke in Auswhal. Otto Clemen, ed., in collaboration with Albert Leitzmann. Berlin, 1912–1933. 2nd ed., 1959–1967.

PRIMARY SOURCES IN TRANSLATION

Luther's Works. Jaroslav Pelikan and Helmut T. Lehmann, eds. Philadelphia, 1955 ff.

Texts Available for Students

Hutten, Müntzer, Luther. Werke in zwei Bänden. Berlin und Weimar, 1970.

SECONDARY SOURCES

Atkinson, James. *The Trial of Luther.* New York, 1971.

Bainton, Roland. *Here I Stand: A Life of Martin Luther.* New York, 1950.

Beintker, Horst. "Zu Luthers Anteil an der Sprachwerdung des Neuhochdeutschen." *Muttersprache,* 76 (1966), 228–34.

Bluhm, Heinz. "The Literary Quality of Luther's Septembertestament." *PMLA,* 81 (1966), 327–33.

Bornkamm, Heinrich. "Luther als Schriftsteller." *Formenwandel, Festschrift für Paul Böckmann.* W. Müller-Seidel and W. Preisendanz, eds. Hamburg, 1964.

————. *Luther und das alte Testament.* Tübingen, 1948.

Burger, Heinz Otto. "Luther im Spiegel der Tischreden." *GRM,* 23 (December, 1973), 385–403.

Dickens, Arthur G. *Martin Luther and the Reformation.* London, 1967.

Doermann, Ralph W. "Luther's Principles of Biblical Interpretation." In *Interpreting Luther's Legacy.* Minneapolis, 1969, 14–25.

Engelsing, Rolf. *Analphabetentum und Lektüre. Zur Sozialgeschichte des Lesens in Deutschland zwischen feudaler und industrieller Gesellschaft.* Stuttgart, 1973.

Erikson, Erik H. *Young Man Luther.* New York, 1958.

Ettinghausen, Walter. "Luther: Exegesis and Prose Style." *German Studies Presented to Professor H. G. Fiedler.* Oxford, 1938, 174–86.

Hillerbrand, Hans Joachim. *The World of the Reformation.* New York, 1973.

Holl, Karl. *The Cultural Significance of the Reformation.* New York, 1959.

————. *Luther*. In Holl, *Gesammelte Aufsätze zur Kirchengeschichte*, 3. Tübingen, 1921 ff.

Iserloh, Erwin. *The Theses Were Not Posted: Luther Between Reform and Reformation*. Boston, 1968.

Kawerau, Peter. *Luther: Leben, Schriften, Denken*. Berlin, 1969.

Kooiman, Willem Jan. *Luther and the Bible*. Philadelphia, 1961.

Lilje, Hanns. *Luther and the Reformation: An Illustrated Review*. Philadelphia, 1967. (Magnificent contemporary illustrations.)

Lortz, Joseph. *The Reformation in Germany*. 2 vols. New York, 1968.

MacLuhan, Herbert Marshall. *The Gutenberg Galaxy*. Toronto, 1962.

Martin Luther Lectures. Roland Bainton, Jaroslav Pelikan, Warren Quanbeck, et al, eds. Decorah, Iowa. (*Luther Today*, 1956; *More About Luther*, 1957; *The Mature Luther*, 1958; others.)

Schwiebert, E. G. *Luther and His Times*. St. Louis, 1950.

Smith, Preserved. *The Life and Letters of Martin Luther*. Boston, 1911.

CONTEMPORARY DRAMAS

Forte, Dieter. *Martin Luther und Thomas Müntzer oder die Einführung der Buchhaltung in Deutschland*. Berlin, 1970.

Osborne, John. *Luther*, a play. New York, 1961.

11

Reaction and Revolution: Antihumanism and the Reform Movements

Duncan Smith

.

Praise of the movement known as humanism has become virtually traditional in scholarly circles. Humanism is seen as a harbinger of the Renaissance and precursor of modern humanist traditions. Indeed, there is much evidence to support some of this enthusiasm for the intellectual movement in fourteenth-, fifteenth-, and sixteenth-century Europe that in the seventeenth century came eventually to be referred to by the high-sounding term "humanism." But at the time of its appearance, the movement, both as a minor intellectual manifestation of modernity in thought and as an important basis in praxis of a new ontology, had wide opposition. Despite the fact that its earliest adherents were most frequently churchmen, the church itself was disinclined to look favorably upon many aspects of the movement, particularly those that, under the guise of various heresies, threatened the stability of the theocracy of medieval Europe.

The evidence that has survived, and that gives us today our views of humanism as a movement, is generally favorable to the humanist position. Its disintegration into various hostile religious

movements in both the Protestant and Catholic camps is, furthermore, not usually seen as a natural result of the intellectual
direction of humanism. It is thus sometimes difficult to point out
how, in fact, the doctrines that humanism frequently espoused
were themselves to produce what casual observers might take to
be chaotic conditions in intellectual and political life during the
Reformation.

Nowhere in Europe is that difficulty so manifest as in "Germany," which by the end of the fifteenth century had become the
center of what had earlier been the Italian Renaissance and
humanist traditions. Contemporary observers of German states in
the fifteenth and early sixteenth centuries agree on the vistas of
prosperous cities and fertile fields and on the apparent wealth
and contentment of the population. A number of German universities had been founded and were rivaling the older established universities of Paris and the Italian cities in all faculties
save perhaps in medicine. The introduction of so-called "Roman
Law" into Germany was by this period almost accomplished, and
the growth of the monopolies in cities like Augsburg, Nürnberg,
and other southern German towns made Germany the financial
center of Europe, competing with declining Venice and Genoa as
well as Amsterdam, Antwerp, and Ghent.

However much this period has traditionally been held in
disdain by modern scholarship, German letters and German
Latinists were flourishing, and at the time of the publication of
Sebastian Brant's great work, *Das Narrenschiff* (The Ship of
Fools) in 1494, German literature was a European-wide phenomenon, translated into all major European languages and
popular in a way never to be approached again, even in the
present day. Works of this European stature include the Latin
poetry of a host of German authors, some of whom, like Sebastian
Brant (1458–1521), wrote in the vernacular as well. The most
famous German literary works in the vernacular include the Low
German epic *Reinke de Vos* (Reynard the Fox, ca. 1498), *Till
Eulenspiegel* (ca. 1450), *Historia von D. Johann Fausten* (1587),
as well as numerous important Reformation dramas.

It is thus easy to see why the general phenomenon of humanism has come to be regarded as a positive development in German cultural and political history. Its later supposed decline in favor of more parochial German interests coincides with the end of the medieval and the beginning of the modern period in German history. In the seventeenth century, Italy, France, and England, even Spain, possessed flourishing cultures whose works are still read and admired by scholars, students, and interested lay people to this day. But it is difficult indeed to find interest on any large scale for the cultural manifestations of Germany, save in music, in this same period. Thus humanism has come to be regarded as the last great climax of medieval Germany's cultural traditions, and the reasons for the subsequent rapid decline of that culture are sought by scholars in such disparate phenomena as the Thirty Years' War (1618–1648), the Religious Wars accompanying the Reformation and Counter Reformation, or the lack of a single German literary language.

But humanism in Germany as in Europe was also a phenomenon with a real and material background. That is, the ideas that adorn the reputations of the European humanists from Petrarch (1304–1374) through Thomas More (1478–1535) and Erasmus (1466–1536) and that touch Luther (1483–1546) and the brilliant but caustic theologian and Greek scholar Melanchthon (1497–1560) long-time collaborator and friend of Luther, are not merely plucked from the air but must have arisen, as do all intellectual conceptions, from actual events in the contemporary history of Europe. Since the humanistic or Renaissance phenomenon was European-wide, touching even the most extreme eastern and northern boundaries of what was then Europe, the real basis must also have been as broad in its implications. That phenomenon—out of which humanism arose and which then practically determined the course of later European intellectual history far beyond the point at which its influence in Germany, at least, is said by scholars to have subsided and finally disappeared—is the economic and social upheaval undergone by Europe from the thirteenth through the sixteenth centuries. Humanism was an effective articulation of the ideas of a new kind of human being, devoted as never before to self-development and various realistic ramifications of the meaning of that term. These new ideas were also at the heart of the new economic system that later came to be called capitalism.

Despite the outward appearances of those walled cities and fertile fields, economic conditions in Germany at the time of the fourteenth through the beginnings of the sixteenth centuries were not uniformly stable for much of the population. The growth of business or commercialism as a major factor in late medieval life altered significantly, even relentlessly, the tone of that life. The replacement of a barter economy on a local scale by a money economy on a national or international scale was accompanied both by the accumulation of tremendous wealth located uniformly in the new urban centers and by a decline in the quality of life on the land for two major social classes, the peasantry and the lower nobility, the so-called free or imperial knights. One of these, in the figure of Goethe's Götz von Berlichingen, has been idealized as a symbol of the quest for "freedom" from the growing constraints on the ideal of individualism of the old society. In reality Götz was little more than another opportunistic robber-baron of the old style, who for a brief time made common cause with the peasantry in the hope of furthering a return to the "good old days." He and his peers were greatly troubled by the changes that late medieval society was undergoing, changes they neither understood nor had the power to prevent. Their eventual resort to arms coincided in part with the famous German peasant uprisings in 1525, and their extirpation by the alliance of princes and cities under the auspices of the imperial government has been used occasionally in German literature as a symbol of this longing for "freedom." In reality, according to modern interpretations, it was more reactionary than progressive.

The first stirrings of discontent are hard to identify, for medieval society was forever torn by some form of radicalism, usually under the umbrella of theological rebellion. These movements, referred to as heresies by the orthodox church, began almost as soon as any notion of orthodoxy had been established. Some of these heresies were minor and focused on what may

today seem like a neurotic quirk in the makeup of their adherents. Some, however, are evidently genuine rents in the fabric of
medieval society, demanding either immediate repair of that
fabric or its replacement by a new spiritual garment. The inertia
of the *status quo*, always a powerful force in politics, was very
much a factor in medieval life and law, where the past was the
chief precedent. It is accordingly not surprising that few of these
movements made any real gains. The most dangerous of them,
the Cathar movement, culminated in the famous Albigensian
heresy of the thirteenth century, located for the most part in
southern France. Its destruction was the combined work of the
orthodox theocracy and the centralizing power of the French
monarchy. The Albingensian Crusade (ca. 1213) succeeded in
destroying the movement as a political force, but it did not root
out all aspects of the Cathar heresy, particularly those having to
do with the notion of the priesthood of all believers.

Some historians see the Waldensian movement, or the Poor
Man's heresy, of southern France as a continuation of the Cathar
movement. Its adherents preached the rejection of material
wealth and devotion to the life of poverty and innocence. This
led eventually to the Franciscan movement, which also advocated
poverty and a return to a more spiritual way of life in the church
and in society as a whole. This movement was incorporated into
the orthodox religion by a clever pope, Innocent III, who realized that regularizing an order to be called the Franciscans
was preferable to having a new and genuine spirituality rampant
throughout Europe among a population very sympathetic to the
new movement's ideals. Since the reputation of the church had
suffered so much from the period of the so-called "Babylonian
Captivity" (1305–1378), when the papacy was divided and its
major seat was at Avignon, not Rome, and from the quality of
the popes who followed the great Innocent III (1198–1216), the
Franciscan order grew to be the movement that for a time re-
established the spiritual leadership of the church. But the movement soon became split, for as its prestige grew so did its wealth
and power, until at last a group of Franciscans, to be called later
the Spirituals to distinguish them from the Conventuals or tradi-

tionalists, demanded a return to the way of life of the founder,
St. Francis (1182–1226), a way characterized by denial and
renunciation, not by gratification through material acquisition.
To a considerable degree this split in the Franciscan order marks
the end of traditional medieval society and culture.

The cries for reform, and for a return to the values and life
style of the early church, had long resounded through Europe,
particularly during times of plague, famine, or warfare. The
outbreak of the Black Death in 1348 witnessed a great return to
spirituality. Within the Franciscan order there had also appeared
scholars whose investigations into the nature of reality led them
to reject many tenets of Catholicism and linked them to the
growing inquiry into the nature of the God-human relationship
and thus into the nature of the state as a reflection in real terms
of that relationship. William of Ockam (d. 1350), an Oxford
Franciscan, came to be the founder of a new ontological and
epistemological view called nominalism, the forerunner perhaps
of empiricism, for the nominalists insisted that the so-called
universals—ideas defined by words—had no real life of their own
as the realists had claimed, but were only given names by human
reason, albeit with the aid of God. The political importance of
Ockam's thought is underscored by his eventual flight to the
protection of the court of Louis the Bavarian (1314–1347), who
had opposed the primacy of the papacy in temporal matters.
Marsiglio of Padua, an Italian political writer with views similar
to those of Louis, was also protected by that court, and the new
ideas of power were thus set in opposition to the traditional
views of church-state relationships. The nominalist-realist controversy—out of which, to a great extent, grew the new humanism siding with the nominalist position—is the central philosophical controversy of the later Middle Ages. It introduces the
principle of human reason as a dominant philosophical tool or
pragmatic mode of inquiry into the nature of the physical world.
The eventual victory of the nominalists set the stage for genuine
scientific inquiry; it led, among others, to Galileo, who chal-
lenged the dominance of a misrepresented Aristotle, and above
all continued the line of skeptical reasoning so brilliantly and

tragically begun by Peter Abelard (1079–1142), who had dared to view man as a being with divine reason long before this view was acceptable. The humanists were to continue this tradition, insisting on the right of the individual to determine more and more how to think about the nature of physical reality.

Such challenges to the established order gave rise to reactions like the Inquisition and to an attempt to reestablish orthodox thinking, but the real physical conditions of the material world were increasingly on the side of the nominalists, as were the secular authorities who opposed the continued dominance of the church in matters of state and society. The abuses of the orthodox religion by many of its adherents also contributed to the discredit into which this religion's theology had fallen. The growth of the new economic system, with its emphasis on self-development, on the need to know through empirical reasoning how to accomplish a number of technical marvels—for this was also a period of major scientific and technical advance in areas like navigation, an offshoot of the new transoceanic trade routes —pushed the orthodox religion and its social system more and more into a defensive posture. The steady decline in the prestige of the church as a moral instrument of God's will on earth led to such rational investigations into the nature of morality as were captured, for example, in Marlowe's brilliant drama *Dr. Faustus* (ca. 1590) and reflected as well in the low-German epic *Reinke de Vos* (1498). The decline of spirituality and the recognition of "real" reality exacerbated the area of conflict within the society, and from heresy came actual armed rebellion.

Such rebellions had occurred before in medieval history. The English peasants under Wat Tyler had rebelled in the early fourteenth century and for a brief time came close to overthrowing the aristocratic regime. Their loyalty to a king (Richard II, 1377–1399), who they imagined embodied hope for their class, proved their undoing; his betrayal of their trust led to devastating destruction of the peasants' lives and property by the terrified and enraged nobles.

In central Europe the Hussite wars were another example of rebellion fomented by social unrest, the principles of which were embodied in religious tenets. Jan Hus (ca. 1369–1415) rector of the university at Prague, was heavily influenced by the doctrines of the English priest John Wyclif (1320–1374) and his Lollard followers. They had preached the priesthood of all believers, the centrality of God's word as it could be found and read in their translation of the Bible, and had thus threatened the fabric of the English theocracy. In England Wyclif had been protected, much as Luther was later to be, by the nobility who saw not only the wisdom of his teaching but their own self-interest in reducing the church's power and holdings. But Hus's teachings coincided with attempts in Europe to weld together again the foundering and partitioned papacy, which had boasted at one brief time three separate popes, each one excommunicating the others and his followers. Hus had not only supported the wrong claimant; he had also denounced papacy and church and had been supported in this by the Bohemian aristocracy, which wanted to rid itself of the German overlordship in Bohemia. The force of nationalism early entered into the Hussite or Taborite (so-called because its spiritual center was at Mt. Tabor) movement. Hus was burned as a heretic at the Council of Constance in 1415, a council to which he had gone under a safe conduct issued by the church leaders (leading to Luther's healthy skepticism of all such safe conducts when they were offered to him). But the Hussite movement in Bohemia became an open civil war, the principle issue of which was the question of Bohemian nationalism and not merely the religious question. The Hussites were eventually defeated and the Bohemian separatist movement crushed, not reviving until the nineteenth century. But the fire was to break out again elsewhere.

Under the general umbrella of religious dissidence were hidden a number of issues that today appear to be so blatantly political as to make us think of late medieval religious reformers as hypocrites who used religion as a cloak for their political ideologies. This is not so, for the ability to separate the religious issues from the political was at that time still very difficult. It is only with the hindsight of history that such a division can be attempted. It is not clear whether religious reformers of both reactionary and progressive ideologies were able in the late Middle Ages to split issues so cleanly. That ability characterizes later ages, though to a great extent its beginnings lie with the great Italian humanist Niccolò Machiavelli (1469–1527), who, however, contrary to the current popular image of him, was despised and exiled for his views and his politics.

When the Hussite wars had ceased to preoccupy central Europe and when the papacy was at last restored both to Rome and to a measure of superficial holiness, there was a slowly rising awareness of economic issues as factors in the proper relationship between God and humans and among people, i.e., the nature of the political state. Though the religious issue was never to go away, and was indeed always a central part of the debates, economic and political problems were more and more clearly added to them and became the source of much humanist and anti-humanist intellectual preoccupation. Once again, these new ideas were the result of giving voice to changing social praxis, and were to lead in definite directions toward new forms of praxis.

It is sometimes difficult to distinguish, among the various movements of reform and revolt, which of them might now be referred to, with hindsight, as reactionary in their intention and which might be seen as progressive, i.e., as intending a revised or radically altered form of the state with more benefits possible for more of the population. By its call for changes in the attitude toward the individual, that is, a call for the increasing view of the self as the paramount philosophical and economic unit in a culture and society, humanism was intellectually allied with what has come to be thought of in historical terms as progressive rather than reactionary political thought. The humanists themselves, however, have often been seen, particularly in Germany, as showing evidence of the intellectuals' inability to take a pragmatic stance *vis à vis* real social problems; the legend of the ivory tower is probably literally to be traced back to this period. In fact, a number of humanists did take courageous stands for and against the issues of the Reformation, but the classic or traditional attitude was that of an Erasmus who chose to bend a bit with the wind of change from whichever direction it might blow.

The reform movements, heresies, and revolts, were at times both reactionary and progressive. Nowhere is that more evident than in the famous German peasant wars that swept through southern Germany in particular in 1524–1525. The causes were predictable.

On the one hand, the peasantry by the fourteenth century had begun to decline from its relative prosperity of the high Middle Ages. (In speaking of the medieval peasantry, despite some pronouncements of historians about the well-being of that class, one must always refer to their *relative* prosperity, for it certainly never was on a class-wide basis anything remotely connected with our ideas of prosperity or with their own age's idea of that happy lot.) The rise of commercialism had brought hardship to the landed peasantry. Most of these were, in Germany, what is known as *Hörige*, that is, they were nominally "free," but paid oppressive dues, fees, and taxes to the landlord for the right to use the land. These fees had begun to rise in response to pressure on the landlords brought about by the increasing shift from a rural to an urban economy. As the lords felt this pressure in their own finances, they immediately passed it on to the peasants and began to resurrect the old duties that earlier peasant reforms as well as general prosperity had successfully abolished in the twelfth and thirteenth centuries. To these were now added new duties. The *Frondienst*, or service to the lord done on the lord's lands, was increased or reinstated, and the death tax (*heriot*), by which one half to all of a peasant's property might be taken by the lord upon the former's death, was increased.

The landlords were frequently the large monasteries rather than particular patriarchal lords or knights, and religious issues entered into the arguments about who owed what to whom at an early stage. The peasants' revolts took the form of cries for reform through reestablishment of the older master-serf relations based on German law of a by-gone day, which had governed relations between lord and peasant in a "friendlier" and more personal manner. The hatred and resentment of the newer Roman law, which had done away with the common or German law—the latter practiced differently in different parts of the

German-speaking territory—had grown to widespread propor-
tions, but attempts to reestablish some versions of the common
law were everywhere a failure. Hatred for the lawyer soon began
to equal the scorn felt for the doctor, though for opposite reasons.
The doctors of the Middle Ages were by and large simply ignorant and powerless, while the lawyers, perhaps ignorant in a
certain sense, were all-powerful. The harvests, too, were no
longer so bountiful. This was due in part to poor methods of
agriculture, which had exhausted the soil, and to the clearing of
the land, which sent the peasants from their farms into the cities
so that the lords might make different use of the empty lands as
for sheep grazing. Mortgage foreclosures were high in the later
Middle Ages.

Inflation had begun to creep over Europe and had increased
immeasurably at the time when the vast silver and gold reserves
of the Americas, newly discovered, made their way to Europe and
depressed the value of money while creating vast fortunes for
those who understood how to use capital and interest. Impoverished peasants resorted to taking out loans on what would now
be called crop futures and would all too frequently find that
inflation had not only made their crops profitless but that resultant nonpayment of the interest on the loan meant dispossession.
The stream of the poor to the urban centers grew to a torrent.
These urban centers saw the rise of the *Lumpenproletariat*, the
nonbeings who labored by day in order to exist, and this at best
marginally, and from whose ranks grew the violent criminal element of early urban society (see Victor Hugo's *The Hunchback
of Notre Dame* for a brilliant sketch of these people in early
Paris). The causes of inflation were virtually not understood by
the people of that day (nor do they appear better understood by
most of us today), but the consequences were clear enough—
higher prices, a lower quality of life, frequently poverty and
death, though all around could be seen the new palaces of the
wealthy and the great cathedrals. Class distinctions became more
and more obvious as the bourgeoisie grew in size and influence.
Some attempts at social welfare programs were undertaken by the
new class (e.g., the *Fuggerei*, a housing project in Augsburg for

the poorer citizens), but on the whole even minimum standards of life seemed to be declining.

It was perhaps natural, then, for the peasantry increasingly to look back to earlier, more secure times when they as a class and as individuals were happier and better off. Certainly the peasantry never understood in any detail the banking practices that so bedeviled them as a class and that seemed in their eyes to be a means for robbing them of the little money and wealth they had accumulated. The discrepancies that had arisen among the classes were more sharply etched now. Attempts of the peasantry to live like lords at times and in places where their incomes were still good (documented in a work such as *Meier Helmbrecht*, ca. 1270), were unsuccessful for several reasons—want of sound financial planning, envy by the middle classes leading to restrictions on the amount and kinds of wealth a peasant could possess, or the graduation of the successful peasant into the ranks of the bourgeoisie.

The new rich were, for the most part, the result of upward social mobility among those former peasants who, like Luther's father, had chosen a different livelihood like mining or weaving (the ancestor of the rich Fugger family of Augsburg had been a weaver) and hastened to disown and make mockery of their actual social origins. The *Fastnachtspiele*, or carnival plays, of southern German cities in the late fifteenth and early sixteenth centuries are in part middle-class attempts to divorce the new urban artisan and guild classes from their lowly social origins by at times scathingly sarcastic portrayals of "Hinz and Kunz," the archetypal stupid, lewd, vicious, and sacriligious peasants. When these very immediate economic and social pressures are added to the more vague but keenly felt decline in morality and spirituality that accompanied the increased social mobility of all classes based on the new economic system, the peasantry's discontent can be better understood, as can their class longing for a simplification of the way of life that seemed so inimical to them. The immorality of the clergy, the source of witticisms then and now among the educated or sophisticated classes, was an immediate and omnipresent disease, one that could be redressed by some direct action. This direct action seemed all the more warranted when the peasant had to pay his dues and taxes to a clerical overlord, who personified for him the wretched state of the clergy. But it should not be imagined that the peasantry's notion of redress and reform, however violent its occasional manifestations in the past, was necessarily directed at the economic causes or the actual theological problems toward which Luther and later Calvin were to direct their wrath.

The peasants' demands for redress of their grievances did not fill their noble masters' hearts with the same kind of satisfaction as did the words of a Luther or his followers, for the peasantry's claims, if satisfied, could only wreak havoc among the aristocracy. Yet initially the peasants did feel that Luther's activities made him their natural leader. He had attacked the immorality of the church, particularly the papacy; he had demanded not a priesthood of all believers, but instead a priesthood that would and could administer to the spiritual needs of the populace without threat of eternal damnation or promise of the soul's release from the flames of purgatory. Luther had spoken out against the evils of usury and of certain business practices and had appealed to the princes to become truly Christian leaders of the populace. All this seemed to make Luther the natural spokesman for the downtrodden lower class. Furthermore, the fact that through his translation of the Bible and his original and forceful use of the German language he could be well understood, made him into something of an idol for the populace. When the eventual time for action by the peasants seemed to have arrived, sometime in late 1524, the peasantry as a class in southern regions of Germany adopted as their own certain of Luther's apparently political positions and expected the great reformer to support their cause. Their disappointment at the immediate and violent denunciation of that cause, which Luther issued in three major tracts calling upon the rulers to extirpate the vile rebels with every means possible, soon disabused them that any help was forthcoming from the new establishment and made it easier for the truly radical groups on both left and right within their various movements to gain control of the uprisings.

Friedrich Engels has written an excellent survey of the events of the peasant revolts of the sixteenth century in Germany and has provided numerous valuable insights into their causes. He is but one of a number of writers, historians as well as literary people, who have been captivated by this brief and terribly violent upheaval, which seemed almost to have transformed the Reformation into the revolution the medieval heresies had long been foretelling. The actual events can only be mentioned briefly here.

The uprisings had begun as early as 1514 in the "Poor Conrad" movement and continued under the famous banner of the *Bundschuh*, the peasants' footwear displayed on their battle flags. The peasant groups leading the uprisings had something of the character of a secret society. The peasant who participated in them joined a secret organization under the banner of the "Bundschuh" and swore a terrible oath to support the organization against the ruling classes (cf. the Mao Mao uprisings of the 1950s in Kenya, where the same sort of terrible communal oath was required and the same extraordinary violence characterized the struggle).

The sporadic peasant uprisings were never very successful in achieving the desired modifications of the social system, for the peasants' demands—as may be seen from the texts of the twelve articles later adopted as their charter and put before an alliance of princes and cities—were by and large made without any understanding of the actual developments in material reality and often constituted a simple plea for a return to older and more trusted ways. Since such a goal was never at any time achievable, the rebellion might have ended with the simple enforcement of the status quo by the substantial military forces at the command of the alliance of princes and cities led by the brutal Georg Truchsess. But combined with the plea for a return to old ways were the growing radical ideas of certain of the earlier "fringe element." These ideas were not unconnected with the main body of the peasants' demands; they were also concerned with fairer terms for the peasantry with regard to *Frondienst* (labor) and various other duties and taxes. But even the earliest peasant

demands, such as those put forth by the ominous-sounding
Drummer of Niklashausen, had something of social radicalism
about them. If the ruling classes were not persuaded by the legitimate demands of the peasant rebels, then the only choice open
to them, according to the radical and widely held view, was the
overthrow of the ruling class in its entirety and the re-creation
(or creation) of a truly Christian state with definite communistic
aspects.

The nature of these demands depended on the political
ideals of the particular radical leaders. Since the ruling class
indeed refused to make any compromise with the peasants, the
radicals swiftly gained the upper hand, and the rebellion, begun
as a reaction against the new conditions of life became a revolution.

The peasants from the various sections of southern Germany, particularly the Black Forest area, achieved early major
successes. The armed resistance of the princes and the cities was
insufficient to withstand the hordes of seemingly inspired, though
ill-equipped men, and sometimes women, who spread a reign of
terror through the regions they conquered. The violence of the
rebellion was itself a strong weapon in its favor, for cities and
castles that otherwise might have attempted resistance now threw
open their gates to avoid the sack visited upon conquered towns.
These initial successes inflamed the revolt still further, and even
greater areas of southern Germany came under the nominal sway
of the peasant forces. Famous leaders like Florian Geyer and his
Black Troop (later made famous in a drama by Gerhart Haupt-
mann) and Thomas Müntzer, who defended the city of Mühl-
hausen against the attacks of the allied armies, provided brief
rallying points for the peasants. But the extent of their success
far outstripped any organization they possessed, and their pro-
pensity to indulgence in wine and riotous living both weakened
their moral position and cost them potential allies. Much has
been made by middle-class historians of the peasants' tendency to
"liberate" the wine cellars first, then the ladies quarters in castles
and convents, and then perhaps to set up some rudimentary form
of new social organization. It is clear that in the history of war-

fare the forces of the ruling class have always been far more brutal and sophisticated in maintaining order than any rebels have been in attempts at its overthrow. The peasants' proclivity for the wine cellar and for the women of the oppressors was but a reflection of their hatred of the oppressing class, a well-earned hatred, if that class's own records of its treatment of the peasantry can be trusted.

The peasants did not often succeed in introducing some form of self-discipline over their hordelike armies, and when the allied force under Truchsess was eventually strong enough to meet them in pitched battles, the issue was never in doubt. In a few great battles, notably the encounter at Frankenhausen in May of 1525, the peasants were routed, hunted down, and destroyed in vast numbers. At Württemberg, Truchsess defeated another peasant army and within a few weeks all the major cities captured or held by the peasants had been retaken by the allied forces and the trees were dotted with the corpses of executed peasants, as the allies exacted a brutal vengeance. Heavy fines were imposed on the peasants as a class (which they paid), and new and stricter regulations were imposed on their lives. Taxes were by and large made even more crushing, as the ruined nobility sought to regain some of its losses. But the burned castles and sacked monasteries throughout southern Germany testified for many years thereafter to the violence of the peasants' rebellion. It was a revolt not to be equaled in Germany until the mid-nineteenth century, when it again failed of success but served notice that the days of the ruling class might indeed be numbered.

The radical groupings that arose in the peasant wars included the Anabaptist (*Wiedertäufer*) movement, a reform doctrine insisting on the rite of adult baptism. The Anabaptists were everywhere hunted down and their sect persecuted, but under the leadership of Jan Matthys and Jan van Leyden, they made a citadel of the city of Münster and resisted repeated attempts of the allied forces to drive them out. When the city finally fell, the leaders were brutally tortured and executed, and the membership either slain or driven into exile. It is interesting to note that despite intense and continuing persecution throughout Europe, the adherents of the sect were always able to establish flourishing and financially successful colonies in Europe and finally in America, a paradoxical contradiction between their radical tendencies and their ability to adapt to a material world otherwise very hostile to their interests.

The peasant wars can be viewed as both a step forward and a step backward in the history of the German reform movement. They were indeed reactionary in their conception of a return to an older order of things. But when this return was blocked by prevailing social and economic circumstances, reversible neither through their efforts nor the efforts of the lower nobility, one result was the beginning of a radical social movement linked to earlier heresies. Such heresies had long plagued the orthodox medieval society with visions of justice and equality for all and much later gave rise to the radical and atheistic ideals of socialism. Religious fervor was replaced by a secular ideological fervor with strong similarities to the powerful motivation of belief in early religious groups.

More ambivalent is the attitude of those who questioned orthodoxy in the matter of individualism. Earlier in this article it was stated that antihumanism was a medieval reaction to the growing disruption of the idea of a collective community as the basis for society, an ideal that had pervaded medieval social constructs. The new awareness of self was exemplified in the writings of German authors of the late fifteenth and sixteenth centuries in works such as *Reinke de Vos, Till Eulenspiegel,* and the *Historia von D. Johann Fausten,* particularly in the subsequent English adaptation of the latter, as well as in a whole host of the popular chapbooks that extolled, Horatio Alger fashion, the virtues of self-reliance, self-discipline, and self-advancement. Certain of these popular chapbooks, like *Fortunatus* (1509), tried to portray both the new age of money, with its concommitant material benefits, and its negative, guilt-ridden side, for the late medieval or early modern individual was still of two minds as to the virtues of progress, which was a new idea. This new individualism reveals itself still more ambiguously in the emergence of a genuine

human villain in medieval drama, which had previously only
seen sinners and villainous devils. These positive and negative
views of individualism were unquestionably related to the new
economic practices, which made a virtue of self-advancement at
the cost of the collective ideal. The growth of empiricism from its
origins in nominalist thought offered a philosophical framework
for the explanation and adaptation of technological progress.
The new awareness of the possibilities of individualism within
such a framework fit comfortably into the changing economic
system.

Perhaps it can be suggested that in striving to achieve the
truly humanistic human being, the individual *par excellence*
whose all-round accomplishments later identified him in popular
jargon as the "Renaissance man," something essentially human
was lost. Subsequent reform movements and even revolutionary
doctrines all seem to have adopted the idea of the humanist
individual as the goal of their new human societies, but they
failed adequately to measure the impact of the loss of the older
collective ideal in social praxis. The peasants, in their revolt,
may ultimately have been only reactionaries whose utopian
dreams were based on ignorance of the true nature of things in
material reality. But their utopias contained images of the lost
collective identity of human beings, and their anxieties about the
coming extreme individualism, however great its technical and
cultural accomplishments, seem to some extent to have been justi-
fied. Out of their abortive efforts and the fears thus aroused have
come ideas that continue to polarize socialist reform movements
to this day.

Arguments have been reopened as to the meaning of humanism, arguments begun at the end of the medieval period and
initially resolved by the successes achieved by the humanist
bourgeoisie and its allied princes, achieved, it must be noted, only
through the rather unhumanistic force of arms. That force elim-
inated the allegedly reactionary elements without, however, re-
solving the question whether in fact a humanism based on an
elaborate justification of the self, as apart from other selves, has
led or can lead to a more rational, more humane social order.

The late medieval era, seen from this point of view, becomes interesting not only for its factual occurrences but for the use made of them by modern historians, who have elevated humanism to an unassailable virtue. This is a position once more being questioned from both the right and left wings of political and social philosophies.

Selected Bibliography

PRIMARY SOURCES

Anon. *Ein kurtzweilig Lesen von Dil Ulenspiegel.* Stuttgart: Reclam, 1967.

Anon. *Flugschriften des Bauernkrieges.* Klaus Kaczerowsky, ed. In *Texte deutscher Literatur 1500–1800*, Reinbek bei Hamburg: Rowohlt, 1970.

Anon. *Lebensbeschreibung des Ritters Götz von Berlichingen.* Stuttgart: Reclam, 1967.

Anon. *Reineke Fuchs aus dem niederdeutschen.* Stuttgart: Reclam, 1967.

Brant, Sebastian. *Das Narrenschiff.* Stuttgart: Reclam, 1967. (Based on the original 1494 Basel edition.)

Gärtner, Werner der. *Meier Helmbrecht.* Stuttgart: Reclam, 1974.

Luther, Martin. *An den christlichen Adel deutscher Nation. Von der Freiheit eines Christen Menschen. Sendbrief vom Dolmetschen.* Stuttgart: Reclam, 1967.

Manifestations of Discontent in Germany on the Eve of the Reformation. Gerald Strauss, ed. Bloomington: Indiana University Press, 1971.

Sachs, Hans. *Meistergesänge, Fastnachtsspiele, Schwänke.* Stuttgart: Reclam, 1967.

A Sixteenth Century German Reader. W. A. Coupe, ed. Oxford: Clarendon Press, 1972.

SECONDARY SOURCES

Andreas, Willy. *Deutschland vor der Reformation.* Stuttgart: Deutsche Verlags-Anstalt, 1948.

Bainton, Roland H. *The Reformation in the Sixteenth Century.* Boston: Beacon Press, 1952.

Bax, E. Belfort. *The Peasants' War in Germany 1525–1526*. Vol. 2 of *The Social Side of the Reformation in Germany*. New York: 1899. Rpt. 1968 by Russell and Russell, New York.

Engels, Friedrich. *The Peasant War in Germany*. New York: International Publishers, 1926.

12

Humanism
and Popular Culture

Josef Schmidt

That the contribution of the German-speaking countries to humanism and the Renaissance is mainly in the fields of theology, philosophy, the visual arts, and science is a generally accepted fact. The German language and literature of the fifteenth and sixteenth centuries were the poor relatives of the Italian, French, and English. The literature in the vernacular, if understood in a narrow sense, has hardly any counterpart, artistically speaking, to the works of Nicholas of Cusa, of Erasmus, of Paracelsus, and in art to Dürer, the Holbeins, or the Cranachs. With the exception of Luther's works, there was hardly any true tandem development of the vernacular and the Latin language that might have led to a fruitful synthesis or creative culmination.

The popular culture of this period, identified as the tradition in the vernacular, has, however, left a lasting impression on German-speaking countries in terms of tradition and historical self-definition. The popular world of the period was rediscovered by the Romanticists, who were largely responsible for our modern conception of the era (as represented by such works as Goethe's *Götz von Berlichingen*, Wagner's *Die Meistersinger*, or even the collection of fairy tales by the Grimm brothers). For them the main features of this period were a leisurely, bourgeois way of life held together by strong communal bonds, and an earthy and robust population whose main concern was living the life of a good burgher or peasant. Neither the Reformation nor the ensuing religious wars seem to have disturbed this rather idyllic notion. There is, of course, some truth in this concept, but it does not completely describe the period. This article aims to set forth manifestations of the historical development of the popular culture of the Renaissance and of humanism.

Probably the most obvious reason for the dichotomy between popular culture and humanism was the tremendous gap between the vernacular and the classical languages, a situation that differed quite remarkably from the one found in Romance countries (the German word *welsch* was used to describe Italian and French indiscriminately). The transition of many dialects (or even sublanguages) into a supraregional language was inextricably linked to the Reformation and Luther's translation of the Bible. Luther's choice of the social character of his language (*Sendbrief vom Dolmetschen*/On Translation, 1530)—he was taking from and addressing himself to the family circle and the market place—was a polemic one. This can also be seen in the little-known folkloristic caricatures accompanying the first translation of the New Testament (*September Bible*, 1522).

The religious quarrels and battles that spanned a period of many decades were polarized into the fatal equation of Latin equals pope, lies, exploitation by the "Roman" Catholic church; German equals the common man, honesty, pious and genuine concern (e.g., *Karsthans*, a pamphlet of 1521). The potentially uniform language strengthened another process of socialization: the emergence of a new class of important merchants and of self-confident burghers who adapted and transformed the oral tradition of the Middle Ages. The craftsmen, tradesmen, and artisans lived in imperial city-states (Hans Sachs in Nürnberg), or independent cities (Huldrych Zwingli in Zurich), or in residential towns (Cranach in Wittenberg). Their expression of Renaissance culture manifested itself mainly through the vernacular (e.g., treatises, contracts, manuals, regulations). While humanists initially developed an impressive display of activity (e.g., Conrad Celtis in Vienna, Erasmus in Basel), they lost any hope of shaping the social environment through the Reformation when their isolation became a "third force," in the words of historian Friedrich Heer, by the conflicts and tensions following the Reformation.

The student of popular culture in the late fifteenth and the sixteenth centuries is faced with another important feature when analyzing the old traditions and the new trends that emerged during this period: the printing press. While for a long period mass publication was understood only as a process of mechanization designed to ease the tedious work of writing manuscripts by hand, the Reformation brought about a remarkable change. Although the statistics show that even in the period 1520–1530 Latin books were far more numerous than German titles, Luther's success can be attributed in part to his shrewd eye for the effect of the mass medium in a modern sense. His treatise *To the German Nobility* (issued in German and Latin simultaneously, 1520) was published in editions of several thousand copies and sold within ten days. A flood of pamphlets followed his three great treatises of 1520, and the number of German publications rose dramatically. Here again one is sorely tempted to draw one's conclusion from the printed records of the period that have been preserved. Within the context of this article the drawback is obvious: written publications addressing themselves directly to the audience and using the vernacular were often of such poor quality in style and paper that they were destroyed before historians could get their hands on them. The writings of Erasmus suffered no such fate!

However, even with this restriction, the wealth of material is remarkable. The "Gutenberg Galaxy," to use Marshall McLuhan's term, had its own dialectic alley ways. And it seems appropriate to choose a typology of various sectors of popular culture in order to illustrate the peculiar dichotomy of the humanists on the one hand and the laymen on the other. The

examples brought forth are by no means exceptional; they illustrate, however, how humanists could address themselves to the
world of the vernacular, and how burghers, artisans, and trades-
people or even peasants could become recipients of preshaped
Renaissance thought and form, which they would mold into
their own world. It is impossible, however, always to draw a
distinction between an original creation and the putting into
print of that which has had a long oral tradition.

A case in question is the popular song or folksong. It played
a great role in the social life of burghers and peasants alike. One
of the earliest collections, the handwritten *Songbook* (1471) of
Clara Hätzerlein, shows an astonishing range of expression. Rid-
dles, puns, jokes, prayers, and love songs indicate an unbroken
tradition back to the popular song of the Middle Ages of which
we know rather little (certain songs of the *Minnesingers* of the
thirteenth century—the German troubadors—and, of course, the
Carmina Burana). The most important collection of songs, Georg
Forster's *Frisch Teutsche Liedlein* (Fresh German Songs, 1539–
1556), is remarkable in that we find a selection similar to that of
Clara Hätzerlein's *Songbook*. It includes, however, several songs
attributed to Orlando di Lasso (who for some time worked in
Munich).

The ballad was a popular genre, and many songs have become an accepted part of the song tradition of German-speaking
countries, e.g.: *Es waren zwei Königskinder* (There Were Two
Royal Children; adaptation of the story of Hero and Leander?),
or *Heideröslein*. Some even became an expression of political
identity, as in the case of the battle songs of Swiss mercenaries
(Zwingli wrote one on the occasion of the first Swiss religious war
in Kappel).

The popular song as a means of indoctrination can be most
clearly seen in the Reformation in texts that were sung to popular tunes of the time, and their worldly original texts were quietly dropped. This practice of pious parody, of baptizing worldly
songs with religious texts (*Kontrafaktur*), enjoyed great popularity both with Lutherans and Catholics for the next two centuries. The technique was also used, however, in the derogatory

sense for ridiculing or even bedeviling the religious/political enemy; there are at least five known parodies of *Innsbruck, ich muss dich lassen* (Innsbruck, I have to leave you), e.g., *Papst in Rom, ich muss dich lassen* (Pope in Rome, I have to leave you), etc. The *Meistersingers* understood themselves to be direct descendants of the *Minnesingers*. They were mostly craftsmen and tradesmen who organized themselves into circles and schools, developing a refined system of setting tone and text; but their creations tended to be too formal and sober. These songs, however, played an important role in bringing this social group into contact with stories derived from Greek and Roman history (to which they had no access by means of language), although most of their themes were taken directly from their own world.

An indication of the popularity of songs in general can be found in two works written by humanist scholars. *The Letters of Obscure Men* (1516) include numerous references to songs depicting a comic situation directly translated into pedestrian Latin. Johann Fischart's translation (1575) of the beginning of Rabelais's *Gargantua et Pantagruel* contains a "drunk dialogue" (chapter VIII) that consists mainly of the first lines of popular songs. The distance of the popular song to neo-Latin poetry is indicated by this jocular use of it.

The popular drama of the time in addition to the Latin school drama and the dramatized story of the Passion performed on Easter, reaching directly back to the Middle Ages, was increasingly influenced by the poetics of neo-Latin plays. The earliest author whose works have by and large been preserved, and who shows no trace of this influence, is Hans Rosenplüt. His Shrovetide plays (*Fastnachtspiele*, Carnival Plays) were written in traditional doggerel or *Knittelvers*, seldom exceeding 250 verses; the plots of these playlets were drawn almost exclusively from the everyday life of his time. Even as the Reformation was having its full impact, the *Fastnachtspiel* remained true to its traditional function: a jocular play with a satirical tendency. Hans Sachs, however, often used the formal structure of plays found in antiquity; acts and scenes subdivided the plays, and their length increased (to more than 2000 verses). And in the exceptional case

(*Menechmo*, 1548) he even adapted a comedy by Plautus, but his version looks clumsy beside Shakespeare's *Comedy of Errors* (1592).

The indirect influence of Latin poetics can also be observed in biblical plays, especially of the sixteenth century. On one hand there was some experimentation with different meters (Paul Rebhun's *Susanna*, 1535), while on the other everyday characters were introduced, giving the plays a contemporary feature and making the stage a place for discussing controversial issues. The good-for-nothing had the company of mercenaries, merchants, innkeepers, and doctors, and more often than not they were able to transcend the confines of their stereotyped roles.

Pamphilus Gengenbach and Niklaus Manuel are representative of this transformation of the Shrovetide play into vicious satire. Manuel, a genuine Renaissance figure, was a mercenary for some time, a gifted painter by profession who gradually became a statesman in Bern, where he was the leading force behind bringing that city to the support of the evangelical reform movement. A talent for visually effective scenes and a rich experience characterize his "documentary" play *The Great Difference between the Pope and Jesus Christ* (1522); the adaptation of the theme by Lucas Cranach, who made it the subject of a series of woodcuts, shows how appealing this tendentious drama was. The corruptness of the pope is contrasted with certain stages of Jesus' life (e.g., Jesus speaks to the lame and the blind; the pope amuses himself at a tournament with knights and courtesans).

The urge to put the issues of the Reformation on stage by using popular forms of theater is probably the reason why early attempts to familiarize a German-speaking audience with the novellas, the treatises, and the plays of the Italian Renaissance were not successful. Albrecht von Eyb, a cleric who had studied in Italy, translated comedies by Plautus and Ugolino Pisani into German (1474–1511). Niklas von Wyle, diplomat and later city registrar of Radolfszell, had also studied in Italy. His *Translatzen* (1461–1478) included novellas by Boccaccio and Enea Silvio, besides works by Poggio and others. Both authors translated for a courtly audience; the influence of their works was very limited.

The exposure of German-speaking countries to humanists from Italy during the councils of Basel and Constance resulted in direct contacts of German humanists with the Italian Renaissance. Enea Silvio's influence from Vienna had a direct impact on these humanists, too. One of the few successes of this influence in adapting the vernacular to the polished Latin form can be seen in *Esopus* (1476) by Heinrich Steinhoewel. These fables became an extremely popular book. This development must be attributed in part to the self-confident principle of translation that the author expresses in the preface (*sensus de sensu*, according to meaning, not to the letter, a maxim that was to become Luther's creed, too). Steinhoewel really wanted to adapt it for the German people—and not simply render the original in a literal German text. This endeavor was later supported by Luther's enthusiasm for the educational value of the genre. He edited a collection himself, hoping to be able to replace the exempla from the lives of the saints by these secular tales.

The anecdote, found in such collections as Johannes Pauli's *Schimpf und Ernst* (Fun and Earnestness, 1522), and Jörg Wickram's *Rollwagenbüchlein* (Stagecoach Booklet, 1555), reached a surprising level of good entertaining prose. Its informative value with regard to life in the sixteenth century is considerable, especially in the attempt to center a series of anecdotes around one figure in *Dyl Ulenspiegel* (earliest known printing, 1515). The character of the sly rogue who outfoxes everything and everybody may be seen as an early piccaro who questions the values of self-satisfied burghers, clerics, and farmers. A satirical view in a general sense is also found in *The Ship of Fools* (1494) by Sebastian Brant, or in Erasmus's *Moriae Encomion* in which illustrations by Holbein clearly linked the work to the popular tradition of the "mirror of morals."

In the field of legends and collections of miracles, the Counter Reformation caused a bitter fight with regard to their authenticity. A whole generation of writers in the Protestant camp systematically blasphemed these collections as "papal lies" (to use the words of the Protestant preacher Hieronymus Rauscher); at the same time there was a strong desire to embark on a similar description of Luther's Reformation. As early as 1550 the historical character of the movement was already strongly realized. The table-talks of Luther's circle in particular became the source of numerous "legends," and of attempts to incorporate the Reformation into the mainstream of church history. That the Catholics wrote equally polemical biographies of the reformer (e.g., H. Emser), is hardly surprising, and these learned authors at times stooped to the cheapest form of invective, rooted in popular culture (Luther was conceived through the devil, his mother was a whore, etc.).

A dark chapter in the annals of the period was the superstition that existed at all levels. Books about the devil abounded, and the infamous *Malleus Maleficarum* (Hammer of Evildoers, compiled by Sprenger and Institoris, 1487), the legal source for three centuries of innumerable witch trials and sorcery charges, was by no means exclusively an interest of the Inquisition. Broadsheets and a whole extensive pedigree of "devil books" show the central place this facet of superstition occupied in contemporary life. And the best-known popular novel (*Volksbuch*) of that time, *Dr. Faustus* (1587), must also be seen in this light. It was a critique of the demonic powers attributed to the higher realms of knowledge.

Superstition was one of the few common interests of the popular culture and the humanists alike. Agrippa von Nettesheim, who had a decisive influence on Italian humanists such as Giordano Bruno with his *artes magicae*, was only the tip of the iceberg. Johannes (Müller) Regiomontanus published a calendar in 1474–75 that contains a curious mixture of astronomical calculation, astrological forecast, and character typology; the graphic layout is the same used by modern newspapers in horoscope columns. It is not surprising that he did this in the vernacular, for in the following decades there were literally thousands of broadsheets, popularizing such knowledge on a truly trivial level, attributing astrological significance to every odd sunset and every calf with two heads. Such men as Johannes Reuchlin, Luther, and Melanchthon wrote treatises on peculiar phenomena of contemporary history and their importance as a warning sign of the corruptness of the times (e.g., Luther's interpretation of the *Pope-Donkey* [*Papstesel*], and Melanchthon's exegesis of the *Monk-Calf* [*Mönchskalb*], 1523). The broadsheet and the chapbook, with topics ranging from a New Year's wish to the claim of being able to explain the mystery of the world, were the sources of information, sometimes even taking the form of an information sheet, such as the numerous newssheets distributed during the Diet at Worms in 1521. A typical example is Christopher Columbus's famous *De Insulis*, a report about the wonders of the New World that was translated immediately into German (1494–1497). The thirst for sensation was an overriding concern, as can be seen in the learned works dealing with foreign and exotic topics. Sebastian Münster's *Cosmographei* (1550), for example, depicts in great detail the peculiar social customs of the newly discovered Indians (that they supposedly were naked, etc.). Works of this nature were usually written in Latin and shortly afterward were translated, usually by a disciple, into the vernacular—an indication of the demand from a new class of readers. A precise reason is given in the preface of the translation of Georg Agricola's *De Re Metallica* (*On Mining*, 1556–57), an English translation of which was done by the late President Herbert Hoover, who had been a mining engineer. The German translator states the author's wish to make the book accessible to the people who really had to read it out of necessity: miners, engineers, administrators, etc. And the professional language of the work—its illustrative terminology—can be put side by side with Luther's translation of the Bible in terms of excellence.

The attempt of Theophrastus Bombastus Paracelsus to lecture in the vernacular caused a violent protest by his colleagues, who regarded the Latin language as a means of preserving the monopoly of knowledge by their profession. He wrote numerous theological and medical works in German, stating in both his criticism of the bad side of popular culture. Paracelsus defended the value of experience against the unquestioned authority of the treatises on medicine dating from antiquity; at the same time, however, he attacked superstitious beliefs in wonder cures and the trust in quacks. His mystical writings were part of a rich tradition, written almost exclusively in the vernacular. Apart from Luther's edition of the *Theologia Deutsch*, the mystics Sebastian Franck, Schwenkfeld, and Weigel (and, of course, the Enthusiasts, Anabaptists and members of other sects) also developed an astounding continuation of the Devotio moderna. Throughout the Reformation they were regarded with mistrust, and were caught in the middle between orthodox Catholics and Protestants.

Developing out of the practical side of the Reformation and the new constitution of social institutions were many manuals, treatises, regulations, and pamphlets on how everyday life should be reformed (e.g., Eberlin von Günzburg's *XV Buntsgenossen*, The 15 Confederates, 1521). The true meeting place of humanism and popular culture is found in the pamphlets of the sixteenth century. They were normally written by anonymous authors, in a style that reveals schooling in the rules of rhetoric but also shows the author's ostensible difficulty in expressing himself in the vernacular. They were often polemic (Ulrich von Hutten), but they could also be quite above the level of political quarrels. Erasmus's *Querela Pacis* (1517) was quickly translated into German by Leo Jud, and fathered a whole generation of *Frydensbüchlin* (Books on Peace) that gradually adapted the reference sources to a vernacular context. A popular counterpart can be found in the numerous constitutions and demands that were articulated by peasants in the uprising of the early 1520s.

The apparent gap between humanism and popular culture should not hide the fact that the spirit of the Renaissance permeated many works that at first seem firmly rooted in one of these two worlds. Jacob Wimpfeling's *Germania* (1501), in which the author refers not only to Tacitus in giving reasons for the historical identity of a region as one would expect, but to other sources as well, triggered a vivid discussion about the question of cultural identity; with the Reformation this problem was translated into a basic slogan-type classification of German characteristics. The interest in the German tradition also found its way to the "last German knight," Emperor Maximilian I, who had his officials compile an inventory of old German lyrics (*Ambraser Handschrift*) and stylized himself in an epic tale (*Theuerdank*,

1517) as an idealized figure. This attempt at self-representation was reflected in numerous chronicles of lesser territories and in autobiographies of people of a lower class (Götz von Berlichingen, a rebel knight during the Peasants' War), or of persons whose life was really not that extraordinary (Thomas Platter, a self-taught humanist and craftsman). The burghers gradually expressed their self-confidence in ever-increasing ways. Sebastian Brant, for example, published two lawbooks in the vernacular for the layman, citing as a reason not only the burgher's obvious difficulty with the Latin language, but insisting on certain "German" principles of common law, which had to be recorded to insure their proper use in the language in which they were formulated. There is no doubt, on the other hand, that the attempts to adapt the great epic tales of antiquity to a burgher's world (Thomas Murner's *Aeneis*, 1515; Johann Spreng's *Metamorphosen*, 1564, etc.) responded to a real demand of contemporary readers, but in the process they lost too much of their substance.

Recent Marxist studies of this period have undoubtedly overemphasized the emergence of political awareness in peasants and burghers in German-speaking countries. But they are correct in stressing the fact that along with humanism there was a growing acceptance of new ways of life closely identified with what we call popular culture. Several popular novels—*Magelone* (1535), *Die history Troy* (1498), and *Hug Schapler* (1456), which deals with a social climber—reflect this change when compared with the *Knaben Spiegel* (Boys' Mirror, 1554) by Jörg Wickram, a didactic novel on how to behave in society; untouched by the political conflicts, the "trivialization" of heroic tales in the world of the burgher is manifest (the romance *Ritter Galmy* by Wickram, 1539, shows this change too, in spite of the title).

From a modern point of view, the culture in the vernacular was crude, coarse, and inarticulate, particularly if compared to the following historical periods. Formally the records were more often clumsy than not, showing the emergence of a literary language rather than its actual formation. But history has given its verdict by letting the humanist culture of the German-speaking countries fade away, while the popular culture, although not often associated with a particular testimony or personage, has endured the test of time and become a strong image in a tradition that reflects the vitality of the Renaissance period.

Selected Bibliography

SECONDARY SOURCES

Brüchner, Wolfgang, ed. *Volkserzählung und Reformation*. Berlin: E. Schmidt, 1974.

Dickens, A. G. *Reformation and Society in Sixteenth-Century Europe*. In *Library of European Civilization*. London: Thames and Hudson, 1966.

Hess, Günther. *Deutsch-lateinische Narrenzunft*. In *Münchener Texte und Untersuchungen zur deutschen Literatur des Mittelalters*, 41. München: Beck, 1971.

Könneker, Barbara. *Die deutsche Literatur der Reformationszeit: Kommentar zu einer Epoche*. München: Winkler, 1975.

Müller, Günther. *Deutsche Dichtungen von der Renaissance bis zum Ausgang des Barock*. Darmstadt: Wissenschaftliche Buchgesellschaft, 2nd ed., 1957.

Pascal, Roy. *German Literature in the 16th and 17th Centuries*. In *Introductions to German Literature*, v. 2. London: Cresset Press, 1968.

Peuckert, Will-Erich. *Die große Wende: Das apokalyptische Saeculum und Luther*. Darmstadt: Wissenschaftliche Buchgesellschaft. 2nd. ed., 1967.

Spriewald, Inbegorg, ed. *Grundpositionen der deutschen Literatur im 16. Jahrhundert*. Berlin/Weimar: Aufbau, 1972.

Stammler, Wolfgang. *Von der Mystik zum Barock*. Stuttgart: Metzler. 2nd ed., 1950.

Taylor, Archer. *Problems in German Literary History of the Fifteenth and Sixteenth Centuries*. New York/London: *MLA*, General Series VIII, 1939.

Wind, Edgar. *Pagan Mysteries in the Renaissance*. London: Faber and Faber. 2nd ed., 1968.

13

The History
of Dr. Johann Faustus

Marvin S. Schindler

When we consider the body of material concerned with the Faust theme in the sixteenth century—the historical Faust and the legend that rapidly developed around him, the Faust of the German and English chapbooks and of the German puppet play, and finally Christopher Marlowe's *Faustus*, all appearing within a space of less than one hundred years and comprising what can be called the "Faust complex"—we must wonder at the reasons for its astonishing popularity in that century and in those following, indeed, at what was to become the immortality of both figure and theme in the media of Western art, music, and literature. After all, there had been other magicians and other alleged pacts with the Devil extending back to pre-Christian history, and information about them had been duly recorded, embellished, expanded, and transmitted throughout the ages. But none until Faust so completely captured the minds and pens of both contemporaries and of the generations to follow.

To attempt an even incomplete answer to the question, we must review and place in perspective the major cultural and intellectual currents, trends, and developments of the fourteenth, fifteenth, and sixteenth centuries in Europe and particularly in Germany in the hope of catching something of the atmosphere, a distillation of the spirit of the sixteenth century. The sixteenth century itself was an amalgam of various circumstances and events that took place earlier in Southern Europe and, with vigorous, peculiarly German contemporary phenomena as additives, precipitated in the north only in the mid-1500s. By thus placing the Faust complex in the context of its time we can perhaps better understand something of its force and the powerful attraction it held for those who greeted the appearance of the chapbook in Germany in the late sixteenth century.

The rapid growth of and interest in the entire Faust complex and the appearance of the first Faust book itself can be seen in part as a by-product of several powerful forces of the time which, if not working together in harmony, did coexist in Germany, at times seeming to complement one another, at other times sharing in an actual if not intended competition for dominance, and always through their interaction further developing and refining the face and the consciousness of the culture of which they were a part. Chief among these forces were humanism, the Renaissance, and the Reformation, together with the general reaction they generated in the world of the Middle Ages.

Some caution is necessary before we proceed, however, for whenever we attempt to divide history into individual periods or ages, whether from a social, religious, political, or literary standpoint, we run counter to the one overriding and indisputable fact of history, namely, that it is an organic and continuing whole; and if it does yield to such a segmentation from one point of view or on one basis, it is bound at the same time to resist from another. And so we run the risk of overcompartmentalization and fragmentation, tending to place segments of history into separate pigeonholes, giving each its own convenient label and limits in time.

Such an ordering of history *is* convenient, and indeed it may be difficult to make necessary distinctions without such categories; furthermore, a given period of time may be so clearly dominated by a particular style or intellectual thrust or force that attaching an identifying name to it that reflects that dominant spirit may be quite reasonable as well as useful. What is necessary, however, is to guard against cutting into almost mutually exclusive pieces the continuum of history, partitioning too radically one "period" from those that precede and follow.

If such a procedure is appropriate in general, it is particularly important when considering sixteenth-century Germany. For in the short span of time with which we are concerned— roughly from the first recorded reference to the historical Faust by the German mathematician and astrologer Johann Virdung in 1507 to the Frankfurt publication of Johann Spiess of the Faust chapbook *Historia von D. Johann Faustus* in 1587—the Renaissance of the south made a late appearance in Germany, but without anything like the impact of its Italian counterpart two hundred years earlier. At the same time humanism, its intellectual offspring, gained at least a somewhat firmer foothold; and finally the Reformation, whose influence extended far beyond the formal schism in the church that soon evolved and formed its nucleus, burst upon and clearly dominated the scene. As a result, sixteenth-century Germany was a time of confluence and confusion of ideas and beliefs, manifested not only as the projected consciousness and perceptions of the society of that period as a whole, but also in the expressed views, words, and deeds of individuals.

Conflicts and contradictions of such an order are involved that the modern mind may at times find it difficult to accept the fact of their simultaneous existence. The great concern with religion and the religious life, for example, was matched by the display of the crudest aspects of a sensual life-style; the danger of the perversion of religion into magic and superstition among the great masses of the people was ever present, a transformation aided ironically and paradoxically by the new reformed church itself, which counted among its early goals the elimination of much in Catholic dogma and ritual that it considered to be no more than harmful superstition.

The first witchcraft trials took place in Germany in the middle of the fifteenth century and continued for two hundred years. What makes the resurgence of interest in astrology, alchemy, magic, witchcraft, superstition, and the occult in general appear so unusual to the twentieth-century reader is the realization that the same period was one of the great ages of human inquiry and exploration, a time that cultivated the roots of modern scientific method and of the enlightened thought of an age to follow. It was a time that saw the beginnings of the new science, the new philosophy, the discoveries of Kepler and Copernicus, the insights and accomplishments of the "father" of modern medicine, Paracelsus. It was the time of discovery of new knowledge and rediscovery of old, fostered by such eminent humanists as Erasmus and Ulrich von Hutten (see the articles on the latter two in this volume).

We can perhaps best characterize the effect of the belated Renaissance in Germany as the culmination of a process of turning from a medieval world view that hung over Germany long after the institutions upon which it was based had begun to crumble. The latter was a view of life defined by theocentrism, with God at the center serving as the frame for every image. Human life was conceived of as moving from God as the origin to God as the end and the consummation following the allotted passage through a finite existence on earth. Such a view brought about a wonderful synthesis, a union of all things—of the natural and the supernatural, of life on earth and in the beyond, of the material and the spiritual—all revolving around and related to God at the center.

The medieval mode of thought was analogical, a system that sought to comprehend meaning not in things and events themselves but in what they represented, and that saw significance in what was perceived as divinely wrought correspondences among all elements and phenomena of the universe that ultimately linked them all to God. Everything possessed a higher significance, and things were viewed not for what they *were*, but for what they *meant*, with Divine meaning holding all together. Thus man was viewed as the microcosm, a precise reflection in miniature of the greater world of the macrocosm. Like the earth, man too, and his progress through life, were governed by the planets and the stars. Like men, the earth had been born, had developed, and would die—indeed, by the middle of the sixteenth century many reported the belief that the earth was nearing its end, and Martin Luther himself had indicated in his *Tischreden* that the world would end in the year 1560, his calculations being based on biblical data. The ideal way of life was the imitation of Christ, the favorite reading material, the lives of the saints. So long as the world was considered divinely ordered, with God at the center of all activity, that union of all things, a oneness we shall never see again, could be preserved.

Characteristic of the Renaissance, on the other hand, was the search for knowledge for its own sake, rather than as a means to an end or as further proof of, or support for, the authority of the church and traditional Christian religious dogma. This totally different way of thinking was necessary for the development of a secular culture and of a new image of man as a free individual, master of his own fate, potential master of the natural world and of his universe—man who stood firm in the face of transience and mocked death by finding a new kind of immortality through thought and deed on earth. The rediscovery of the art and works of classical antiquity, representing not crumbling ruins and pagan myths, but rather that which had *not* perished in time, which had remained amidst change, towering above chance and binding through continuity, became a symbol for the new man and his culture, and later for the new classical ideal. At the same time, for better or for worse, the old medieval harmony began to come unstuck.

With the search for knowledge came an exposure to and desire for different, more exciting, even dangerous ways of life, accentuated by the possibility of a seemingly limitless expansion in the potential range of human existence. Scientific and technological advances brought with them the ongoing attempt by man to master the natural world, a world to which, in the medieval view, he was not superior, but of which he was a part; it was a relationship soon to be lost forever. Expansion in space was marked by the exploration and discovery of new areas of the world; in technology by such discoveries as gunpowder, the compass, and the printing press, as well as astonishing advances in the sciences; and the expansion in learning encompassed an expansion of time, for the humanists returned to the past to study ancient texts—not in search of support for or explanation of the Bible and of Christian dogma—but to understand them for themselves and in search of moral and philosophical systems and guidelines independent of the church. There was, in general, a renewed fascination with the unknown for minds freed from the restraints of the past.

In the German territories, which were far from united, such development lagged far behind that in the South, partly owing to a lack of national, political, or social focal point. Only humanism, the intellectual offspring of the Renaissance, made a lasting imprint on German culture, though it too was vastly weaker in its effect than was the movement in Italy. If the Germans, in the revival of antiquity, could not exult as did the Italians in the rebirth of their own glorious past, they could at least turn with some pride to the almost forgotten virtues of the Germanic past, rekindling a dormant interest in things German.

United around the figure of Johannes Reuchlin (1455–1522), who was persecuted by the Inquisition for his studies of Hebrew and his search for hidden knowledge in the occult lore of the Jews and the cabala in particular, the German humanists at first supported Martin Luther, whom they must have considered the leader of a form of religion parallel to the secular Renaissance and as a fighter for the same kind of intellectual freedom for which they struggled. But no one could have been more tragically misunderstood than this imposing but basically conservative figure. In great disappointment the humanists later parted from Luther over such issues as man's free will, the existence of which the stern monk denied. Through his destruction of the authority of the priests and of the church hierarchy, and his denial of the efficacy of the sacraments in the doctrines of justification by faith alone, the priesthood of all believers, and the Bible as the source of all religious truth, Luther shook the very foundations of the Catholic church—and, unwittingly and perhaps tragically, of the entire existing traditional social and political order.

The time of the growth of the Faust legend was indeed one of complex intellectual crosscurrents with results which, if they were not foreseeable, are at least comprehensible. For the new science to thrive in this transitional age, it was necessary to accept a new way of looking at things—and it is no accident that man stood directly before the discovery of those tools that forced literally a new way of looking at things and without which modern empirical science could not have progressed as it did: the telescope and the microscope. A system of thought was needed whereby newly discovered scientific truths did not necessarily disprove older, and especially established theological, truths. There would be no need then for God's will and scientific explanations to collide. New truth would supply only the kind of truth demanded, and all things would be reconcilable—belief in God, in the power of human reason, in scientific explanation, the burning of witches, and the existence of the Devil. There was a predictable shift in interest from the significance of things to the things in themselves, as in pure science.

It may be that in modern society we are approaching the ultimate in this direction, coming ever closer to understanding how things work while at the same time losing sight and comprehension of the meaning of things. In any case, in the sixteenth and seventeenth centuries both kinds of questions were still posed, a situation that led to a kind of double truth or double-think as both kinds of reasoning stood side by side, leading to conflicting answers, each acceptable and at the same time quite irrelevant to the other.

Gradually, one kind of truth displaced the other—it could no longer be that when an earthquake struck the religious man asked why, the scientist how, and both answers were acceptable. But in the sixteenth century, Kepler, for example, deserving of his fame as a man of modern science, was at the same time a superstitious mystic who believed in the mystery and the supernatural powers of numbers; in addition, he was a sun worshiper. Paracelsus, with whom we date the beginnings of modern medicine, believed still in the complete correspondence between the parts of the human body and the "body" of the world; he was an alchemist as well as a physician. Sir Thomas Browne, the renowned English physician, believed as firmly in the existence of witches as he did in medical science. And Luther himself, along with countless other brilliant thinkers of his time, including many leading humanists, was committed to a belief in the physical existence of the Devil. We may speak metaphorically today of a person who sold his soul to the Devil, but in sixteenth-century Germany such a statement was accepted at face value.

It is against this background that the meteoric rise in popularity and the unfailing staying power of the Faust complex must be seen. The durability of the theme is certainly due to our natural fascination with the unsolved mysteries and unanswered questions fundamental to the Judeo-Christian beliefs and ethics involved: the relationship of creator and creation, of good, evil, and man's capacity and thirst for knowledge—the same issues raised in the myth of the Garden of Eden. But the impetus for its long-lived development in the sixteenth century surely lies with the social-political-religious conditions of that time.

One of those periods in human history that saw and anticipated the most penetrating and all-encompassing changes in man's conception and perception of himself and his world, the sixteenth century was a time of collapse of the traditions, conventions, and authority that had sustained and maintained him in it for centuries. As is not uncommon for such a time, the growing insufficiency of dying conventions, the faltering capacity of the old system to answer the most pressing existential questions, drove man to the spiritual and the inexplicable for answers, to religion and to the occult. It is a phenomenon we have witnessed to a lesser degree in our own time.

If Luther's challenge to the structure of Western beliefs were not enough, Copernicus was lecturing and publishing already in the year 1500 that the earth was not the center of the universe, and man stood suddenly alone. When the clouds burst, the storms of the Reformation caused major social and political upheavals. Devil worship and black magic grew, fed by the sensationalism of a gossip-laden pamphlet literature spread among the towns, which seized upon unusual and mysterious happenings and magnified them out of all proportion. Together with the perplexing discoveries of the new science, Luther's published convictions, his doubt in the certainty of salvation, removed for many much of the assurance of religion. Out of fear and confusion those who were suddenly deprived of the hope of approaching God or obtaining knowledge of him—absolute knowledge of God being impossible and not to be sought, according to Luther, for such knowledge could be obtained only as it was revealed in the Bible and in the work of Jesus—had little other than the supernatural to bolster their security. At the same time Luther made it clear that knowledge provided from sources other than the Scriptures was a gift of the Devil and could be obtained only through a pact with him.

The life and legend of Faust, modified and enlarged upon with each new retelling, in many ways satisfied the taste and reflected the spirit of the times, so much of which is mirrored in the Faust chapbook. The growing middle classes, attending the new universities at home and abroad, were conscious of their new-found freedom from a medieval world view that condemned all worldly pleasures of life and threatened the partaker with eternal damnation. The spirit of human inquiry rose to new heights; newly aware of themselves and of the beauties of this world, men were moved to praise and examine that world in new ways—and sensed their limitations all the more. What could be more predictable than for man to turn to the occult and to magic, with the ultimate goal of the subordination of nature, or of others, to his will.

The broad masses of the people, on the other hand, distrusted and were confused by the new spirit and by new scientific "truths" they could not comprehend and were warned by the clergy against accepting. Some, clinging to the church and viewing the new scientific activity and spirit of inquiry as a falling away from Christianity and a return to heathenism, were nonetheless fascinated by the supernatural and the occult—which included *both* science *and* magic—and must have taken a vicarious pleasure in the forbidden and the dangerous in following the exploits of a Dr. Faustus. Others, perhaps equally perplexed by the discoveries of science, their faith in God and the church shaken by uncertainties raised by the Reformation, no doubt pursued his career with a more active interest. Among the humanists themselves there were many Faustian natures. But the Faust chapbook was a source of interest for all.

The new reading public of the middle class, at which the *Historia* was aimed, cultivated new and less limited tastes, a situation that would lead soon to the development of the modern novel. Then too, the historical Faust, whom Luther himself spoke of in a discussion with the humanist Melanchthon, was a contemporary of this reading public or at the very least lived in their direct memory. At a time of growing national awareness and social change, the fact that Faust was both a German and the upwardly mobile son of a peasant who gained a degree of respect and even admiration in his legendary life and in the chapbook must have increased the popularity of the book. To this must be added the pure shock effect of the story. Whether the warning that prefaces the *Historia* was meant to be taken seriously or not, it is clear that the author was reacting to all the fears, insecurities, and uncertainties of his intended audience and to that spirit of human inquiry and search for knowledge noted above.

> History of D. Johann Faust, the infamous magician and practitioner of the black arts, how he sold himself in a compact with the Devil for a stipulated time, what strange things he saw, himself arranged, and indulged in during that time, until at last he received his well-deserved reward. For the most part taken and set in print from his own posthumous writings as a fearful and abominable example and sincere warning to all prideful, inquisitive, and Godless persons. "Subject yourselves to God, resist the Devil, and he will flee from you" [James iv]. Cum Gratia et Privilegio. Printed at Frankfurt on the Main by Johann Spies. M.D.LXXXVII.

For those addressed and duly warned were precisely those who, for whatever reasons, were not content with a life lived according to the doctrine of the church, and with the restrictions such a life exacted. And, after all, what damns the Faust of the chapbook is not the pact with the Devil, which is merely symptomatic and symbolic of his downfall. Earlier Christian legend, especially the lives of the saints, is replete with tales of magicians, such as Cyprian of Antioch and Theophilus, who compacted with the Devil only to break the pact and attain salvation through conversion to Christianity or a reaffirmation of faith in God, the latter course also open to but refused by the Faust of the *Historia* in an episode colored with a strong tint of the Reformation.

Rather, Faust's inclination and aspiration, his attempt and desire to break through those limitations which the Reformation and the views his age had inherited from the Middle Ages still considered to have been set by God, condemned him. For when one sees beyond the trivialities of his reported life, that spirit of inquiry and search for knowledge beyond man's ken so characteristic of the Renaissance man—and the reaction to it of the Reformation—is the real reason for his doom. (It is perhaps worth noting as a reflection on the author of the *Historia* that secular biography itself evolved as a distinct Renaissance genre, offering as it does one type of immortality in this world.) It is, after all, a Faust who has scorned his theological training and has become a *Weltmann*, a man of this world, whom we hear of in the first chapters.

For all his shortcomings, and for all the disappointing and trivial matters on which he wastes his powers, the Faust of the *Historia* is much more than the charlatan and rogue who emerges from the reports of the life of the historical Faust—the petty magician and boaster becomes something of a scientist in his own right, a mathematician who writes astronomical treatises and to whom other scientists are said to have brought their questions. He is instructed by the Devil in matters of geography and meteorology, and his whirlwind tour of the world reminds us that it was indeed the age of exploration, discovery, and travel. Like a good humanist, he is concerned with the myths of the ancients and the rediscovery and preservation of their lost writings. All this, of course, is in addition to his less savory dealings and exploits. If such items as the temptation by the Devil, to which Faust succumbs, and the parody of the Last Supper (in the

final meal with and leavetaking from his students) are designed
to project his life as a kind of anti-imitation of Christ, the specifically Lutheran aspects of his downfall are presented with even
less subtlety. For the Luther who denied free will and distrusted
reason as a seductive power that would lead man to the loss of
salvation could easily himself have written those words of Faust,
repeated at the most crucial moments, with which he curses these
two human qualities so highly valued by non-Protestants of that
time and by emerging modern man. And how damning to those
who believed in the Lutheran doctrine of justification by faith
alone must have been Faust's inability to repent and reaffirm his
faith because he despairs of God's saving grace!

Parallels between Faust, the age in which he lived, and the
drive for knowledge of modern man have been drawn too well
and too often to belabor the point here. And yet, one is hard put
to leave a consideration of Faust without pausing a moment.
Man's drive for knowledge for its own sake, to extend the
parameters of his control over his universe, continues in our own
society and time, where it is an accepted fact of the human
condition. The second half of the twentieth century has witnessed the penetration of human inquiry into what Faust would
have called the mysteries and secrets of our universe, the delimi-
tation of man's "natural" or "divinely set" boundaries to an
extent that the readers of the chapbook probably would have
believed impossible of fulfillment. Whether this be accomplished
by Faustian magic, a pact with a real or abstracted Devil, or the
investigative techniques and methods of modern pure science,
the thrust of the questions of the sixteenth century, those posed
by the author of the Faust chapbook—in fact those of the Paradise of Genesis—remain unanswered: does the uninhibited right
to pursue truth necessarily issue in evil? Must the unrestricted
search for knowledge, the fundamental principle and goal of
pure science, freed from the restraints of more conservative moral
and ethical controlling authority, issue in ultimately destructive
and antihuman action? Does the extreme of individuality implied by such a philosophy include the possibility of the destruction of man? For the author of the *Historia* the search itself was

so dangerous that the end for the seeker must clearly be eternal damnation.

Selected Bibliography

PRIMARY SOURCES

Das älteste deutsche Faustbuch. Wilhelm Scherer, ed. Berlin, 1884 (facsimile edition of the 1587 Spiess Faust Book).

Das älteste Faustbuch: Wortgetreuer Abdruck der edition princeps des Spies'schen Faustbuches vom Jahre 1587. Zerbst: E. Luppe's Buchhandlung, 1868; rpt., Amsterdam: Rodopi, 1970.

Das Faustbuch, nach der Wolfenbüttler Handschrift. H. G. Haile, ed. Berlin, Erich Schmidt, 1963.

Historia von D. Johann Fausten. Richard Benz, ed. Stuttgart: Reclam, 1968.

Historia von D. Johann Fausten. In: *Deutsche Volksbücher.* Karl Otto Conrady, ed. Rowohlts Texte Deutscher Literatur 1500–1800. Reinbek bei Hamburg: Rowohlt, 1968.

Historia von D. Johann Fausten. Hans Henning, ed. Halle, 1963.

The History of the Damnable Life and Deserved Death of Doctor John Faustus, 1592. William Rose, ed. Notre Dame: University of Notre Dame Press, 1963.

The History of Doctor Johann Faustus. H. G. Haile, ed. Urbana: University of Illinois paperback, 1965.

Das Volksbuch vom Doktor Faust. Robert Petsch, ed. Halle, 1921 (critical edition).

SECONDARY SOURCES

Faust: Sources, Works, Criticism. Paul A. Bates, ed. New York: Harcourt, Brace, World, 1969.

Faust: Vom Ursprung bis zur Verklärung durch Goethe. Oskar Schade, ed. Berlin: K. Curtius, 1912.

Holborn, Hajo. *A History of Modern Germany: The Reformation.* New York: Knopf, 1967.

Jantz, Harold. "An Elizabethan Statement on the Origin of the German Faust Book." *JEGP,* 51 (1952), 137–153.

————. *Goethe's Faust as a Renaissance Man: Parallels and Prototypes.* Princeton: Princeton University Press, 1951.

Kiesewetter, Carl. *Faust in der Geschichte und Tradition.* Leipzig: Verlag von Max Spohr, 1893.

Kippenberg, Anton. "Die Faustsage und ihr Übergang in die Dichtung." *Jahrbuch der Sammlung Kippenberg,* 6 (1926), 240–262.

Knowles, David. *The Evolution of Medieval Thought.* New York: Vintage Books, 1964.

Kuhn, Thomas S. *The Copernican Revolution.* Cambridge: Harvard University Press, 1957; rpt., New York: Vintage Books, n.d.

Lacroix, Paul. *Science and Literature in the Middle Ages and the Renaissance.* 1878; rpt. New York: Ungar, 1964.

Mason, Eudo C. *Goethe's Faust: Its Genesis and Purport.* Berkeley and Los Angeles: University of California Press, 1967.

Nicolson, Marjorie Hope. *The Breaking of the Circle: Studies in the Effect of the "New Science" on Seventeenth-Century Poetry,* rev. ed. New York: Columbia University Press, 1960.

Palmer, Philip Mason and More, Robert Pattison. *The Sources of the Faust Tradition from Simon Magus to Lessing.* New York: Oxford University Press, 1936.

Peuckert, Will-Erich. "Dr. Johannes Faust." *Zeitschrift für deutsche Philologie,* 70 (1947/1948), 55–74.

Pre-Reformation Germany. Gerald Strauss, ed. London: The Macmillan Press Ltd. 1972; rpt. New York: Harper and Row, 1972.

Reske, Hermann. *Faust: Eine Einführung.* Stuttgart: Kohlhammer, 1971.

Schwerte, Hans. *Faust und das Faustische: Ein Kapitel deutscher Ideologie.* Stuttgart: Ernst Klett, 1962.

Seiferth, Wolfgang S. "The Concept of the Devil and the Myth of the Pact in Literature Prior to Goethe." *Monatshefte,* 44 (1952), 271–289.

Tillyard, E. M. W. *The Elizabethan World Picture.* New York: Vintage Books, n.d.

Wedgwood, C. V. *The Thirty Years War.* Garden City: Doubleday, 1961.

Willey, Basil. *The Seventeenth Century Background.* 1934; rpt. Garden City: Doubleday, n.d.

Wolff, Eugen. *Faust und Luther: Ein Beitrag zur Entstehung der Faust-Dichtung.* Halle: Max Niemeyer, 1912.

14

The Role
of Classical Humanism
in the Copernican Achievement

Robert K. DeKosky

To what degree did Copernican thought incur a debt to classical sources? In particular, did his innovative astronomy-cosmology essentially spring out of a stimulus exerted by ancient Greek thinkers?

That humanist currents influenced Nicolaus Copernicus we cannot doubt. He was born in 1473 into a German-speaking family living in Toruń, a city under the sovereignty of the king of Poland. His father died in 1483, but the young Copernicus was fortunate in that his maternal uncle, Lucas Watzenrode, assumed guardianship of the family. Through Watzenrode's influence, Copernicus enrolled at the University of Cracow in 1491. He matriculated there for several years, but did not obtain a degree.

At Cracow the new humanistic learning had made important inroads, although scholastics on the faculty resisted it stubbornly. Filippo Buonaccorsi, the well-known Italian humanist, had visited Cracow in 1470, and he remained under the patronage of the Polish kings until his death in 1496. The German Conrad Celtis, (1459–1508), active in the revival of German historical and cultural studies, had lectured there on Cicero. Though the Latin translations of Homer, Vergil, and Horace had not become part of the curriculum at the time of Copernicus's period of study, he very probably gained access to these classical works by virtue of their secret circulation in student quarters. No doubt the Cracow experience also triggered Copernicus's interest in astronomy and mathematics, for the university had an excellent reputation for its offerings in these subjects; indeed, it was the only university in central Europe possessing a chair of astronomy at that time.

Copernicus was elected a canon of Warmia in Poland in 1495, apparently through the aid of Watzenrode, the bishop of Warmia since 1489. The appointment carried with it a prebend and therefore freed Nicolaus from future financial concern. He did not assume the duties of this position for about fifteen years, however. In 1496 he followed in the footsteps of his uncle and enrolled at the famous law school of the University of Bologna to study canon law. During his four years at Bologna, Copernicus also pursued his interests in humanistic studies and astronomy. He assisted and studied with the professor of Astronomy at Bologna, Dominico Maria Novara, and he began to learn Greek.

After a brief stay in Rome, Copernicus returned to Warmia in 1501 to request of his chapter permission for two additional years of study. Now he wished to pursue medicine at Padua, the Italian university most famous for offerings in that subject. While at Padua he not only learned medicine; he joined a humanistic circle devoted to the study of ancient philosophy and literature and he improved his knowledge of Greek. Following a common pattern, Copernicus had come from the north to Italy for professional studies, but he participated in humanist activities as well.

In the spring of 1503, Copernicus's prolonged leave from his Warmian chapter was about to end, and he wished to return with a degree—a requirement by statute of his chapter for any canon granted absence for university study. He could not obtain a medical degree, for that required three years of study. In May, 1503, the University of Ferrara conferred on him the doctorate in canon law. Copernicus chose Ferrara because the expense of obtaining the degree was less there than at the universities where he actually had matriculated. Rather than returning to Frombork (the town in which his cathedral chapter was located), Copernicus joined his uncle in Lidzbark in the latter half of 1503. He remained with Watzenrode until 1510, when he returned to Frombork.

During the years at Lidzbark the versatile Copernicus engaged in various activities. As a doctor of canon law, he performed important advisory and administrative services for his uncle. Though he had had only two years of medical study, Copernicus became Watzenrode's personal physician. Indeed, his contemporaries accorded him great respect for his medical ability: Tiedemann Giese (1480–1550), a close friend of Copernicus who later became bishop of Chelmno, related that "in medicine Copernicus was honored like a second Aesculapius" (the ancient Roman god of healing). Nicolaus also maintained his strong interest in classical scholarship. While at Lidzbark he worked off and on translating into Latin the Greek *Letters* of Theophylactus Simocatta, a seventh-century Byzantine. The *Letters* was a collection of moral, rustic, and amatory epistles. Copernicus's translation, published at Cracow in 1509, was the first Latin rendition of a Greek author independently printed in Poland. Though a modest achievement when set against the classical scholarship of an Erasmus, Copernicus's effort was an important contribution to the spread of humanism in his homeland. The publication takes on added significance when one considers that the University of Cracow did not even offer Greek in its program of studies until 1520.

But during these years Copernicus also persisted in his astronomical work—his life's passion. By the end of the stay at Lidzbark he had attained a first-rate competence in technical astronomy. He may even have embraced the heliocentric cosmology for which he would achieve lasting fame.

We know that Copernicus had envisioned a heliocentric system by 1514. In that year he circulated a short unsigned tract among a select few individuals that contained an elucidation of the new cosmological arrangement. The *Commentariolus*, as historians have come to call it, was to remain unpublished during

Copernicus's lifetime. Not until the end of his life, pressured by friends, did he submit to publishing his views in the famous *De revolutionibus orbium coelestium* (On the Revolution of the Heavenly Spheres, 1543). In all probability, Copernicus refused to publish the new astronomy for decades because he did not wish to experience the expected abusive reactions from conservative theologians and university professors of (natural) philosophy.

The impact of humanism on Copernican astronomy shows up in the criteria to which Copernicus appealed in defense of his novel outlook. But we must not overemphasize Copernicus's humanism at the expense of his interest and achievements in technical astronomy. Though influenced by the ancients, Copernicus was no blind adherent of any classical philosophical or cultural tradition. His decision to opt for the theory of a moving earth instead of the traditional medieval alternative did not derive merely from his discovery that Aristarchus (310–230 B.C.) and certain ancient Pythagorean philosophers had put the earth in motion. Indeed, in the *Commentariolus* he commented that the Pythagoreans had "asserted the movement of the earth for no good reason." He would rest his own preference in an astronomical model on substantial mathematical and astronomical reasoning.

In order to gauge properly the effect of humanist currents on the Copernican achievement, we must discuss briefly the medieval scholastic approach to understanding the phenomena of the heavens. From the thirteenth century—following translation and assimilation of Greek and Islamic scientific-philosophical writings into the Latin West—up to the generation of Copernicus, Western thinkers considered accurate description of heavenly movements and explanations of celestial motions as two separate areas of endeavor. To the astronomer fell the task of formulating geometrical models, complex to be sure, which could correlate closely with the apparent movements of planets against the background of the stars and accurately predict future planetary positions.

The astronomer's function was indispensable for valid calendar reckoning and for the purposes of astrology. He patterned his approach after that of the *Almagest*, the great treatise on astronomy fashioned by Claudius Ptolemy of Alexandria in the second century A.D. Utilizing a basic theme actually derived from Plato and the Pythagoreans, Ptolemy had conceived models in which combinations of simple circular motions generated resultant complex motions similar to those followed by the planets. For example (Figure 1a), he would imagine a point p moving circularly about another point f which, in turn, simultaneously moved circularly about a third point e; he would combine such circular motions judiciously in attempting to reproduce a planetary movement against the stellar background as viewed from point e, assumed as the position of the earth. Ptolemy, as would his later counterpart in the medieval Latin West, had no pretensions that the intricate combinations of circular motions he conceived were physically real; he did not offer them as true component motions of the complex resultant astronomers perceived through observation. Ptolemy did not view his task as physical explanation of heavenly motions. Rather he endeavored to describe accurately and to predict apparent celestial movements through the use of hypothetical models similar to Figure 1a.

In two basic ways, the approach of the medieval natural philosopher to heavenly phenomena agreed with its astronomical counterpart. Like the Ptolemaic astronomer, he assumed the earth to be central and absolutely immobile in the cosmos, and he too grounded his explanations on the belief that circular motions were proper to celestial bodies. But the natural philosopher looked to the writings of Aristotle (d. 322 B.C.) for his inspiration. Concerned primarily with theorizing about the structure of the cosmos and with accounting for the causes of celestial movements, the Aristotelian envisioned that heavenly bodies were embedded in solid, transparent, concentric crystalline spheres that rotated about an unmoving earthly center. But while the crystalline-sphere model of the heavens satisfied the quest for physical explanation, it could only approximate the overall motions of the planets; the theory of concentric spheres was inadequate for covering detailed planetary movements against the stars.

Though he obviously would have wished for a reconciliation

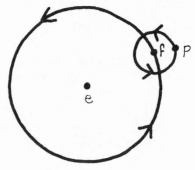

Figure 1a

•
e

Figure 1b

Figure 1b shows a part of the resultant motion of point p, while p moves according to the model of figure 1a. From point e (the position of the immobile earth) the motion of point p (the planet) would appear irregular, because the motion of p is a resultant of two uniformly circular motions. By properly assigning sizes and angular velocities to combinations of uniform circular motions similar to figure 1a, Ptolemy attempted to reproduce the irregular movements of planets against the background of the stars.

of astronomy and the physics of the heavens, the medieval intellectual was less disturbed about the gap between these two areas
than we might at first think. The so-called nominalist current,
deeply rooted in medieval philosophy, discouraged belief that
the human mind could attain certain knowledge of relationships
among individual objects and beings. In its classic expression in
the thought of the brilliant theologian and logician William of
Ockham (1290–1349), nominalism allied easily with a theological accentuation on God's unrestricted omnipotence.

According to Ockham, both the nature and the existence of
individual objects depended on the inscrutable will of God. As
absolutely omnipotent, God could have made things entirely
different from the way they are. No set universal patterns or
relationships bound His creativity; rather, we must assume that
each individual thing in the universe possesses its own uniqueness. To be sure, individuals evince similarities, but God's ability
to create anything that does not involve a logical contradiction
impels us to stress the singularity of each and every thing in the
universe.

Ockham's theory of knowledge, uncompromisingly empirical, did indeed emphasize the uniqueness of individual objects.
He held that through what he termed "intuitive cognition," the
human mind apprehends an individual object *immediately* and
directly. Our recognition of what appear to be universal relationships among individual things is subsequent and secondary to
comprehension of the individual. In fact, the mind cannot attain
certainty of universal relationships among individual objects, because knowledge of one existence does not allow the certain in-
ference of the existence of another thing or event that has not
been directly experienced.

This trend significantly affected fourteenth-century attitudes
toward "science" or natural philosophy, by their very natures
concerned with the discovery or formulation of general causes,
laws, or theories. Leading figures such as Jean Buridan (d. 1360),
the influential master in the Philosophy Faculty of the University
of Paris, and Nicole Oresme (d. 1382), Buridan's pupil and later
Bishop of Lisieux, inclined toward viewing theories of nature as

hypothetical and avoided claiming them to be absolutely "true": they termed physical generalizations "probable," in the sense of being empirical hypotheses that cannot be proven with certainty. A strictly hypothetical astronomy utilized "to save the phenomena" (i.e., to describe and predict apparent celestial movements accurately), and claiming no insight into the actual structure, component motions, or causal mechanisms involved in the heavenly process, meshed well with the critical nominalist attitude toward human knowledge. In fact, nominalists allowed Aristotelian cosmological principles only "probable" status, denying that the theory of an absolutely immobile earth had been or could be demonstrated with certainty. However, both Buridan and Oresme did allege that a geostatic earth was more probable than any geokinetic counterpart. The result of all of this was that medievalists tolerated the rift between astronomy and cosmology, affected as they were by a nominalist current that forsook the belief that the human mind could apprehend with certainty the true physical and geometrical relationships among heavenly bodies.

At the outset of his *Commentariolus*, Copernicus plainly indicated that his aim would be to fabricate a mathematical astronomy at once accurate and true to physical reality. In this he renounced the hypothetical nature of mathematical astronomy so characteristic of the Ptolemaic *Almagest* tradition. Stimulated by humanist currents, he exuded an optimism that the human thinker could achieve a certain grasp of the genuine system of the universe, in evident opposition to the spirit of his medieval predecessors. The new attitude emerged as Copernicus began the attack on traditional astronomy by repudiating a geometrical tool—the "equant"—which Ptolemy had invoked in his effort to reproduce geometrically the movements of planets. For any given planet, Ptolemy had employed a combination of circular motions, the complex resultant of which was to trace out the apparent movement of the planet against the stellar background. Ptolemy had found, however, that he could achieve a desired level of accuracy only if he had one of the component circular motions—the equant circle—move with uniform angular motion relative to a point removed from its center. Thus, while the other circular motions encompassing a planetary set would appear to move at uniform speed as viewed from their own centers, the equant motion would be irregular relative to its center; the equant motion was not a *uniform* circular motion.

Copernicus was able to dispense with the Ptolemaic equant because he had hit upon a way to reproduce its effect through a particular combination of three *uniform* circular motions. This equivalent to the equant had been formulated in the fourteenth century by the Islamic astronomer Ibn al-Shātir (1304–75). Copernicus may well have gained access to the construction during his sojourn in Italy through a translation or paraphrasing of al-Shātir of which we do not have knowledge. At any rate, the elimination of the traditional equant construction removed what in Copernicus's view was a major barrier to the formulation of a physically plausible and true astronomy.

As *Commentariolus* reveals, Copernicus's conception of heavenly physics still focused on the traditional notion of rotating spheres carrying the planets. Prior to the elimination of the Ptolemaic equant construction, however, the wedding of technical astronomy to cosmology had seemed implausible, because the spherical equivalent to an equant motion would have entailed a nonuniform rotation about the spherical axis. Indeed, the fifteenth-century astronomer Georg Purbach—whose *Theoricae Novae Planetarum* (New Theory of the Planets) was the primary astronomical textbook of Copernicus's student generation—attempted to formulate accurate astronomical models in terms of rotating spheres. Nevertheless, Copernicus himself had remained cool toward what he felt to be Purbach's physically inconceivable application of nonuniform spherical rotations. But now Copernicus could envision sets of uniformly rotating spheres—combining motions by virtue of connections similar to those linking the two spheres in Figure 2—which could accurately reproduce the apparent movement of a planet assumed to be embedded in the smallest sphere, as viewed by an observer at point 0.

When *Commentariolus* brushed aside the equant as "neither perfect enough nor sufficiently in accordance with reason," it

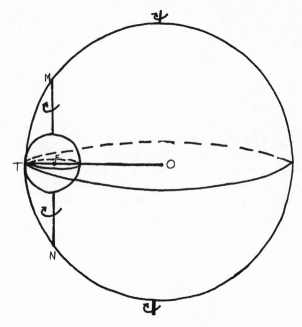

Figure 2

divulged criteria stemming from Copernicus's humanist interests as well. After all, was he not going back to a purer astronomical ideal of uniform circular motion—the paradigm of the Pythagoreans and of Plato—by rejecting a subsequent scheme sullied by violations of it? We should not ignore in Copernican thought the psychology of a return to a more ancient (and therefore more genuine) prototype, so typical of the humanist temper. Moreover, under the impact of his acquaintance with a Pythagorean philosophy of nature, Copernicus held a strong faith that the human intellect could formulate a true, mathematically couched, physically explainable astronomy "in accordance with reason." As had the Pythagoreans, he believed that exact mathematical relationships were inherent in the celestial process. Consequently, he held that exact knowledge of the principles underlying heavenly movements was accessible to the human mind, in direct opposition to the attitudes of the medieval astronomer and the nominalist natural philosopher, both of whom had denied to the human thinker any certain knowledge of the relationships governing celestial motions.

We must be clear on a critical point. The confrontation between Copernican astronomy and traditional perspectives did not center on the question of greater accuracy of description or prediction of planetary movements. Copernicus claimed only that he had formulated more "perfect" and "more reasonable" constructions *equivalent* to Ptolemaic devices. He did not and could not assert his constructions as intrinsically more accurate than Ptolemy's. To be sure, he was dissatisfied with the accuracy of prevailing astronomical tables (based upon the Ptolemaic constructions), but improvement in accuracy was to occur by virtue of more accurate observation and more judicious assignment of parameters. Copernicus's objection to Ptolemy's constructions was not that they were inherently inaccurate, but that they were philosophically intolerable.

Like his decision to eliminate the Ptolemaic equant, Copernicus's choice of a heliocentric astronomy entailing a daily rotation of the earth on its axis and a yearly revolution of the earth about the sun was not dictated by considerations of predictive accuracy. Here again, Copernicus had no reason to believe that the traditional geocentric model was less likely to provide the geometrical basis for accurate astronomical tables than a heliocentric counterpart. We should also note that the question of systems was independent of the equant issue, since either system had to account for the irregularity in planetary motion for which Ptolemy had applied the equant. Copernicus's substitution of three combined spherical rotations in *Commentariolus* for Ptolemy's equant was applicable to both systems. (Thus, in Figure 2—showing two of the spheres of a planetary set—point 0 would be the earth in a geostatic model, or it would be a position close to the sun in a heliocentric model.)

With the choice of astronomical systems ultimately hinging on philosophical considerations, a humanist impact also contributed to Copernicus's decision to opt for the theory of a moving earth. We cannot do full justice to all important factors involved in the controversy within the scope of this discussion, but can briefly indicate the pros and cons of heliocentrism. Theological, physical, and astronomical difficulties faced a theory of a moving earth. It violated the literalist sense of several key passages in Holy Scripture. It appeared inconsistent with a commonsense interpretation of the motion of freely falling bodies: should not the earth rotate eastward underneath a rock falling from a tower, so that one would expect to observe the rock's point of impact *west* of the tower's base? But the rock always falls to a point directly underneath the tower top. Thirdly, if the earth moves through space, the astronomical observer should expect to note changes in the angular separations between stars over the course of the year (stellar parallax). But no stellar parallax had ever been detected (and would not be until 1838, with the aid of the telescope).

Copernicus said nothing of the Scriptural or the physical problems in *Commentariolus*. Later on, in Book I of his magnum opus, he would make only a half-hearted attempt to confront the physical difficulty, speculating that perhaps the air surrounding the earth rotates with it and "pushes" the falling body to the east at the same rate as the earth during the period of the body's fall.

This was an inadequate solution to the difficulty. Galileo would eventually meet the problem with his novel inertial physics. Finally, the only response Copernicus could make to the lack of observed parallax in defending the proposition of a moving earth was to argue that the diameter of the earth's orbit was insignificant relative to the distance between the earth and the stars, and that therefore the parallax effect was indetectibly small.

Against the formidable drawbacks of heliocentric astronomy, however, stood what Copernicus held to be more weighty advantages. Instead of having to posit separate causes and motions for the overall daily east-to-west movements of celestial objects, one motion of daily earthly rotation about its axis would suffice; here the allegation of diurnal axial rotation of the earth enjoyed an advantage from the standpoint of intellectual economy, a consideration both Buridan and Oresme had recognized back in the fourteenth century. Furthermore, Ptolemy had had to offer special constructions to account for the prominent periodic "retrogressions" in planetary drift relative to the stellar background. Copernicus recognized, however, that no separate devices were necessary to explain this phenomenon in the heliocentric system (Figure 3): with the earth and another planet moving about the sun in different orbits and with different orbital velocities, the terrestrial observer must expect to note what appears to be retrogression of the planet against the background of the stars, but what in reality is an effect deriving from changing orbital positions of both the viewer and the viewed object.

Moreover, Ptolemy also had needed to invoke ad hoc and highly implausible assumptions to explain why inferior planets— Mercury and Venus—never appear to move more than 26° and 48°, respectively, from the sun (i.e., why Mercury and Venus are observed only during the periods of time immediately surrounding sunrise or sunset). But here again Copernicus realized that if he assumed the orbits of Mercury and Venus centered on the sun and *inside* the orbit of the earth, no special explanation for the phenomena of the inferior planets was necessary; just because the two planets were closer to a motionless and central sun than the earth, with all three planetary orbits approximately coplanar,

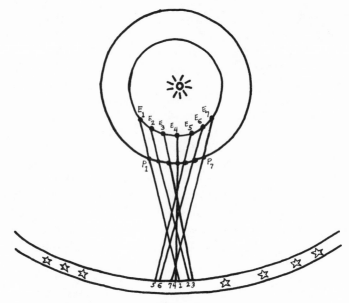

Figure 3
Explanation of Planetary Retrograde Motion According
to the Copernican Heliocentric Arrangement

An observer on the earth (E) viewing the positions of a planet (P) at
successive times 1 to 7 must expect to perceive the planet's direction of
movement against the stars to change or retrograde. Note that against
the stellar background the planet moves retrograde between time 3 and
time 4, and then resumes its original motion against the stars between
time 5 and 6. The time span from positions 1 to 7 in this diagram is
about three months, as the earth has traversed about ¼th its orbit
around the sun.

apparent restriction of the movements of Mercury and Venus relative to the sun as viewed from the earth was an inevitable consequence.

Yet of all the factors Copernicus cited to defend the theory of a moving earth, one in particular evidences the effect of his humanist education. Unlike the Ptolemaic perspective, the very geometry of the heliocentric model permits determination of both the order and the relative sizes of planetary orbits. Ptolemaic astronomy supposed observation to originate from an unmoving *central* position; the observer—perceiving only angular velocities—had no means of determining distances of bodies moving about himself as a fixed reference. Though Ptolemaic astronomers had formulated convenient rules for estimating relative diameters of the planetary orbits, there was nothing intrinsic in the geometry of geocentrism that allowed definitive determination of orbital sizes. Indeed, even the means they utilized could not provide wide agreement as to the relative sizes of the orbits of the sun, Venus, and Mercury.

As Copernicus came to recognize, supposing the sun central enables the astronomer easily to obtain the order and sizes of the orbits of Mercury and Venus. At maximum elongation from the sun (Figure 4), he can determine the distance PS relative to ES (the distance between earth and sun), since angle EPS = 90° and angle PES is directly measurable. PS, of course, is the average radius of the inferior planet's orbit around the sun. Assuming the heliocentric system, the order from the center is sun, Mercury, and Venus; measurement of the maximum angles of elongation from the sun for Venus (48°) and Mercury (26°) absolutely fixes the relative sizes of the orbits of the two planets by the Copernican geometrical relationships.

Copernicus likewise could determine the order of the superior planets from observation presuming the heliocentric model, though the means of determination is not as straightforward as in the case of the inferior planets. No doubt the fact that the geometry of the heliocentric construction specified the planetary order appealed to Copernicus's sense of systematic proportion, which surely had been heightened by the Platonic-Pythag-

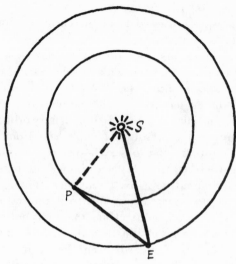

Figure 4

orean influences of his Cracow and Italian educations. In the heliocentric arrangement he perceived "an admirable symmetry in the Universe and a clear bond of harmony in the motion and magnitude of the orbits." (*De revolutionibus*, chapter 1, p. 10).

In his attitude toward the relationship between human intellectual constructs and physical reality and in the criteria he applied to defend heliocentrism, Copernicus evinced the humanist influence. His veneration of Platonist-Pythagorean sources—though not uncritical hero-worship—assumed no small part in his criticism and transcendence of medieval astronomy-cosmology. One can certainly argue with justification that his rigid adherence to the paradigm of uniform circularity in astronomical models implied more an emphasis upon a pristine classical ideal than a revolutionary step in astronomy. Stressing this line of argument, Johannes Kepler (1571–1630), who would break with the circular ideal and allege (correctly) that planets move about the sun in simple *elliptical* orbits, deserves credit for "revolutionizing" astronomy along with Copernicus. Moreover, Copernicus called up the opinions of Sophocles and Philolaus to bolster his theory of the cosmic arrangement in *De revolutionibus*. Referring to the ancients for support, he indicated at once his own respect and the esteem of his reading public for the thought of classical antiquity.

It was fitting that Copernicus should select as his personal seal the image of Apollo playing a lyre. The god of the sun and the symbol of his music aptly represented the reverence Copernicus felt for the central body in his own cosmos and the harmonious (mathematical) relationships he believed to endure among the planetary and stellar movements.

Selected Bibliography

Note: A definitive and annotated bibliography of the literature concerning Copernicus up to 1970 appears in Edward Rosen, *Three Copernican Treatises* (New York, 1971), pp. 199–312. For subsequent writings on Copernicus, one should consult the annual critical bibliography of *Isis*, the journal of the American History of Science Society.

PRIMARY SOURCES

Swerdlow, Noel. "The Derivation and First Draft of Copernicus's Planetary Theory: A Translation of the *Commentariolus* with Commentary." *Proceedings of the American Philosophical Society*, 117 (1973), pp. 423–512. (Indispensable rendition and commentary on Copernicus's work.)
Copernicus, Nicolaus. *De revolutionibus orbium coelestium*. Nuremberg, 1543. Facsimile edition New York, 1965.
———. *On the Revolution of the Heavenly Spheres*. Transl. by C. G. Wallis. In *Great Books of the Western World*, vol. 16. Chicago, 1952, pp. 479–838.
———. Book I of above. Transl. by J. F. Dobson and S. Brodetsky in *Occasional Notes of the Royal Astronomical Society*, vol. 10, May, 1947.

SECONDARY SOURCES

Africa, Thomas. "Copernicus' Relation to Aristarchus and Pythagoras." *Isis*, 52 (1961), pp. 403–9.
Armitage, Angus. *Copernicus, the Founder of Modern Astronomy*. New York, London, 1957.
Bienkowska, Barbara, ed. *The Scientific World of Copernicus*. Dordrecht, Boston, 1973.
Dobrzycki, Jerzy, ed. *The Reception of Copernicus' Heliocentric Theory*. Dordrecht, Boston, 1973.
Grant, Edward. "Late Medieval Thought, Copernicus, and the Scientific Revolution." *Journal of the History of Ideas*, 23 (1962), pp. 197–220.
Koyré, Alexandre. *The Astronomical Revolution*. Transl. by R. E. W. Maddison. Ithaca, 1973, pp. 15–116.
Kuhn, Thomas. *The Copernican Revolution*. New York, 1959.
Lesnodorski, Boguslaw. "Copernicus the Humanist." In *Mikolaj Kopernik: szkice monograficzne*. Józef Hurwic, ed. Warsaw, 1965, pp. 237–79.
Mossakowski, Stanislaw. "The Symbolic Meaning of Copernicus' Seal." *Journal of the History of Ideas*, 34 (1973), pp. 451–60.
Neyman, Jerzy, ed. *The Heritage of Copernicus: Theories "More Pleas-*

ing to the Mind." The Copernican Volume of the National Academy of Sciences. Cambridge, Mass., 1974.

Prowe, Leopold. *Nicolaus Copernicus.* Berlin, 1883–84; rpt. Osnabrück, 1967.

Rosen, Edward. *Three Copernican Treatises,* pp. 313–412. (See note above; gives the most reliable and up-to-date treatment of the details of Copernicus' life.)

———. "Copernicus." In *Dictionary of Scientific Biography,* vol. 3. New York, 1971, pp. 401–411.

———. "Copernicus' Quotation from Sophocles." *Didascaliae: Studies in Honor of Anselm M. Albareda.* New York, 1961, pp. 369–79.

Transalpine Humanism:
A Chronology

I.	**1340–1400**	**Early chancellery humanism (Prague)**
	1347–1437	Luxemburg dynasty
	1333–1356	Petrarch in Germany
	1348	Prague University founded by Charles IV
	1348–52	Plague sweeps Europe
	1350–52	Rienzi in Prague; Chancellor Johann von Neumarkt (died 1380), fourteen years of correspondence with Petrarch
	1360s–1520	Devotio moderna
	1365	University of Vienna founded
	1386	University of Heidelberg founded
	1400	*The Plowman from Bohemia*
II.	**1400–1475**	**The Italian vogue**
	1414–18	Council of Constance
	1415	Jan Hus burned
	1419–36	Hussite wars in Bohemia: destruction of budding German humanism

1431–49	Council of Basel, defended by Nicholas of Cusa (died 1464) and Enea Silvio Piccolomini, later Pius II (1458–1464). In 1437 Pope Eugenius IV pronounced its dissolution, but the council refused to accept the decision and remained in session.
1434–56	Luder in Italy and Greece
1438	Founding of the Hapsburg dynasty (Vienna)
1442	Silvio poet laureate; Silvio remains for eleven years at the Imperial Chancellery
1450	Johann Gutenberg's printing press
1451	Silvio introduces humanistic studies in Vienna
1452–93	Emperor Friedrich III
1453	Constantinople conquered by the Turks
1456	Luder's inaugural address at the University of Heidelberg
1460	University of Basel founded
1462	Niklas von Wyle translates Silvio's *Eurialus et Lucretia*
1472	Schlüsselfelder translates Boccaccio's *Decamerone*
1487	Conrad Celtis poet laureate
1502	Celtis, *Quattuor libri amorum*

III. **1475–1525**   **Patriotic humanism**

1509	Erasmus, *The Praise of Folly*
1515–17	*Epistolae obscurorum virorum* (Rubeanus-Hutten)
1517	Luther's theses: the Reformation begins
1519–56	Charles V (introduction of Roman law)
1521	Diet at Worms
1522	Luther, *New Testament*; Johannes Pauli, *Schimpf und Ernst*
1524–25	Peasants' War
1528	Death of Albrecht Dürer
1534	Luther's *Biblia*
1536	Death of Erasmus
1546	Death of Luther
1587	*Historia von Dr. Johann Faustus*

Index